Also by the same author

ng from Hampstead: The Story of Henry and Lucy Stedall and children (Book Guild Publishing, 2002)

*-volume history of Mary Queen of Scots:

Challenge to the Crown, Volume I: The Struggle for Influence in eign of Mary Queen of Scots 1542–1567 (Book Guild Publishing,

urvival of the Crown, Volume II: The return to Authority of the sh Crown following Mary Queen of Scots' Deposition from the e (Book Guild Publishing, 2014)

of Substance: The London Livery Companies' Reluctant Part in the ation of Ulster (Austin Macauley Publishers, 2016)

Queen of Scots' Downfall: The Life and Murder of Henry, Lord ey (Pen & Sword Books Limited, 2017)

oots of Ireland's Troubles (Pen & Sword Books Limited, 2019)

beth I's Secret Lover, Robert Dudley, Earl of Leicester (Pen & d Books Limited, 2020)

Queen of Scots' Secretary, William Maitland: Politician, Reformer Conspirator (Pen & Sword Books Limited, 2021)

ite: www.maryqueenofscots.net

ELIZABET

FINAL YE

H
th

A

Th
th
20

Th
Sc
Th

Me
Pla

Ma
Da

The

Eli
Sw

Ma
and

Wel

ELIZABETH I's FINAL YEARS

HER FAVOURITES AND HER FIGHTING MEN

ROBERT STEDALL

PEN & SWORD **HISTORY**

AN IMPRINT OF PEN & SWORD BOOKS LTD.
YORKSHIRE – PHILADELPHIA

First published in Great Britain in 2022 by
PEN AND SWORD HISTORY
An imprint of
Pen & Sword Books Ltd
Yorkshire – Philadelphia

ISBN 978 1 39908 315 7

Typeset in Times New Roman 11.5/14 by
SJmagic DESIGN SERVICES, India.
Printed and bound in the UK by CPI Group (UK) Ltd.

Pen & Sword Books Limited incorporates the imprints of Atlas, Archaeology,
Aviation, Discovery, Family History, Fiction, History, Maritime, Military, Military
Classics, Politics, Select, Transport, True Crime, Air World, Frontline Publishing,
Leo Cooper, Remember When, Seaforth Publishing, The Praetorian Press,
Wharncliffe Local History, Wharncliffe Transport, Wharncliffe True Crime and
White Owl.

For a complete list of Pen & Sword titles please contact
PEN & SWORD BOOKS LIMITED
47 Church Street, Barnsley, South Yorkshire, S70 2AS, England
E-mail: enquiries@pen-and-sword.co.uk
Website: www.pen-and-sword.co.uk

Or
PEN AND SWORD BOOKS
1950 Lawrence Rd, Havertown, PA 19083, USA
E-mail: Uspen-and-sword@casematepublishers.com
Website: www.penandswordbooks.com

Contents

PART II: DEVELOPMENT OF MILITARY AND COURTLY SKILLS

PART III: THE ARMADA AND ITS AFTERMATH

PART IV: HONING DEVEREUX AMBITIONS

PART V: FURTHER CAMPAIGNS AGAINST THE SPANISH

Contents

List of Illustrations
(in colour section)

Preface

This is my eighth history book (excluding a narrative on my family while living in Hampstead with their horses from about 1890 to 1935). Of these, four cover the period of Mary Queen of Scots in Scotland, two provide a broad span of Irish history, and this is my second covering the reign of Elizabeth I, seen through the eyes of her favourites.

It might be thought that there is not much new to uncover about Mary and Elizabeth in this well-trodden period of Tudor history, but I have been amazed to unearth areas and personalities that I knew little about. Conventional history books tend to take the form of meticulously researched biographies written with a single-minded focus. With biographers having a natural love (or very occasionally hatred) for their subject, they tend to highlight those facets of their subject's personality which fit best with their underlying thesis. Biographies have the advantage that they can be written chronologically and once the research has been done, they are, from my own experience, relatively easy to commit to writing.

In this book, I have set myself a different challenge. My objective has been to explore the lives of all the key favourites surrounding Elizabeth, both at court and elsewhere. This has enabled me to portray the interplay among them and with both Elizabeth and her political advisers, particularly William Cecil, Lord Burghley, and his son Robert. As many of them aspired to military glory as their route to political authority, one or other of them became involved in almost all the campaigns making up a fairly continuous period of war with Spain in many different arenas following on from the Spanish Armada. This narrative thus provides an outline of the later period of the Anglo-Spanish wars, the first part of which is covered, albeit superficially, in *Elizabeth I's Secret Lover*, my biography of Lord Robert Dudley, Earl of Leicester. It is not always a glorious period of English military prowess, which may be the cause of its events being bypassed in English classroom history, despite them often being more threatening to the nation's security than the Armada. To provide a more complete story, I have also summarised the career of the battle-scarred Sir Francis Vere, who was most certainly not a 'favourite', but was the great Elizabethan general in the Low Countries during this period.

With this narrative having several different parallel strands, it cannot be written entirely chronologically without losing individual storylines. My focus has always been to present each story so that it flows, even if it means that the chronology jumps about a bit.

Perhaps inevitably in writing the history of different personalities, there are those who, as an author, seem admirable and those who do not. It is difficult to be dispassionate about one's 'children', although each should be loved equally. I have found myself less and less attracted to Elizabeth in her latter years, and there is almost nothing to respect about James I while on the English throne, despite his extraordinarily successful, if devious, reign while still in Scotland. Notwithstanding his undoubted bravery, Robert Devereux, 2nd Earl of Essex, comes across as little more than a spoilt prig, wholly unsuited to high command, suffering from fits of depression and lacking in judgement and stability under pressure. If there is a hero (or heroine), it is his sister Penelope Rich, much admired by Sir Philip Sidney. She was probably the most delightful dinner companion of her day, but unhappily locked into an arranged marriage to Robert, 3rd Lord Rich. In addition to her courtly accomplishments, she was the Devereux family's political lynchpin, developing her family's close association with James VI in Scotland. She also became the mistress of Charles Blount, 8th Lord Mountjoy, whose military achievement in Ireland may be little known, but he stands out, after Essex's failure there, as one of the great English generals of all time.

All the stories that we know about Sir Walter Raleigh doffing his cape to the queen and importing potatoes and tobacco from North America for the first time can be shown to be fantasy. Despite his brilliance with his pen, he was also an inveterate liar, embellishing the not inconsiderable achievements of his expeditions at every turn while demeaning those of others. He shared none of Essex's popularity, but remained remarkably resilient during long periods spent in the Tower of London as part of the gross mistreatment meted out to him by James I.

Although Burghley has received copious praise as the great Elizabethan statesman, I have said elsewhere that I can only see him as devious to the detriment of those of his contemporaries whom he saw as a threat. He had the advantage of commissioning the great contemporary histories of the period, particularly by William Camden, resulting in plaudits for his political achievement from Victorian biographers such as Martin Andrew Sharp Hume. This has caused Lord Robert Dudley, Earl of Leicester, and Mary Queen of Scots to receive a bad press. While it is the ambition of every serious historian to research original sources, it has to be recognised that many of them are biased or even falsified, just as they are by the present-day press. Too often contemporary sources are accepted at face value. With so much praise for Burghley and even for his son, the despicable Robert Cecil, it is the favourites who have tended to come off worst. This is not a story designed to uncover great heroes, although some of them were, but none of them was free from fault.

My principal sources are outlined in the bibliography, but I am obliged to five in particular. Sally Varlow's *The Lady Penelope* is far more than a biography of Penelope Rich. She is a proponent of the view that Lettice Knollys was a granddaughter of Henry VIII and draws attention to the devious nature of the Cecils. Steven Veerapen in *Elizabeth & Essex* engrosses us in the political aspects of the period and provides a masterclass in succinct writing. Anna Beer's *Patriot or Traitor* provides a far more detailed account of Raleigh's life than I have had space to do, particularly to highlight the quality of his extraordinary poetry and writing. Cyril Falls, in his *Mountjoy – Elizabethan General,* first published in 1955, provides a comprehensive account of his subject's military achievements, even if he is less assured on his life at court and relationship with the Devereux family. Finally, Sir Clements R. Markham's remarkable *Sir Francis Vere* reads as if it were written yesterday, but the narrative dates from 1878. It is based on Francis's personal account of his various campaigns, providing maps of each action to encompass the war in the Low Countries in extraordinary detail. Perhaps inevitably, their various accounts of the Island Expedition to the Azores conflict with each other, largely

Preface

because of the embellishment given to original sources by their individual narrators.

I am greatly indebted to Claire Hopkins at Pen & Sword for all her support, and to Karyn Burnham who has edited and improved the narrative. I would also like to thank Liz who remains incredulous that I should write books, but then wonders how else I would be able to occupy my time.

Robert Stedall
October 2021

1. Devereux Family Tree (sourced from www.stirnet.com)

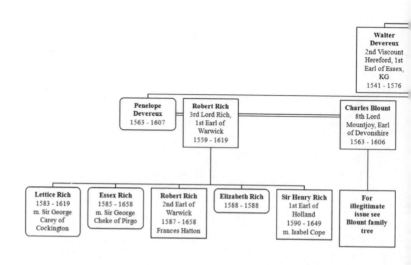

	William Bourchier 1st Earl of Ewe - 1420

Walter Devereux 2nd Viscount Hereford, 1st Earl of Essex, KG 1541 - 1576

Penelope Devereux 1563 - 1607 — **Robert Rich** 3rd Lord Rich, 1st Earl of Warwick 1559 - 1619 — **Charles Blount** 8th Lord Mountjoy, Earl of Devonshire 1563 - 1606

Lettice Rich 1583 - 1619 m. Sir George Carey of Cockington

Essex Rich 1585 - 1658 m. Sir George Cheke of Pirgo

Robert Rich 2nd Earl of Warwick 1587 - 1658 Frances Hatton

Elizabeth Rich 1588 - 1588

Sir Henry Rich 1st Earl of Holland 1590 - 1649 m. Isabel Cope

For illegitimate issue see Blount family tree

Family Trees

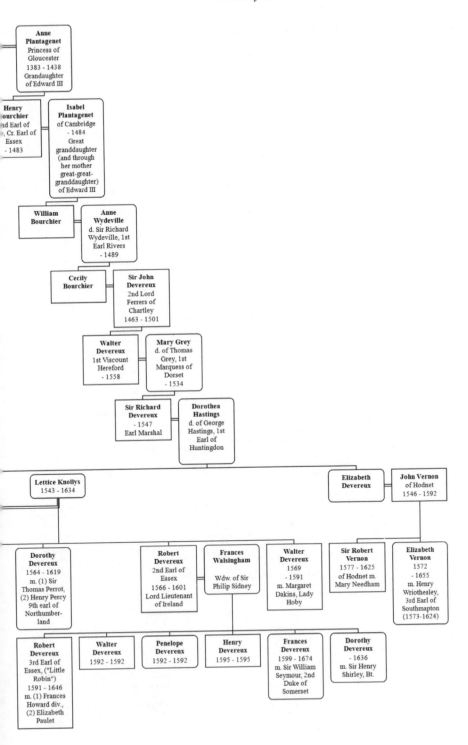

Anne Plantagenet Princess of Gloucester 1383 - 1438 Grandaughter of Edward III

Henry ¦ourchier ¦nd Earl of ¦, Cr. Earl of Essex ¦ - 1483

Isabel Plantagenet of Cambridge - 1484 Great granddaughter (and through her mother great-great-granddaughter) of Edward III

William Bourchier

Anne Wydeville d. Sir Richard Wydeville, 1st Earl Rivers - 1489

Cecily Bourchier

Sir John Devereux 2nd Lord Ferrers of Chartley 1463 - 1501

Walter Devereux 1st Viscount Hereford - 1558

Mary Grey d. of Thomas Grey, 1st Marquess of Dorset - 1534

Sir Richard Devereux - 1547 Earl Marshal

Dorothea Hastings d. of George Hastings, 1st Earl of Huntingdon

Lettice Knollys 1543 - 1634

Elizabeth Devereux

John Vernon of Hodnet 1546 - 1592

Dorothy Devereux 1564 - 1619 m. (1) Sir Thomas Perrot, (2) Henry Percy 9th earl of Northumber-land

Robert Devereux 2nd Earl of Essex 1566 - 1601 Lord Lieutenant of Ireland

Frances Walsingham Wdw. of Sir Philip Sidney

Walter Devereux 1569 - 1591 m. Margaret Dakins, Lady Hoby

Sir Robert Vernon 1577 - 1625 of Hodnet m. Mary Needham

Elizabeth Vernon 1572 - 1655 m. Henry Wriothesley, 3rd Earl of Southmapton (1573-1624)

Robert Devereux 3rd Earl of Essex, ("Little Robin") 1591 - 1646 m. (1) Frances Howard div., (2) Elizabeth Paulet

Walter Devereux 1592 - 1592

Penelope Devereux 1592 - 1592

Henry Devereux 1595 - 1595

Frances Devereux 1599 - 1674 m. Sir William Seymour, 2nd Duke of Somerset

Dorothy Devereux - 1636 m. Sir Henry Shirley, Bt.

2. Blount Family Tree (sourced from www.stirnet.com)

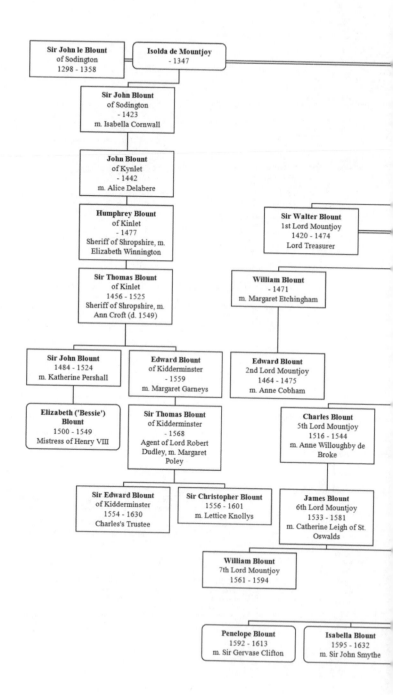

Family Trees

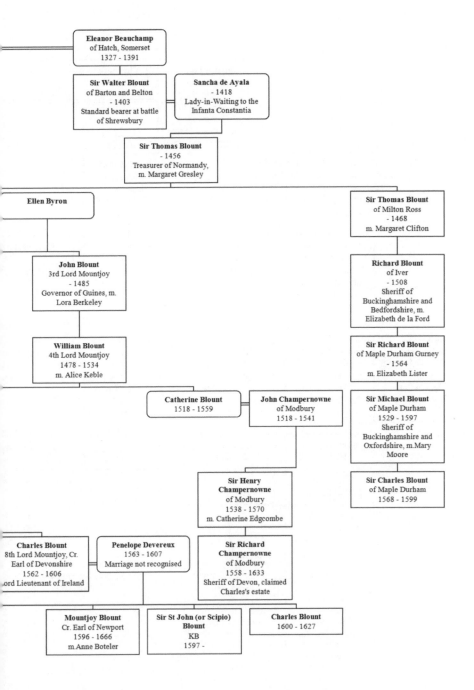

Eleanor Beauchamp
of Hatch, Somerset
1327 - 1391

Sir Walter Blount
of Barton and Belton
- 1403
Standard bearer at battle
of Shrewsbury

Sancha de Ayala
- 1418
Lady-in-Waiting to the
Infanta Constantia

Sir Thomas Blount
- 1456
Treasurer of Normandy,
m. Margaret Gresley

Ellen Byron

Sir Thomas Blount
of Milton Ross
- 1468
m. Margaret Clifton

John Blount
3rd Lord Mountjoy
- 1485
Governor of Guines, m.
Lora Berkeley

Richard Blount
of Iver
- 1508
Sheriff of
Buckinghamshire and
Bedfordshire, m.
Elizabeth de la Ford

William Blount
4th Lord Mountjoy
1478 - 1534
m. Alice Keble

Sir Richard Blount
of Maple Durham Gurney
- 1564
m. Elizabeth Lister

Catherine Blount
1518 - 1559

John Champernowne
of Modbury
1518 - 1541

Sir Michael Blount
of Maple Durham
1529 - 1597
Sheriff of
Buckinghamshire and
Oxfordshire, m.Mary
Moore

**Sir Henry
Champernowne**
of Modbury
1538 - 1570
m. Catherine Edgcombe

Sir Charles Blount
of Maple Durham
1568 - 1599

Charles Blount
8th Lord Mountjoy, Cr.
Earl of Devonshire
1562 - 1606
ord Lieutenant of Ireland

Penelope Devereux
1563 - 1607
Marriage not recognised

**Sir Richard
Champernowne**
of Modbury
1558 - 1633
Sheriff of Devon, claimed
Charles's estate

Mountjoy Blount
Cr. Earl of Newport
1596 - 1666
m.Anne Boteler

**Sir St John (or Scipio)
Blount**
KB
1597 -

Charles Blount
1600 - 1627

3. Howard Family Connections (sourced from www.stirnet.com)

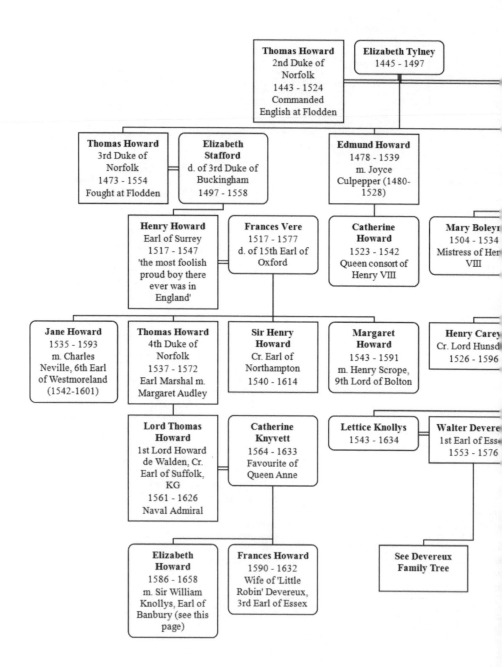

Family Trees

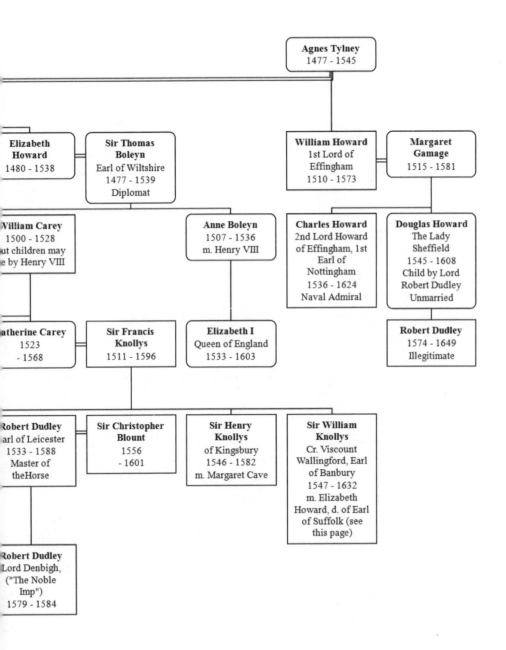

4. Grey family connections (sourced from www.stirnet.com)

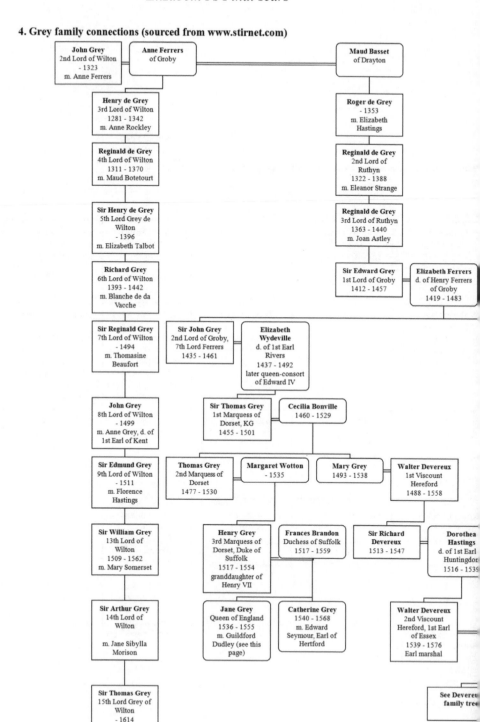

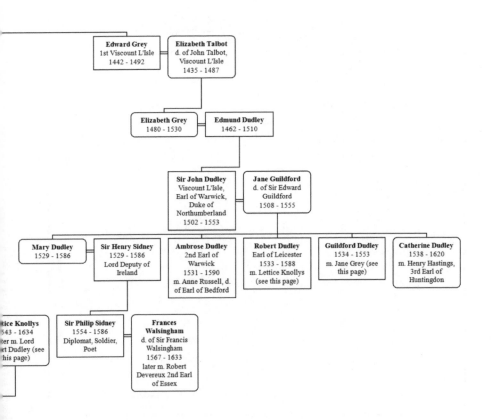

Edward Grey
1st Viscount L'Isle
1442 - 1492

Elizabeth Talbot
d. of John Talbot,
Viscount L'Isle
1435 - 1487

Elizabeth Grey
1480 - 1530

Edmund Dudley
1462 - 1510

Sir John Dudley
Viscount L'Isle,
Earl of Warwick,
Duke of
Northumberland
1502 - 1553

Jane Guildford
d. of Sir Edward
Guildford
1508 - 1555

Mary Dudley
1529 - 1586

Sir Henry Sidney
1529 - 1586
Lord Deputy of
Ireland

Ambrose Dudley
2nd Earl of
Warwick
1531 - 1590
m. Anne Russell, d.
of Earl of Bedford

Robert Dudley
Earl of Leicester
1533 - 1588
m. Lettice Knollys
(see this page)

Guildford Dudley
1534 - 1553
m. Jane Grey (see
this page)

Catherine Dudley
1538 - 1620
m. Henry Hastings,
3rd Earl of
Huntingdon

tice Knollys
543 - 1634
ter m. Lord
rt Dudley (see
his page)

Sir Philip Sidney
1554 - 1586
Diplomat, Soldier,
Poet

Frances
Walsingham
d. of Sir Francis
Walsingham
1567 - 1633
later m. Robert
Devereux 2nd Earl
of Essex

The Low Countries

THE
AZORES
ISLANDS

Corvo

Flores

Graciosa

São Jorge

Terceira

Faial

ANGRA

HORTA

Pico

São Miguel

PONTA DELGADA   VILLA FRANCA

Santa Maria

100 miles

The Azores

Ireland

Introduction

This book stands on its own, but can be read as a sequel to *Elizabeth I's Secret Lover* covering the period from the death of Elizabeth's great 'favourite' Lord Robert Dudley, Earl of Leicester in 1588 until the early part of the reign of James I.

Having taken the heart-wrenching decision in about 1566 not to marry Leicester, Elizabeth's romance with him fizzled out and he began to 'play away', anxious to provide an heir for the titles and wealth he had amassed as the perquisites of his long-running romance with an infatuated queen. If Elizabeth could not marry her 'Sweet Robin', the love of her life, then she would not marry at all. She parried all her government's increasingly desperate efforts to cajole her into a political marriage with a Continental suitor to provide a Tudor heir. Instead, she became obsessed with the company of beautiful men, twenty or even thirty years her junior, showering them with the resources to enable them to appear in all their finery and positioning them to do her bidding.

Elizabeth strung her 'favourites' along in a refined game of courtly love, in which they played out a role as suitors using chivalrous verses larded with classical metaphor to extol her virtues. They were expected to display all the courtly graces, dancing to reveal the full extent of their elegant legs expensively attired in silk stockings. It was 'an eroticised political relationship'.[1] She relished her ability to maintain their attention by playing one off against another with half-promises of preferment either financial or political. This wrinkled and latterly gap-toothed old harridan, plastered with make-up, moulded them into the sixteenth-century equivalent of box office superstars to provide her with the sensations of eternal youth. In this uncomfortable existence, they were expected to exude sexuality in a court which she professed to believe was a haven of morality. When dressed in all their finery, they would sport conveniently detachable jewel-encrusted codpieces (from 'cod', a bag or scrotum), padded out to enhance the wearer's virility. For those young ladies surrounding the queen, a favourite's presence often became irresistible, sometimes leading to children being conceived out of wedlock. Such indiscretion shocked the aging queen, not only because it tarnished the court's good name with visiting ambassadors, but it meant that her favourites were failing to provide her with their undivided, albeit platonic, attention.

It was not just sexuality. Favourites had to be able to play cards, to show dexterity on the tennis court and demonstrate all the martial arts and equestrian skills, both in the tiltyard and riding out beside their queen to show her off to good effect. To underline their bravery, they flocked to take their chance as soldiers of fortune or on naval expeditions to demonstrate their military prowess. The enemy was always the Spanish, whether in the Low Countries, the Americas, Ireland, France or in mid-Atlantic, where there might be a heavily laden Spanish treasure ship to plunder. Very often, favouritism gained for them commands ahead of career soldiers, who naturally felt demeaned to be placed under the supervision of inexperienced courtiers. Perhaps because favourites very often took the lead, it was not always a glorious period of English military success, despite their efforts to embellish the facts. Essex saw military glory as his route to political advancement. There is no doubt that his derring-do gained him great popularity, but Elizabeth saw this as a threat to her own appeal.

Favourites needed to watch their backs. While away from court, they often faced criticism from competing interests. With Elizabeth reluctant to provide finance for projects to the extent they believed necessary, there were ample opportunities for politicians and rivals to backbite. This caused the absent favourites to be left short of the resources they considered necessary, even forcing them to subsidise expeditions from their own pockets. With few expeditions achieving their planned objectives, favourites became adept at providing reports with a spin, which embellished their achievements, while glossing over shortcomings. There was no need for the truth to interfere with a good story. Very often it is difficult to unravel an expedition's real achievements from the differing commentaries provided by competing interests.

Favourites also used poetry. Writing poetry was not just the language of romance and chivalry, but the means of disseminating political satire without blatantly divulging one's true intent. Leicester's coterie of brilliant poets had included Philip Sidney and Edmund Spencer, as 'fluent propagandists' on political issues to impart subtle criticism of rivals.

Even after Leicester's romance with Elizabeth had run its course, he remained the person from whom she would seek advice. William Cecil, by then Lord Burghley, always turned to him to help resolve her indecision when faced with a difficult course of action, such as the execution of Mary Queen of Scots. Although she took solace in the company of Sir Christopher Hatton, he was Leicester's friend and protégé and was careful never to overstep the mark with his mentor. By the time of Leicester's death in 1588, Hatton was aged 48, leaving him well over the hill in comparison to younger men now clamouring for preferment. He wisely stepped back from the limelight to adopt a political persona that led to his appointment as Lord Chancellor. There was now an extended period, during which Sir Walter Raleigh gained Elizabeth's heart. Despite being exceptionally handsome, an accomplished poet and writer and a great adventurer, he was not of aristocratic stock and found knives being poised to assist his fall from grace, so that he was eventually playing second fiddle to rival claims for her affection. Nevertheless, he amassed a great fortune from royal perquisites which he enhanced by investment in privateering ventures.

It had generally been assumed that Philip Sidney would step into his uncle's shoes as Elizabeth's favourite, allowing Leicester to continue to provide political and military advice in the background. Sidney was the paragon of his age, an accomplished diplomat despite his youth, even being offered the hand of two European princesses, which he was obliged by Elizabeth to turn down. His undoubted bravery was demonstrated with tour de force performances bedecked in blue armour in the lists and his heroic military exploits in the Low Countries. He was the most brilliant poet of the Elizabethan age providing his *Arcadia* for his sister Mary, Countess of Pembroke, as a commentary on contemporary life, and *Astrophil and Stella,* his sonnet sequence revealing his unrequited passion for Penelope Devereux, soon to be betrothed and married to Robert, 3rd Lord Rich. Sadly, Philip lacked the manly beauty, which was the prerequisite for a favourite, as his face was blemished by smallpox contracted in his youth. He also crossed Elizabeth by criticising her proposed marriage to Francis de Valois, Duke of Anjou, and she found his burgeoning success as a diplomat on the Continent to be threatening.

While many favourites, just as Leicester had done, aspired to political greatness, they found their route to supreme authority blocked by Burghley, the great architect of Elizabeth's Protestant Reformation and government. Burghley was thirteen years older than Elizabeth, academically brilliant and politically unchallengeable. He had been sufficiently pragmatic to survive the reign of Mary I and had shown all his devious skills to remain unsullied as Elizabeth's leading minister. He employed a comprehensive spy network to unearth scandals to embarrass his less careful opponents. In foreign policy, his objective was to position England as the balance of power in Europe and to needle the Spanish at every opportunity to divert their focus away from an invasion of England in the guise of a Counter-Reformation. Defeating the Spanish was never a realistic option and would have allowed France to re-emerge as an alternative threat.

Burghley never missed an opportunity to feather his own nest, receiving commissions for granting government contracts of all kinds, as was the norm for a head of state. By taking under-the-table handouts from merchants seeking the right to provision expeditions, he was able to control and even limit the successes of overly ambitious favourites. While Elizabeth provided her favourites with generous perquisites, such as monopolies on the distribution of sweet wines, the real plums, such as the role of lord treasurer or master of the wards went to Burghley. The role of master of the wards was particularly lucrative, providing the income of every deceased aristocrat during the minority of his offspring in return for arranging his children's upbringing and education. This allowed him to sell wardships to the highest bidder, reserving those with the most glittering prospects for marriage with his own children. On reaching his or her majority, a ward who found the marriage arrangements made on their behalf to be distasteful, was heavily fined to enable the commitment to be unwound. It was through these means that Burghley was able to lavish a fortune on his magnificent homes at Burghley and Theobalds.

The younger favourites held Burghley, the elder statesman, in great awe and, as his ward, Essex lived for a period in his home. Their respect for him did not extend to his younger son, Robert, who succeeded his father in all his political roles and perquisites to their detriment. Robert was a little runt of a man and a hunchback who, at 5ft tall, was known affectionately by Elizabeth as her 'pigmy' or her 'little elf'. The favourites had little time for him, but he remained close to the queen, whispering in her ear at their shortcomings. While they risked their lives on military and pioneering expeditions, Robert adopted his father's policy of keeping them starved of resources.

Despite all the shortcomings, there were two great heroes of this period of the Anglo-Spanish wars. One was the career soldier, Sir Francis Vere, who was everything but a favourite, and the other was Mountjoy, who most certainly was. Elizabeth described Vere as 'entombing the spirit of a brave soldier in the corpse of a less sightly courtier', with scars as the legacy of his exploits commanding both Dutch and English forces in the Low Countries.[2] His achievement was to curtail Spanish efforts to subsume the Dutch under their rule. Mountjoy undertook the task of defeating the Irish rebels supported by Spanish allies after Essex's ignominious failure (in what was an untenable situation for him). Both Vere and Mountjoy showed a military genius that marks them out as two of the great commanders of English history.

By the time of James's accession to the English throne, Essex had already been executed as a traitor following his ill-fated rebellion against Robert Cecil's government. Both Mountjoy and Raleigh fell foul of James. Mountjoy's misdemeanour was attempting to marry Penelope after her divorce from Rich, but they both died soon after. Raleigh's fall from grace was more drawn out. He spent fifteen years in the Tower, for his perceived involvement in the Main Plot in 1604. He then embarked on one more failed treasure hunting expedition to the Orinoco before his ultimate execution. (His tragic end is briefly outlined in Endnote 5.)

Background

Walter Raleigh (Ralegh or Rawley) was born in about 1554, the fifth son of a family of minor gentry in Devon. His family had connections with many other similar Devon families such as Carew, Hawkins, Gilbert, Drake and Champernowne. His only close relative among those who served Elizabeth was his aunt Kat Champernowne, who had been Elizabeth's governess and senior lady-in-waiting until her death in 1565. This meant that their times in Elizabeth's service did not overlap. Raleigh was destined to become a soldier, and in 1569, while in his mid-teens, was at Moncontour near Poitiers, fighting for the Huguenots, possibly as a mercenary in the service of Lodowick of Nassau, but he seems to have returned to England after the Peace of St Germain in August 1570. After landing at Margate, he set out for Richmond Palace in the hope of sighting Elizabeth, who was planning Christmas there after her recent excommunication by the Pope.

In 1572, Raleigh matriculated at Oriel College Oxford and was later at the Middle Temple but became better known there for his satirical verse than his proficiency in the law. In 1576, he wrote a verse in praise of George Gascoyne's *The Steel Glass,* with words redolent of his own future:

> For whoso reaps renown above the rest,
> With heaps of hate shall surely be oppressed.[1]

In 1577, while living in Islington, he faced three charges for brawling. This was a long step from Richmond Palace. In 1579, Captain Raleigh, commanding one hundred men levied in London, joined the Irish Lord Deputy, Arthur, 14th Lord Grey de Wilton, who had raised a total of 2,500 additional troops to combat the so-called Desmond rebellions. These had broken out in Munster and had the support of an expeditionary force from Catholic Europe.[2] Grey needed to act decisively. He attempted a naval blockade to prevent the arrival of further rebel reinforcements. In October 1580, Italian and Spanish mercenaries, who were occupying a small earthen fort at Smerwick, were forced into surrender after a naval bombardment from Admiral William Wynter. Although the mercenaries were spared, Raleigh and his men had the gruesome task of executing any Irish prisoners with them and laying nearby crops to waste. As Edmund Spencer was to explain, famine was the surest and quickest way to pacify the Irish.

While in Ireland, Raleigh had a further role. He provided Francis Walsingham, Elizabeth's Secretary of State, with intelligence in letters which demonstrate his growing confidence. He even offered political advice on the shortcomings of Thomas Butler, 10th Earl of Ormonde, who had been appointed President of Munster. He did not miss the opportunity to hint at his own heroism as a selfless leader and called for a further one hundred men to deal with the rebels' guerrilla tactics. He needed these men to replace those of his 'miserable creatures' who had become too unwell to serve, despite needing to be paid and fed. It made a good story, but his later letters advocated protection for the Irish rather than forcing them into subservience, a philosophy which he would follow in his later colonial ventures.

Despite being able to show his military qualities, Raleigh hated being stuck in an Irish backwater. On 26 August 1581, he wrote to Leicester from Lismore to offer his services. When he returned to England in December with dispatches, his good looks caught the queen's attention. She wanted this eloquent and handsome 6ft-tall man in personal attendance, and he remained at court as an esquire to the body. His Devon brogue soon gained him the nickname of 'Water'. He may have been of humble origin, but he was 'sharp and enterprising' – and 'impossibly handsome'.[3] His 1585 portrait miniature by Nicholas Hilliard, shows a somewhat effeminised 'dark-haired man, with flowers in his hair', a neat beard and upturned moustache.[4] In 1589, he was 'framed in so just a proportion and so seemly an order, as there was nothing in him that a man might well wish to have been added or altered'.[5] Such physical attractiveness was hard to dislike.[6]

*****

Francis Vere, born in about 1560, was the second son of the fourth son of John de Vere, 15th Earl of Oxford, a title granted by Matilda to his ancestor, Aubrey de Vere, in 1141. The 15th Earl, who died in 1540, was Henry VIII's Great Chamberlain, and was succeeded in this role by his son, also John, the 16th Earl. When the 16th Earl died in 1562, he left, among many other legacies, £20 to his infant nephew Francis. His son, Edward, was aged only 12 when he succeeded his father as the 17th Earl, becoming a ward of the queen. She immediately sent him to live in Cecil's household. In 1571, Cecil arranged his marriage to his daughter, Anne. To Cecil's great disappointment, he dissipated much of his patrimony to the detriment of the whole Vere family.

Geoffrey Vere, Francis's father, occupied Crepping Hall in Essex, but, following his early death, his widow, Elizabeth Hardekyn, moved with her four sons and a daughter to Kirby Hall, which was held on long lease from the Oxford estates surrounding the Castle of Hedingham. With John, Geoffrey's eldest son, inheriting the lease over Kirby Hall, he continued in occupation with his mother, while his younger brothers, Francis, Robert and Horace, were destined for military careers. This did not deter Cecil from trying to recover control of the lease on his wayward son-in-law's behalf.

In 1585, with Leicester planning his expedition to the Low Countries, Francis, who was now 25, volunteered to joined him. He was about six years younger than Sidney and Raleigh, and older than Charles Blount by four years and Essex by six years. Being without employment on arrival in the Low Countries, he travelled to the Hague to meet up with Peregrine Bertie, 11th Lord Willoughby of Eresby, who was married to his cousin, Mary de Vere, Oxford's sister.

Willoughby, who had been sent on a diplomatic mission to Frederick II in Denmark, was now detailed to take command of a troop of horse. He was a man of standing, being a son of Katherine Willoughby, Baroness of Eresby in her own right (and the widow of Henry VIII's soulmate (and brother-in-law), Charles Brandon, Duke of Suffolk). When he was granted the government of the important fortified town of Bergen-op-Zoom, he took Francis into his service. Very soon, Francis was involved in a successful skirmishing attack on a Spanish supply train and then in the capture of Axel, in which Willoughby's small force joined with Sidney and the young Count Maurice of Nassau. Francis later acquitted himself well in the action at Zutphen, in which Sidney was mortally wounded and, in the autumn of 1586, was promoted captain with command of a company.

*****

The Devereux family probably took its name from Évreux in Normandy and 'was of high rank'.[7] Following the Norman Conquest, it was granted lands in Wales and created a power base at Carmarthen Castle, building 'up vast estates in the Marches, Wales and Staffordshire ... wielding almost royal power over all who lived on their lands'.[8] The heads of the family enjoyed a long list of titles and could 'boast the largest private army in the country'. Penelope Devereux's great-great-grandmother, Cecily Bourchier, who had married, Sir John Devereux, 2nd Lord Ferrers of Chartley, was a great-granddaughter of Edward III three times over. (See Family Tree Chart 1) Penelope's great-grandmother, Mary Grey, was a granddaughter of Elizabeth Wydeville, Edward IV's consort, by her first husband, the 7th Lord Grey of Groby, and an aunt of the 'ill-fated' Lady Jane Grey. (See Family Tree Chart 4) Her grandmother, Dorothea Hastings, was a daughter of George, 1st Earl of Huntingdon, whose wife, Anne, was the daughter of Henry de Stafford, Duke of Buckingham, another descendant of Edward III and of John of Gaunt. Penelope's mother, Lettice Knollys, was a daughter of Catherine Carey and a granddaughter of Mary Boleyn. It is sometimes claimed that Catherine Carey, who, through the Boleyns, was a cousin of Queen Elizabeth, was sired by Henry VIII, making Penelope his great-granddaughter. Certainly, Catherine was appointed by Henry to the prestigious role of maid-of-honour to Anne of Cleves, a role generally reserved for a royal princess. Further evidence for Catherine being Henry's daughter is set out in Endnote 1.

It was in the service of Anne of Cleves that Catherine met Francis Knollys, a young courtier 'who had been sent to escort the new queen on her inauspicious entry into London'.[9] By the standards of Penelope's other ancestors, the Knollys family was 'new' gentry, only rising to prominence during the reign of Henry VII. Nevertheless, they had acquired Grey's Court near Henley-on-Thames as their principal residence in addition to other properties including the leases of Wallingford Castle and Ewelme Park. Francis continued the family's upwardly mobile trajectory as a successful courtier and politician, gaining a knighthood from Henry VIII, becoming Master of the Horse for Edward VI and later a trusted servant of Elizabeth at Hatfield. By 1553, after thirteen years of marriage, he and Katherine already had ten children, of which Lettice was their second and their eldest daughter.

Being a leading Protestant, Knollys removed himself to the Continent during Mary Tudor's reign, and Catherine later brought five of their children to join him in Frankfurt. Elizabeth sorely missed her, writing from Hatfield and signing herself: 'Cor Rotto [Broken-hearted]'.[10] In a singular demonstration of affection for Catherine's daughter, Lettice, who enjoyed a striking resemblance to her, Elizabeth retained her as a member of her household at Hatfield from the age of 10 until she was 16, despite her parents' absence abroad.

In 1558, on becoming queen, Elizabeth reappointed 'the old flock of Hatfield' into positions as her advisers and attendants. Knollys and Catherine rushed back from Frankfurt to take up salaried posts as part of this inner circle. Knollys became Vice Chamberlain, Catherine was made a Lady of the Bedchamber, while Lettice was appointed a maid of the privy chamber.[11] Their return to royal service did not end Catherine's pregnancies, and her youngest child, Dudley, who did not survive infancy, was only born on 9 May 1562, after Lettice was already married to Walter Devereux, Viscount Hereford.

The Devereux family had enjoyed an illustrious past. Walter's grandfather, also Walter, had been created Viscount Hereford in 1550 after proving himself both politically and militarily. Having married Mary Grey, a sister of the 2nd Marquess of Dorset, he became a confirmed Puritan and a close ally of John Dudley, Duke of Northumberland, the Protector for Edward VI, after supporting him in the coup which ousted the king's uncle, Edward Seymour, Duke of Somerset. Nevertheless, after backing Protector Northumberland's efforts to promote Jane Grey as queen, he spent a period in the Tower of London until his eventual release to his home at Chartley, in Staffordshire. This did not prevent his grandson, Walter, who succeeded as 2nd Viscount Hereford in 1558 when he was 19, being described by Camden as 'a very excellent man' in whom 'honesty of manners strived with nobility of birth'.[12]

Walter (the 2nd Viscount) was determined to make his name with the new queen who much admired his good looks and fashionable clothing. On arrival at court, he was soon captivated by Lettice, and they were married in the late summer of 1560 when he was about to be 21 and she still 16. This was a marriage that suited them both. Lettice was now a viscountess, married into the old nobility. With her mother remaining a Lady of the Bedchamber, Walter had forged a link with a respected family, whose close access to the Crown should advance his career.[13]

Walter's efforts to ingratiate himself with the queen brought the couple into great favour. As soon as they were married, he was given the honour to act as proxy for a foreign dignitary receiving the Order of the Garter. He then escorted Lettice on a tour of his extensive estates. She was presented to the people of Carmarthen before moving on to the old Bishop's Palace at Llanfydd (anglicised by the family to Lamphey) in Pembrokeshire, occupied by Walter's widowed mother. This had been acquired by his father in 1546. It was a luxurious residence, housing a fine library, and set in fields and woodlands which ran down to the sea. Walter had spent much of his childhood there and Lettice's children seem to have holidayed there each summer, despite the long hike on difficult roads from Chartley. It was to become a much-loved retreat for their eldest son, Robert, when not at court.

From Lamphey, Walter and Lettice detoured through the Devereux estates in Herefordshire and Staffordshire where Lettice visited their moated manor house at Chartley, which was to become their principal home when not in London. In was at Chartley that Penelope, their eldest child, was born into their devoutly Protestant household in January 1563. With Walter being there for the birth, he sent a proxy on 12 January to attend Parliament in his place. The birth did not signal Lettice's retirement from court, and she remained on the list of the queen's unpaid gentlewomen.[14] Elizabeth became Penelope's godmother, sending a handsome gilt cup with a cover as a christening gift. Other children soon arrived. Dorothy was born in September of the following year and Robert on 10 November 1565. Another son, Francis, died young and Walter (known as Wat) was born on 31 October 1569.

Penelope and Dorothy received a careful Protestant education under the Cambridge scholar, Mathias Holmes, who remained until Penelope was 15. Lettice also acted as a foster mother for Gabriel de Lorges, Count of Montgomery, a French Huguenot of Scottish extraction, whose father's shattered lance had, in 1559, caused the death of Henry II in a jousting accident. Although he was absolved of this crime, he was later executed for his militantly Huguenot stance against Catholicism. It was the young Montgomery's influence which fostered Robert's later affiliation with French Huguenot interests. It also resulted in Penelope speaking 'perfect' French, in addition to fluency in Spanish and speaking some Italian. She also learned to play 'the flute "divinely", dance gracefully and sing like a nightingale'.[15]

*****

The Blount (or Le Blount) family (pronounced Blunt) was also closely associated with the Norman and Plantagenet kings, both as soldiers and courtiers. Robert Le Blount from Picardy, born in 1029, had commanded William the Conqueror's fleet during its landing in England, holding the title of 'Dux Navium Militarium', and he was granted estates at Ixworth in Suffolk by a grateful king. In 1367, Sir Walter Blount (his seven times great-grandson) accompanied Edward, the Black Prince, and his brother John of Gaunt, Duke of Lancaster, as their standard bearer, in their support for Peter, King of Castile and Leon ('Pedro the Cruel') to regain his throne. As a part of this Anglo-Spanish alliance, it was agreed that Peter's daughter, the Infanta Constantia, should marry John of Gaunt. This resulted in him succeeding his father-in-law as King of Castile. When she arrived in England to become his bride, she was accompanied by her lady-in-waiting, Sancha de Ayala, daughter of Don Diego Gomez de Toledo, whose wife was connected to the royal houses of Aragon and Leon. In 1373, Sir Walter was granted the honour of marrying her. Perhaps benefiting from a handsome dowry, he was able, in the following year, to acquire estates in Derbyshire from his elder brother. Tragically, he was killed in 1403 at the Battle of Shrewsbury after donning Henry IV's apparel to confuse those seeking out the king. Having found the story in Holinshed's Chronicles, Shakespeare wrote:

> A gallant knight he was, his name was Blunt,
> Semblably furnished like the King himself.[16]

Sir Walter's third son by Sancha, Sir Thomas Blount, who was appointed Treasurer of Normandy, had an eldest son, another Walter, who fought with the victorious Yorkists at Towton. Having been appointed Lord Treasurer, he was created the Lord Mountjoy (the surname of his paternal great-grandfather's first wife's Anglo-Norman family) and a Knight of the Garter. (See Family Tree Chart 2) Edward IV granted him the forfeited lands of the Earl of Devonshire, who had been killed while on the losing side at Towton. By the time of Walter's death in 1474, he had developed a taste for letters, a quality inherited by his charismatic grandson, William, the 4th Lord Mountjoy. In 1496, when William was 18 and already married, he travelled to Paris where he developed a warm attachment to Erasmus, then aged 29, who was on a lecture tour to promulgate humanist doctrine. William invited Erasmus to England to stay with his father-in-law, Sir William Saye, at Bedwell in Hertfordshire. 'You would have seen me in Italy', wrote Erasmus in 1499, 'if Lord Mountjoy had not carried me with him into England. Whither would I not follow so humane, so kind, so amiable a young man!' He was captivated, writing to his friend Faustus:

> Your friend Erasmus gets on well in England. He can make a show in the hunting field. He is a fair horseman … The English girls are divinely pretty – soft, pleasant, gentle and charming as the Muses. They have one custom which cannot be too much admired. They kiss you when you arrive; they kiss you when you go away; and they kiss you when you return. Go where you will, it is all kisses, and, my dear Faustus, if you had once tasted how soft and fragrant those lips are, you would wish to spend your life here.[17]

William, who was about thirteen years older than Prince Henry (later Henry VIII), became his 'page' to act as his tutor. This enabled Erasmus to meet both the prince and Thomas More. He also travelled to Oxford, delighting in its academic environment. When Henry became king, William invited Erasmus back to England. On his arrival in October 1509, William, who was not wealthy, provided Erasmus with a liberal pension of £60. He was involved in a further display of extravagance in 1520 by accompanying the king to the Field of the Cloth of Gold.[18] William's son Charles, who inherited as 5th Lord Mountjoy on his father's death in 1534, maintained his father's friendship with Erasmus, who, in about 1531, dedicated a new edition of his *Adages* to the young man. John Leland also dedicated poems to him, implying that Charles sponsored their publication.

Despite the Mountjoys' glittering history of royal service, albeit with some decline in family fortune, Charles's son James, who inherited as 6th Lord Mountjoy in 1544, was not of similar calibre. He lived at Canford Manor in Dorset and was appointed Lord Lieutenant of the county on Elizabeth's accession to the throne in 1558. Despite his marriage to the wealthy Catherine, daughter and heir of Sir Thomas Leigh of St Oswalds, he was continuously short of money. Between 1561 and 1563, he disposed of estates in Yorkshire, Lincolnshire and St Giles-in-the-Fields, received as part of his wife's dowry. In 1562 and

1563, he sold lands at Burnham-on-Crouch in Essex (by coincidence, to Richard, 1st Lord Rich of Leighs). His financial difficulties stemmed from investments in mining ventures, ever hopeful of finding English sources of metals to relieve dependence on overseas' supplies. He was not alone; both Leicester and Cecil had some success with investments in such projects. Unfortunately, the 6th Lord seems to have been a victim of a scam, while attempting to free himself from debt. He turned to alchemy, believing that gold manufacture out of base metals would restore his fortune.

If this were not bad enough, James's eldest son, William, who inherited as the 7th Lord in 1581, was involved in costly lawsuits with the Huntingdons over land ownership and, in 1594, his death was 'hastened ... by debauchery' while still unmarried.[19] This left his younger brother Charles, born in 1563, to inherit a 'decayed and impoverished house' as the 8th Lord Mountjoy. On sitting for his portrait, he was depicted with a trowel in his hand, with the inscription: '*Ad reaedificandam antiquam domum*'. [For the restoration of an ancient house.][20] '[He] was ambitious, eager for place and power; his house was ancient and honourable; it was also in sore need of restoration.'[21] To emulate 'his great-grandfather and grandfather, the friends of Erasmus, ... he had to earn what they had enjoyed'.[22]

PART I

THE DUDLEYS AND
THE DEVEREUXES

Chapter 1

Leicester's flirtation with Lettice Knollys, 1565–76

While Lettice enjoyed an apparently idyllic life as a young wife moving between her various Devereux homes, her mentor Queen Elizabeth, ten years the elder, was juggling Continental marriage suits proposed by her government in their single-minded effort to protect English independence. Elizabeth was most reluctant. She had become besotted with her childhood friend, Lord Robert Dudley, who had done much to support her during the reign of her sister, Mary Tudor. On her accession, Dudley was appointed to the important role of Master of the Horse, requiring him to spend much of his time in her presence. In 1552 he had married Amy Robsart of a well-to-do, but not ennobled, Norfolk family; she had failed to provide him with children and was suffering from breast cancer. It seemed that Elizabeth and Dudley were only waiting for her death to enable them to marry.

Although they remained on socially cordial terms, Cecil (later to become Lord Burghley), now Elizabeth's Secretary of State, strongly opposed Robert's marriage to Elizabeth. In part, this was because he wanted her to make a dynastic marriage to provide England with security, but he also considered Robert to be politically unreliable. Elizabeth did not help his standing with her ministers by encouraging him to undermine any marriage suits they were proposing. Nevertheless, it was also recognised that England's independence as a Protestant nation depended on her providing an heir.

When Amy Robsart died after falling down a couple of steps and breaking her neck at her lodging at Abingdon in Oxfordshire, Cecil had only to ask if she were pushed. With Robert having been with the court at Windsor, there is no serious modern suggestion that he was implicated in her death, and he was completely exonerated at the independent inquest.

Nevertheless, Elizabeth concluded that she would greatly damage her standing by marrying him. Furthermore, Cecil persuaded her to test his integrity. When she asked Robert to seek Spanish support for their marriage in return for them backing a Counter-Reformation, Robert unashamedly made the proposal to the Spanish ambassador. With Robert being a leading Puritan, she now knew that his ambitions were greater than his religious and political conscience. Although she realised that she could never marry him, it did not end their close association. It is probable that their affair became intimate, and he continued to believe that she could be won round – and would have been, if she had become pregnant.

It was perhaps a coincidence that in 1565 Robert began paying attention to Lettice. She was already pregnant by her husband, but Robert was persuaded by Sir Nicholas Throckmorton that the flirtation would make Elizabeth jealous and would force her hand. There is no doubt that Robert was attracted to Lettice, but it was, at that time, no more than harmless banter. There is no mention of her facing any royal hostility, and Robert seems to have struck up a friendship with her husband, becoming a godfather to their son, who was born in the following November and named Robert in his honour. Such was Elizabeth's reconciliation with Robert that at the end of 1565 she granted him the use of Durham Place, previously occupied by the Spanish ambassador, and appointed him to the lucrative role of Chancellor of the County Palatine of Chester.

When Robert gave Elizabeth an ultimatum to make up her mind by Christmas, she promised to let him know by Candlemas (2 February 1566). The ambassadors were certain that 'Cecil … would resist to the last the marriage of the queen with [Robert], under the patronage of France or Spain'.[1] Candlemas came and went without any word of marriage and, although his suit eventually petered out, he remained the love of her life.

In 1569, following the death of her wealthy husband, John, 2nd Lord Sheffield, Robert began a secret affair with Douglas Howard, the daughter of the 1st Lord Howard of Effingham. To protect his standing with Elizabeth, Robert managed to keep this relationship hidden and always made clear to Douglas that he could not marry her. In August 1574, Douglas gave birth to a son, Robert, who took the surname Sheffield; after the child's birth, however, it seems that Robert's relationship with Douglas had run its course. He conveniently arranged for her to marry

3

Sir Edward Stafford, who became the English ambassador in Paris and provided her with a pension of £700 per annum. By now, his roving eye had again chanced upon Lettice.

By this time, Walter had begun to make his name as a soldier, having arranged a muster of men at arms around Chartley to secure the imprisonment of Mary Queen of Scots at Tutbury. This followed the launch of a Catholic rebellion in the North led by the Earls of Northumberland and Westmoreland with the prospect of Spanish support. Their plan was to release Mary and to arrange her marriage to the Duke of Norfolk. A further motive was an attempt by the 'old' nobility to reduce the power of the 'upstart' Cecil. With Cecil having Elizabeth's complete backing, Walter maintained mounted soldiers at Tutbury to deter Mary's escape and escorted her south to the relative security of Coventry. He immediately returned north to challenge the rebels, proving himself a born leader by mustering a further 3,000 men at Lichfield and linking up with Lettice's uncle, Henry Carey, Lord Hunsdon, and her brother, William Knollys, under the overall command of Leicester's brother, Ambrose Dudley, 3rd Earl of Warwick. On Leicester's recommendation, Walter was appointed High Marshal of the Field. Warwick told the privy council: 'I never saw a nobleman in all my life more willing to serve his prince and country.' On 20 December, the rebel leaders fled to Scotland, but Walter's reprisals on their supporters demonstrated a bloodthirsty bent that was to recur when he was later in Ireland. Nearly 800 rebels were executed, leading, in April 1570, to Elizabeth's excommunication by the Pope. In the summer of 1571, to recognise his zeal in service, Walter was created a Knight of the Garter, and Elizabeth confirmed his claim to the earldom of Essex and viscountcy of Bourchier, titles previously held by his Bourchier ancestors.[2] In January 1572, he was one of twenty-five representative peers who sat at Norfolk's treason trial.

Elizabeth's excommunication seemed to threaten further outbreaks of Catholic rebellion, but with her religious tolerance having made her popular, English Catholics generally preferred her as a Protestant English queen to the prospect of a foreign Catholic one. In January 1572, with the French also in fear of Habsburg aggression, they proposed that Elizabeth, who was 39, should marry Francis, Duke of Alençon, the 17-year-old youngest brother of Charles IX. Elizabeth enjoyed the romance of it all, even though he was by repute 'short, puny and pitted with smallpox', marvellously ugly and with a curvature of the spine.[3]

She named him her 'frog', or more politely as 'Monsieur'. Although Leicester initially played along with the match, he was horrified when Elizabeth seemed to take it seriously. Nevertheless, it seemed to be brought to an abrupt end in August when news arrived from Paris of the Guise-inspired Massacre of St Bartholomew, during which many of the leading French Huguenots attending the marriage of Henry of Navarre (later Henry IV) to Margaret de Valois, Alençon's sister, were assassinated. Nevertheless, the suit drifted on. When Charles IX died in 1574, Alençon fell out with his brother Henry, now king of France. Although he remained Catholic, he sided with the Huguenots, forcing the French crown into the very one-sided Edict of Beaulieu. This resulted in him being granted the dukedom of Anjou. Furthermore, his Huguenot affiliation made him far more acceptable as a spouse for Elizabeth.

With the Spanish threat continuing, it was recognised that their most likely bridgehead for an invasion of England was through Catholic Ireland, which remained rebellious. To prove 'his good devotion to employ himself in the service of her Majesty', Walter – now Earl of Essex – approached Elizabeth with a plan to subdue and colonise an area of eastern Ulster dominated by the O'Neills.[4] Elizabeth welcomed any opportunity to plant more settlers but had been reluctant to fund their military protection. In August 1573, having mortgaged his estates to underwrite a borrowing of £10,000 from the Royal Exchequer, Essex set out from Liverpool to occupy an area covering most of County Antrim. Despite this being in direct contravention of the rights of the Ulster clans, Elizabeth funded half his cost of settling 1,000 men. After a stormy crossing in which his ships became scattered, he reached Carrickfergus, but the new arrivals, many of whom were Irish in Essex's pay, were poorly equipped and proved unreliable. In the face of mounting local hostility, many returned to England. Sir William Fitzwilliam, the Lord Deputy, who had not been warned of the expedition in advance, disapproved of the venture and proved uncooperative. When some of Essex's supporting troops threatened to desert for want of better pay, he hanged them and became involved in mindless acts of cruelty in the locality. Far from reproving this, Elizabeth appointed him as Governor of Ulster and praised his 'good services'. He reported to her: 'I will not leave the enterprise as long as I have any foot of land in England unsold.' With his project under great pressure, he needed Council funding for it to continue. In December 1575, he returned home but was unwell and retired to Lamphey to recuperate. He was facing financial ruin with debts of more than £25,000 in addition to the £10,000 borrowed from the Exchequer, and was forced to sell a large part of his English estates.[5]

Essex did not attend Hampton Court for the court's Christmas celebrations, but needed to find the right moment at the end of the festivities to plead with Elizabeth for help. He blamed many of his difficulties on her prevarication over providing financial support. His only way out was to return to Ireland and to make a success of his project. Elizabeth supported this, as he had shown himself to be the kind of ruthless leader that she considered necessary, but Sir Henry Sidney (the father of Sir Philip), recently restored as Lord Lieutenant with increased powers, had no respect for his bloodthirsty treatment of the Irish and lacked confidence in him.

Meanwhile, Lettice continued to attend court. In July 1575, she was present when Elizabeth came with the court to visit Leicester's newly refurbished country estate at Kenilworth. The party lasted eighteen days with every aspect being sumptuous in its extravagance. There were masques specially written for the occasion, music, dancing, water pageants, spectacular food and wines and magnificent fireworks. Lettice came without her husband, who was still in Ireland, and Douglas Sheffield was not there. It is apparent that Lettice was by then enjoying a relationship with Leicester, as at one stage Elizabeth threatened to leave, and it seems that her nose had been put out of joint. If her husband did not already know it, Lettice also attended hunting parties there and stayed at Leicester's London residence, Durham Place, while attending court. This heralded a massive row. The Spanish ambassador, Antonio de Guarás reported: 'As the thing is publicly talked about in the streets, there is no objection to my writing openly about the great enmity which exists between the Earl of Leicester and the Earl of Essex.'[6] The ambassador spiced it up by suggesting that Lettice had produced two children by Leicester while her husband was in Ireland. While this is certainly untrue, it seems that she had not been enjoying domestic harmony with Essex for some time, despite their four handsome children. This made his absence abroad convenient.

It was through Leicester's intercession that Essex was restored to Ireland, receiving what Camden described as 'the empty title of Earl Marshal' of Ireland.[7] Leicester seems to have wanted him kept out of the way while he developed his relationship with Lettice. He pressurised

Sidney, his brother-in-law, to be more effusive in seeking Essex's reappointment.[8] Sidney was suddenly fulsome with praise, describing him as 'so noble and worthy a personage', and 'complete a gentleman'.[9] It took until the following May, 1576, for the terms of Essex's return to Ireland to be agreed. He was granted Farney in County Monaghan and Island Magee in County Antrim to compensate for the loss of estates in England that had had to be sold. He was still unwell and signed a will at Chartley on 14 June, in which he granted handsome dowries of £2,000 each to his daughters Penelope and Dorothy. A few days later he set out for Dublin. It is not clear if Lettice came to Chartley to see him off, but she soon joined Leicester in London and accompanied him north when he went to Buxton to take the waters.

Chapter 2

The 1st Earl of Essex's death and his children's education, 1572–81

While in England, Essex had renewed his acquaintance with Philip Sidney, having always held him in great affection. Even while Philip was still attending Shrewsbury School, Essex had provided him with the gift of a horse. By now, Philip was already a budding diplomat, having spent time on the Continent while Essex was in Ireland. In 1572, he had visited Paris, staying with Sir Francis Walsingham, the English ambassador, during the Massacre of Saint Bartholomew. He later gained considerable prestige while travelling in Protestant Europe, after being taken under the wing of the diplomat Hubert Languet, who was promoting the development of a Protestant league to combat Catholic aggression. Not only did Philip's poetry show that he was cultivated and cultured, but he had diplomatic flair. His father was the Lord Deputy of Ireland and President of the Council of Wales, and he was likely to become the heir to his uncles, the Earl of Warwick and Earl of Leicester. This made him quite the most eligible young Englishman on the Continent.

When Philip returned home in mid-1575 he attended Leicester's great pageant at Kenilworth with his parents, but he was far less well-known in England than on the Continent, where he was already recognised as 'the paragon of the age'.[1] In his absence his elder sister Ambrosia had died, after which Elizabeth had written a most sympathetic letter to the Sidneys offering, if it would suit them, to take their younger daughter Mary, then 14, into a position at court. Her offer was gratefully accepted. She shared all her brother's charm and, within a year, had become betrothed to the widowed 42-year-old Henry Herbert, who had succeeded his father as Earl of Pembroke in 1570. The Sidneys were delighted at this glittering prospect for their 15-year-old daughter, despite having to borrow from their relations to find the required £3,000 dowry.

After setting out back to Ireland, Essex was held up in Holyhead while his ship waited nearly a month, until 26 July 1576, for a favourable easterly wind. It is probable that Philip, who wanted to visit his father, travelled with him. Sir Henry, who was campaigning in Galway, returned to Dublin to greet them after being instructed by Walsingham, and probably by Leicester, to remain on good terms with Essex. He then returned with Philip to Galway to search out rebels, but without great success.

While father and son were away from Dublin, Essex had been enjoying a drink with his page and a third person, when all three were stricken with dysentery. Believing he had been poisoned, Essex decided to return to Lamphey to recuperate, but was too unwell to travel and realised that he was dying. On 22 September, at the age of 36 and only two months after arriving back in Ireland, he succumbed.[2] Although Sir Henry ordered a post-mortem, Essex's secretary confirmed that there was no evidence of foul play. Two days before dying, Essex managed to dictate a letter to Elizabeth bidding her farewell and asking her 'to be a mother unto' his children, but with no similar request to support his widow. Elizabeth always took great interest in the children's welfare and politely offered her condolences to Lettice but provided her with no practical help.[3] Essex also wrote to Sir Henry with a message for Philip:

> Tell him I send him nothing, but I wish him well, and so well, that if God do move both their hearts, I wish that he might match with my daughter. I call him son; he is so wise, so virtuous, and godly; and if he go on in the course he hath begun, he will be as famous and worthy a gentleman as England ever bred.[4]

On receiving it, Philip, 'with all the speed he could make, went to him but found him dead before his coming in the castle at Dublin'.[5]

Essex's will also confirmed his wish that Penelope should marry Philip, despite their nine-year age difference. Although his secretary, Edward Waterhouse, wrote to confirm this, Sir Henry was unenthusiastic, writing privately to Leicester, that he 'could not brook' Essex. He reported that a better man might have been more successful in Ulster and urged the queen to promote 'the introduction of collonys of English and other loyal subjects, whereby a perpetuall inhabitation

9

would have ensued to be a recompense as well of that which was spent' and to build up the 'strength of the country against all forreyne invasion'. He argued that this was 'no subject's enterprise, a prince's purse and power must do it'.[6] Sir Henry was also concerned that the depleted state of the Devereux finances would make Penelope's promised dowry of £2,000 difficult to meet.[7]

Sir Henry had always been impoverished, so it was important that Philip's marriage should bring financial benefit. If Philip were to follow his father's diplomatic career, his credentials needed to be developed on another grand tour on the Continent. Setting him up in marriage to Penelope was beyond his means, and the couple had had few opportunities to meet, with Philip having gone abroad aged 18 in 1572 when Penelope was 9. She had probably not attended Leicester's pageant at Kenilworth as a 12-year-old, and, having been away from London completing her education, they are unlikely to have met until 1581, when she was already betrothed to Robert Rich.

With Essex's body having been brought back to England, he was buried in late November 1576 near the Devereux estate at St Peter's, Carmarthen. His son, the 11-year-old Robert, now 2nd Earl of Essex, was not considered sufficiently robust to undertake the arduous journey from Chartley to attend the funeral. Significantly, Lettice was not made an executrix of her husband's will, despite her having managed his estates while he was in Ireland, and was not left a jointure over Chartley, their principal home.[8] After some argument, she was forced to move out.[9] Nevertheless, she carried on a determined correspondence to maintain her entitlement to a liferent over one-third of the estate and took legal action to gain an extra £60 per annum.[10] Despite the estates being heavily encumbered, she persuaded Burghley, as a trustee, to grant her a life interest in Benington on the borders of Hertfordshire and Essex.[11] Whatever her husband may have come to think about his errant spouse, he did 'bequeath a quantity of jewels, plate and properties "to my right well beloved wife"'.[12]

The will's principal concern was for the care of the Devereux children. Robert, who inherited Chartley, was placed under the supervision of Burghley and Thomas Radcliffe, 3rd Earl of Sussex. His father had expressed a wish for him to join Burghley's household and marry his daughter Anne (although this never happened). His move to live there did not happen immediately. With Lettice attending court over the Christmas season in company with Leicester, the young Essex remained at Chartley with his siblings, but they all visited her in London after the New Year. He then adhered to his father's will by living partly at Cecil House in London and partly at Theobalds in Hertfordshire. While there, he will have met Robert Cecil, Burghley's second son, who was two years older but sadly deformed and a hunchback. It is thought that Essex's ill-concealed contempt caused lasting antagonism.

Burghley soon noted Essex's aptitude for study, reporting 'that at the age of eleven he could "express his mind in Latin and French as well as in English [and was] very courteous and modest in his bearing, disposed rather to hear than to answer, greatly given to learning"'.[13] In early 1577, he attended Trinity College, Cambridge, under the supervision of its Master, the Reformist John Whitgift, who was to become Archbishop of Canterbury in 1583.[14] That spring, he wrote to thank Burghley: 'for your lordship's care in placing me here in the university where, for your lordship's sake, I have been very well entertained by the university and the town'.[15] It was usual for the civic authorities of Cambridge to play host to young noblemen. (Even at the age of 12, he seems to have courted popularity.)[16] He did not forget his studies, so that 'his accounts for 1577 include charges for his meals, a standing desk, his ink and quills, and a selection of books'.[17]

The 1st Earl's will called for his younger children to be sent for their further 'maintenance' to the care of the Huntingdons at King's Manor, York, where Huntingdon was living as President of the Council of the North. Catherine Huntingdon, who was a sister to both Leicester and Sidney's wife Mary, had no offspring, but, as ardent Puritans, she and her husband were much respected for their devotion in overseeing the education of children of noble families. Although young Wat seems to have moved to York in early 1577, Penelope and Dorothy remained for a time with Lettice. With Chartley no longer available to them, they moved with a small band of servants to her father at Grey's Court, where the two girls settled down to their lessons with Mathias Holmes. They also made an extended visit to Sir George Digby, who had children of a similar age at Coleshill. Sir George had been a ward of Sir Francis Knollys and was a prominent Dudley supporter. Perhaps Coleshill was chosen as it was only ten miles from Kenilworth, where Lettice made several visits for buck hunting, sometimes with Penelope and the Digbys.

11

By October 1577, Lettice and her daughters were in Hackney, where Essex called on them from Cambridge. His good beginnings there seem to have given way to overspending and absenting himself without leave. On arrival in the capital, he was greeted in the City of London with a handsome gift of £500. He then came with his mother and sisters to Whitehall Palace to attend the 1577 Christmas revels at court, for which he needed better clothing. He was soon in possession of a new 'broad riding hat' and 'five pairs of shoes'.[18] 'Her Majestie showed him great countenance.'[19] In his fluster, on seeing the queen for the first time, he doffed his hat, but failed to put it back on his head, even when requested by her to do so and, to her amusement, refused her offer to kiss him. When the festivities moved to Hampton Court, the Devereux children made a second visit, again paying their respects to the queen. Such extravagance did nothing to conserve their father's depleted estate.

At the end of the court's new year festivities, Essex returned to Cambridge, while Penelope and Dorothy moved to join Wat with the Huntingdons. Suddenly their 'daily life revolved round morning and evening family prayers'.[20] Lady Huntingdon trained them in every aspect of their expected future role in managing a large household. This was very mundane after the merry-go-round with their mother, and Penelope seems to have rebelled against a regime designed to develop her inner piety.

During the following winter, when Essex sought to join the Huntingdons to spend Christmas with his siblings, he was required by both Burghley and Leicester to spend the festive period at Cambridge as he had been away from his studies for too long. To his credit, he seems to have settled back once again to his four-year degree course to provide him with a grounding in 'learning, piety (however assumed), grace and wit', which would later stand him in good stead with Elizabeth.[21] He proved an able scholar and in July 1581, at the age of 15, he graduated and received his MA.

Chapter 3

Philip Sidney – the moulding of a renaissance diplomat, 1576–82

Philip Sidney spent most of 1576 at court, at the end of which he became a royal cupbearer but was never established as one of Elizabeth's favourites. He had no opportunity during this time to meet Penelope, who was undertaking her studies away from London, generally at Grey's Court. He fulfilled several domestic engagements, attended the baptism as godfather to Elizabeth, Lady Russell's daughter, at Westminster Abbey, gave advice to his brother Robert, who had just matriculated from Oxford, and offered his diplomatic services to James VI in Scotland.

By 1577, the 22-year-old Philip was being encouraged by Languet to return to the Continent to continue his diplomatic training and perhaps to see some military action. In that February, Elizabeth chose him, despite his youth, to travel to Austria to offer condolences following the death of Maximilian, the Holy Roman Emperor, and to offer a Garter knighthood to Rudolf, the new Emperor, notwithstanding the mistrust for Rudolf's Catholic bias. On arrival, Philip took the opportunity to meet up with his old university friend, Edmund Campion, now a Jesuit, who was teaching at the University at Prague. His probable purpose was to seek advice on how to approach Rudolf, but associating with a known Jesuit was considered unwise. He rejoined Languet and again discussed the prospect of forming a Protestant league. It was even suggested that he might make a suitable spouse for a Protestant European princess, probably Ursula, the sister of the Elector Palatine. Philip backpedalled, not wanting to commit Elizabeth to a European alliance without her full approval. He was then asked to act as Leicester's proxy at the baptism of Elisabeth, daughter of William 'the silent' of Orange, for whom Leicester had been invited to become godfather. Such was Philip's success on this visit that William proposed that Philip should marry Mary of Nassau, his 20-year-old daughter by an earlier marriage. Having two royal marriage proposals eclipsed any further thoughts of him espousing the juvenile Penelope.

On Philip's return to England in June he went straight to Greenwich, where he received great praise for his briefing to Elizabeth and senior Councillors on the advantages of a Protestant league. Nevertheless, Elizabeth was nervous of promoting Sidney and Dudley ambitions and feared that a European marriage for Philip could lead to English military involvement on the Continent. On 21 April, during his absence, his beloved sister Mary had married Pembroke and now lived in great style between Pembroke's London residence at Baynard's Castle in the City, and his idyllic country seat at Wilton in Wiltshire. With Philip feeling the need to absent himself from court, he took advantage of Mary's hospitality during August and September for an extended visit to her rural and wooded retreat at Wilton and was there again in December. The Wiltshire countryside provided him with an ideal environment in which to write poetry.

By August 1577, both Leicester and Walsingham were in support of the formation of a European Protestant league as Philip envisaged, but it needed to be of sufficient strength to compete against the combined power of France, Spain and the Holy Roman Empire. They disagreed with Burghley, who had worked assiduously to avoid conflict by maintaining England as the balance of power between Catholic nations to deter them from combining against Protestantism. The ever-cautious Elizabeth always supported Burghley, but they both realised that defeat of the Dutch in the Low Countries would place England next on the Spanish agenda. Despite their differences, Leicester and Cecil respected each other and remained on cordial terms socially, not least because they were both utterly loyal to Elizabeth.

Through Philip's introduction, Leicester established a friendship with Duke John Casimir, the second son of the Elector Palatine. Casimir had raised a mercenary army ready to march into Flanders to challenge the Spanish. In April 1578, he requested that Philip should come to negotiate, in the hope that an English force would be sent to his support. Although Elizabeth prevaricated, she recognised the imperative of preventing a Dutch defeat. Nevertheless, Philip's impending departure to the Continent greatly concerned Sir Henry in Ireland, as he needed his son's negotiating skills to defend his imposition of a 'cess' tax, which was making him extremely unpopular, even though it was his only means of paying troops to maintain control. With Elizabeth being inundated with complaints from Ireland, she recalled Sir Henry, despite the more general plaudits for his governance coming from every side.

On 5 June, Philip was called to court by the Council to receive Elizabeth's instructions for his embassy to the Continent, and Howard of Effingham was required to ready six ships to carry 'three standards' of infantry as an escort. It seemed inevitable that Elizabeth would be pressurised into sending him, but she again prevaricated as she did not want to be seen to be making an overt challenge against the Spanish. She eventually ordered Philip to set out in August, but again lost her nerve and asked him to meet Casimir privately, although not as her representative. Even now, she changed her mind. She had heard rumours that Casimir was claiming to have English support for an invasion of Flanders. As her whole purpose was to disguise England's involvement, she instructed Philip to tell Casimir that he would not receive English support. Leicester was furious and persuaded her that, if Philip were sent only as her messenger, his credibility would be destroyed after his initial encouragement for the formation of a Protestant league.

With the Spanish stepping up their aggression against the Dutch, Anjou expressed an interest in becoming the Low Countries' protector. In late 1577, he blundered into the conflict as their champion. With Casimir's support having been stalled, William had little option but to accept Anjou's offer by signing a treaty with him in August. Elizabeth needed to establish whether he was acting personally or with French Government support. She considered a French annexation of the Low Countries to be just as detrimental to English interests as one by Spain. When Anjou admitted that he was acting without Henry III's support, he was suddenly far less dangerous. In July 1578, Elizabeth offered him clandestine backing and rekindled their romance. The Council was split, with Leicester warning that the prospect of a French king of England would destroy Elizabeth's popularity, while Burghley and Sussex supported Anjou's suit, probably as a means of reining in Leicester. Philip was another vehement opponent of the marriage but was neutralised by being sent to Paris to facilitate the arrival of Anjou's envoy, Jean de Simier, who appeared on 5 January 1579 with instructions from Anjou to negotiate its terms.

During this time, Casimir had been stuck in Flanders with 12,000 mercenary troops which he could not afford to pay. With Leicester's and Philip's encouragement, he made a last-ditch effort to gain English support and arrived on 22 January with a retinue of twenty-five advisers including

15

Languet. With Philip back from Paris, he was commissioned by Elizabeth to join Leicester in welcoming Casimir. Having escorted him for an audience at Whitehall, he was lodged at Somerset House, and the City of London gave him the full VIP treatment, including a chain and plate worth 2,000 crowns. He visited Leicester at Wanstead and was entertained by Sir Henry, now back from Ireland, on Philip's behalf. Although Elizabeth appointed him as a Knight of the Garter, she had no interest in reaching an agreement with him while engrossed in 'lapping up the attentions' of Simier.[1] Casimir's effort was to no avail, and he returned to Ghent without English support. This forced Languet to transfer his services to William of Orange.

In retrospect, we can see that Elizabeth's objective with Anjou was to take her courtship to the brink so that English support for him was seen to be serious, but without ever quite committing herself. She rather enjoyed Leicester's discomfiture. The Council remained deeply divided. Anjou's efforts in the Low Countries had already become a 'series of embarrassing fiascos'.[2] Many of his troops deserted or defected and he withdrew to France, from where he decided to come to England to see Elizabeth himself. Leicester did his best to undermine Simier, and according to William Camden, it was Simier who, in June, told Elizabeth of his secret marriage to Lettice. (See Chapter 4) This suggests that Anjou was being pursued out of jealousy, but it is now generally believed that she had become aware of the marriage before his arrival.

On 17 August, Elizabeth greeted Anjou at Greenwich and genuinely enjoyed his company, despite the Leicester faction's strong opposition to him. Philip even threatened to duel against Cecil's arrogant son-in-law, Oxford, who had befriended her 'Frog'. With Philip already in trouble for this high-profile offence, he attended a dinner with the Leicester faction at Baynard's Castle, Pembroke's London home. With Leicester being forced into silence after his marriage to Lettice, the dinner guests agreed that only Philip had the 'silver tongue' necessary to explain the shortcomings of the Anjou marriage to Elizabeth, although there is no doubt that several guests had a hand in his letter. It was couched in terms of loyal affection and concern for her safety but warned her that Anjou's fickle nature would increase the Protestant/Catholic divide, causing her the contempt of her subjects who had hitherto loved her. It would bring no advantage and would end any prospect of forming a Protestant league. The letter was widely circulated and Languet considered Philip brave for speaking out, fearing that it would make him an enemy of Anjou, who was still trying to assist the Dutch.

With William of Orange writing to Elizabeth to defend Philip's stance, he does not seem to have suffered unduly, and remained at court over the winter of 1579/80. His New Year gift to her of a gold cup was accepted with good grace. Nevertheless, he spent much of 1580 at Wilton, working on his most famous poem, the *Arcadia*, dedicated to his sister. Despite its pastoral and romantic style, it is a highly political text, venting his frustrations and provoking questions without always providing answers.[3] With its content so sensitive (although at this distance scholars dispute its meaning), it was not widely circulated, but Wilton was now the gathering point for those opposing the Anjou marriage.

After spending months in the wilderness, Philip believed he should return to London. At New Year 1581, he presented Elizabeth with a small gold whip set with diamonds and seed pearls in token of his penitence and took part in a spectacular chivalric tournament in the tiltyard on 22 January, where he acted out the role of the Blue Knight to reinforce his submissive persona. He did not spend much time at court as he was sitting as member of Parliament for Shrewsbury.

Meanwhile, on 23 January, Anjou accepted the sovereignty of the Low Countries and reinvigorated his suit to marry Elizabeth. Plans were soon being made for his return to England at the head of a new French mission, and Whitehall Palace was sumptuously redecorated. On his appearance on 17 April, there was feasting, dancing and entertainment. Leicester and Pembroke were most pointedly detailed to greet the royal party and Philip participated in another chivalric joust.

Despite having greeted Anjou in great style, Elizabeth needed an elegant means of wriggling out of any commitment to marriage. Eventually she loaned him £60,000 (which she paid to the States-General), so that he could return to the Low Countries in support of the Dutch. On 1 February 1582, a fleet of fourteen vessels escorted him to Holland with an entourage of 600 hand-picked men, including Leicester and Philip. On arrival, the English exerted pressure on the Dutch to install him as Duke of Brabant, but William of Orange was unimpressed. In January 1583 Anjou left for France, completely discredited after trying to wrest control of Antwerp from his Flemish allies. When he died on 10 June 1584, England had lost its much-needed French alliance with which to combat the Spanish, but Elizabeth quickly cultivated solidarity with Henry III and his heir, the Huguenot Henry of Navarre, soon to become Henry IV.

Chapter 4

Lettice's relationship with Leicester, 1577–79

Following her husband's death in Ireland, Lettice's clandestine relationship with Leicester blossomed. Being overweight, Leicester made regular visits to the spa at Buxton, hoping also to cure intermittent bouts of malaria. Lettice did not go there with him, as the cure required men to remain chaste from women. Nevertheless, she often stayed at Kenilworth for buck-hunting. Being firmly established as lovers, they deemed it wise to remain away from the limelight at court and, by the second half of 1577, they were contemplating marriage. In early 1578 she became pregnant, and they entered into a secret betrothal or marriage ceremony at Kenilworth, although its details are unknown. He immediately acquired Wanstead, a property in Essex, to provide her with a home outside London. In May, Elizabeth decided to visit it while Leicester was at Buxton. Although she fretted at his absence, he reported to Walsingham that he would not be able to greet her as he was finding the waters beneficial. With Lettice wanting to keep out of sight, Philip was called away from negotiating a diplomatic mission to the Low Countries to act as Elizabeth's host, writing a masque, *The Lady of the May,* to be performed in her honour. This was an allegory on her dilemma over sending troops to support the Dutch.

With Elizabeth (officially at least) unaware of Leicester's relationship with Lettice, Sir Francis Knollys was determined that he should make an honest woman of his daughter. He insisted on a full marriage ceremony before witnesses. This took place on 21 September, and was conducted secretly at Wanstead by Robert's chaplain, Humphrey Tyndall. To provide irrefutable evidence, Knollys insisted on written depositions being provided by the witnesses under oath to confirm their attendance. Tyndall even had to confirm details of his ordination. Two days later,

Elizabeth visited Wanstead for a second time. Although she met Lettice, by then all trace of the celebration had disappeared. Leicester dared not risk any loss of standing and continued to insist that Elizabeth should not be told.

It is not clear when Elizabeth first learned of the marriage. Lettice had certainly been in favour with her at the New Year of 1579 as she received a gilt cup and cover from the queen, but by mid-1579 Elizabeth had become desolate at Leicester's involvement in a passionate marriage with her pregnant kinswoman. Lettice was now seen as a 'she-wolf' and was never forgiven. Although she had been pregnant at the two marriage ceremonies she must have suffered a miscarriage, as no child survived. Nevertheless, on 6 June 1581, she was safely delivered of a son, Robert, known as 'the Noble Imp', and the witness statements of the marriage confirmed the child's legitimacy. (See Endnote 2) The Noble Imp's arrival severely dented Philip's hopes of inheritance. At a stroke, he was no longer either Leicester's or Warwick's principal heir.

Most tragically, the Noble Imp fell suddenly ill at Wanstead in July 1584 and died within a fortnight. Robert and Lettice were distraught. With Leicester now aged 52 and Lettice 41, they had no realistic expectation of more children. Their attention was now focused on his illegitimate son, Robert; on Lettice's eldest son, Essex; and on her two beautiful daughters, Penelope and Dorothy. Although Philip now resumed his position as heir to the Earldoms of Leicester and Warwick, he remained under a cloud with Elizabeth for criticising her romance with Anjou, and it was the more glamourous Essex, who was cast by Leicester in the role of favourite to enable him to maintain his influence at court.

Chapter 5

Penelope's arrival at court and marriage to Lord Rich, 1580–90

Despite Elizabeth's hatred of Lettice, she never took her animosity out on her children, treating them with 'extraordinary tolerance and partiality'. In late 1580, she offered her godchild, Penelope, who was just 18, a post in the royal household.[1] Lady Huntingdon escorted her south and presented her to Elizabeth at Whitehall Palace on 30 January 1581. Although Dorothy probably came south with them, she did not attend court and was housed with Lettice (who was then four months pregnant with the Noble Imp) at Leicester's house in the Strand.

Penelope's arrival at court caused a sensation. Her 'beauty, charm and grace' would become legendary. 'Her impact on a court already thronged with celebrities – sophisticated, talented, rich and beautiful people – was extraordinary. Her large dark eyes and golden hair, her sweet voice and lute playing, her dancing, languages, and her good nature captivated them.'[2] She wanted to enjoy herself and was soon introduced to gambling, playing cards and board games, which had been forbidden in the Puritan piety of York. Although court etiquette was formal, she was no longer constrained.

Philip may not have met the blossoming Penelope initially, and she will have missed his participation as the Blue Knight in the tournament eight days beforehand. Nevertheless, he was soon recording her rosy cheeks as of 'fair claret'.[3] He was not alone. William Byrd wrote:

> Her beauty great had diverse gods enchanted,
> Among the which Love was the first transformed.
> (From *Weeping full sore*)[4]

John Dowland wrote dances for her and Charles Tessier, the French lutenist, dedicated his first book of songs to her.

20

Flirtation and courtly love were the order of the day. It did not always stop there. One of the queen's maids of honour, Anne Vavasour, gave birth to a son. It turned out that Oxford (who was married to Burghley's daughter) was the father, but when he tried to leave the country, he was arrested and thrown in the Tower. Penelope was granted Anne's position as a maid of honour and from now on was at Elizabeth's beck and call in what was the most eligible marriage market in the land. Although Lettice could not join her daughter at court to ensure her well-being (and her pregnancy would have made her appearance problematical), Leicester paid Penelope great attention, providing handsomely decorated rooms for her when she was able to join Lettice and Dorothy at Leicester House, Wanstead or even at Benington. It was at this time that the double portrait of Penelope and Dorothy, hanging at Longleat, was painted.

Within a month of Penelope's arrival, the Huntingdons were giving consideration to her marriage. Despite her late father's hope that she might marry Philip, their age disparity and Sir Henry's opposition did not bode well. With Catherine Huntingdon and Mary Sidney being Leicester's siblings, it is probable that it was a family decision not to encourage Philip, whose future inheritance was now threatened by the imminent arrival of Lettice's baby. He hardly knew Penelope, and both would need wealthy spouses. Nevertheless, they now met at court and on family occasions.

Meanwhile, Catherine Huntingdon heard rumours that the eminently wealthy Robert, 2nd Lord Rich of Leighs, was on his deathbed (he died on 27 February). He was a leading landowner in Essex and his eligible son, also Robert, was just three years older than Penelope. He was recognised as a stalwart Puritan with an income of £5,000 per annum (three times that of the Devereux estates). The Rich family had come to the fore as successful lawyers. Richard, 1st Lord Rich, who had been Solicitor General and later Lord Chancellor under Henry VIII, had a reputation for corruption and greed, enhancing his fortune from the sale of monastery lands. Most famously, he had brought about Sir Thomas More's execution by providing evidence which confirmed More's denial of royal supremacy over the church. The Devereux family may have been aware that the 2nd Lord Rich had taken troops to support the 1st Earl of Essex in Ireland in 1573, but had been one of the first to desert him as winter set in.[5] Showing no concern about their unsavoury background, Lady Huntingdon wrote to her husband at York, and, on 10 March 1581, he solicited Burghley and Walsingham to gain the queen's approval for Penelope to marry the 3rd Lord Rich. The family undoubtedly approved but struggled to raise the £2,000 dowry out of the Devereux estates. It was Knollys who saved the day by advancing £500.

The couple probably became betrothed in April, and Lady Huntingdon agreed to a November wedding date in London. Elizabeth confirmed her approval, not least because she enjoyed hunting in the deer parks at Leighs and found Rich's lack of royal ancestry unthreatening. At some point, probably after Penelope's betrothal, Philip realised what he had let slip through his fingers. He had undoubtedly become better acquainted with her and was very soon writing *Astrophil and Stella* about his unrequited love for her. This is a sequence of 108 sonnets about the love of Astrophil [Philip – the star-lover] for Stella [Penelope – the star], although 'Stella' also becomes a synonym for immortal beauty.[6] Philip's compositions span a considerable period, some sonnets being written soon after her betrothal and some relating to events occurring in the following year, when she became 'Perfection's heir'.[7] In sonnet 37, Astrophil states:

> Towards Aurora's Court a Nymph doth dwell,
> Rich in all beauties which man's eye can see:
> Beauties so far from reach of worlds, that we
> Abase her praise, saying she doth excel
> Rich in the treasure of deserv'd renown,
> Rich in the riches of a royal heart,
> Rich in those gifts which give th'eternal crown:
> Who though most rich in these and every part,
> Which make the patents of true worldly bliss,
> Hath no misfortune, but that Rich she is.[8]

The reference to her 'royal heart' is yet another hint of her being a great-granddaughter of Henry VIII. (See Endnote 1) Sonnet 41 records the encouragement he gained when she watched him at the lists:

> Stella look'd on, and from her heavenly face
> Sent forth the beams, which made so fair my race.

Nevertheless, Sonnet 86 shows that she rebuffed his advances when they were alone together, gently pushing his hand away in deference to her honour:

> There his hands, in their speech, fain
> Would have made Love's language plain;
> But her hands, his hands repelling,
> Gave repulse all grace excelling.

Being betrothed, Stella explains:

> Trust me, when I thee deny,
> In myself the smart I try;
> Tyrant honour, doth thus use me,
> Stella's self might not refuse thee.

Astrophil and Stella ends touchingly on this moral note, but when Penelope married Rich in November 1581, Philip could not bring himself to attend. He took his leave of the queen and left London for a month. No one was more excited about Penelope's marriage to Rich than the 16-year-old Essex, who appeared from Cambridge. He was growing up and was now 'athletic, vigorous and flamboyant'.[9] He spent over £40 on two suits of clothes for the occasion, and kitted out his servants with new Devereux badges, showing an extravagance that did not please his mentors.

There is no hint of Philip's relationship with Penelope being anything other than unrequited. Had there been more to it, we can be sure that the gossips at court would have known. His poem remained hidden until 1591, five years after his death. In 1581, he may have represented a courtly episode in Penelope's life, but if she felt any romance, it was stifled. Two years later, he wed Walsingham's daughter, Frances, in another arranged marriage. Although Frances was beautiful and caring, she was perhaps second best. At least Walsingham was able to settle Philip's not inconsiderable debts. They initially enraged the queen by failing to consult her in advance. She considered it demeaning for Philip to marry the daughter of her spymaster, of whose shadowy methods she disapproved. Nevertheless, she ultimately became godmother to their daughter, who was named Elizabeth in her honour.

Although Robert Rich was an extremely good catch financially, he had little in common with Penelope. He was a poor linguist with little interest in literature and lacked her sophistication and charm. For Penelope, 'The glorious party was over.'[10] As a stalwart Puritan, he disapproved of church ritual, play-going, dancing, gambling and music. As the dominant landowner around Leighs Priory, he caused great friction with Bishop Aylmer of London when he determinedly promoted Puritan ministers to livings in his giving.[11] He also promoted nonconformists to the seats under his control in Parliament. Penelope was not attracted by Puritanism or by his chaplain, the religious radical Ezekiel Culverwell, appointed to Leighs in 1586, who disapproved of her 'frivolous' interests, until temporarily suspended by Aylmer.[12]

Marriage had its compensations. It would always be more bearable for Penelope so long as she continued to attend court. It was here that she had sparkled after her dreary existence at York. Court life also suited Rich, anxious to display his 'trophy wife'.[13] Nevertheless, she could no longer be a maid of honour and would miss the flirting and flattery. She was there for the Accession Day tilt on 17 November 1581 in which Philip again took part and did not want to miss the celebrations on Anjou's visit to court Elizabeth. She remained close to her siblings, using her presence at court to help to restore Devereux standing. Rich cultivated a warm relationship with Essex, visiting him at Cambridge in July, soon after he had graduated, and provided him with a gelding. The brothers-in-law remained on friendly terms until Essex's death in 1601.

Another great compensation was the beauty of Leighs, a former Augustinian priory, which had been brick-faced by the 1st Lord to make it into 'a worldly paradise, a heaven on earth'.[14] Its great hall had been the nave of the former priory church. 'Tall fantastical ornate chimneys' had been added and the gardens contained 'summer houses, streams, a bowling green, banqueting house and walled private garden'.[15] One visitor commented: 'My Lord, you had need make sure of heaven, or else when you die you'll be a great loser.'[16] It was an ideal location to offer hospitality to foreign dignitaries. Rich entertained the Polish prince Count Laski in April 1583 after his arrival at Colchester and then escorted him to London.[17]

Leighs was also a wonderful family home and a place for Penelope to dote on her children as they started to arrive. Her eldest two were daughters, Lettice (known as Lucy), named after her grandmother in defiance of Elizabeth's hostility, and Essex, born in about 1583 and 1585 respectively. They were followed by Robert, born in 1587. The arrival of a male heir caused great rejoicing, and Penelope was soon back at court with her husband to greet those returning from the Low Countries. With only three children in the first five years of her marriage, it can be implied that she kept Rich at a distance when she could, perhaps to enjoy court life, but she then seemed to produce children on a regular annual basis. After Robert's birth, she was soon pregnant again, and Elizabeth agreed to stand as godmother to her daughter, born in 1588 and named Elizabeth, although, very sadly, the child soon died. After Henry's birth in early August 1590, Rich helped in her attempts to improve her brother's standing with Elizabeth. In return, Essex approached Henry of Navarre, newly enthroned as Henry IV of France, to become a godfather for the new arrival.[18]

Penelope's mother was now conveniently only thirty miles away at Wanstead and remained wholly supportive after her marriage to Leicester. Penelope also enjoyed the company of trusted staff members, particularly Jeanne de Saint-Martin, her Huguenot lady-in-waiting, with whom she conversed in French. She wrote to her:

> Since I first knew you, I have borne you such affection that neither time nor absence will ever blot out the recollection of your great merits. ... [There is] no fault in the world that I hate more than inconstancy and I assure you that you will never find it in me but on the contrary a friendship unchangeable and perfect that will last all my life.[19]

In 1582, Leicester employed Jean Hotman, an eminent Huguenot scholar, as his private secretary. He had arrived in England to study at Oxford, and when Penelope visited Leicester House and Wanstead, Jean was able to meet Jeanne. To her great delight, they married in October.

Despite all the charms of her marital home, Penelope's 'role as a country hostess, supporting her husband as a local landowner, was never going to content her. However much she loved her children, managing a large household and hunting in the local forests, her ambitions for her family ranged wider than Lord Rich's Essex estates.'[20] Nevertheless, there is no contemporary evidence to suggest that she was desperately unhappy from the outset, as later suggested by Charles Blount. On the contrary, *Astrophil and Stella* implies that she rejected Philip's pass before her marriage. Although Rich later gained a reputation for being ineffective, he was wealthy and titled and his shortcomings were not initially apparent.

Although Penelope later became besotted with Charles Blount, there can be absolutely no doubt that her first five children were born in what seems to have been a harmonious, if not passionate, relationship with Rich, and Henry, her youngest child by him, was not born until 1590. In 1618, after Rich's creation as Earl of Warwick, the title passed to Robert, his eldest son, and later to Henry's descendants. There can have been no contemporary question about Henry's paternity.

Chapter 6

Dorothy Devereux, 1583–94

Although there is no evidence that Penelope's relationship with Rich was initially unhappy, her sister Dorothy was determined to avoid being forced into an arranged marriage. Within three months of Penelope's wedding, Leicester seemed to be regretting that he had not done more to promote his nephew, Philip. He drew up a new will offering Philip and Dorothy £2,000 if 'such love and liking might be betwixt them as might bring a marriage'.[1] This was never likely to succeed. With the Noble Imp still living, Philip was not Leicester's heir and Dorothy was not attracted to her sister's rather earnest cast off. In 1583, Leicester tried once more to find his beautiful stepdaughter a suitable spouse. By then he was working with Walsingham to foster a closer relationship with James VI of Scotland as Elizabeth's potential heir. Without consulting Dorothy, he proposed to James that by marrying Dorothy and giving an assurance not to change his religion, 'they would have him declared by the judges to be the heir to the Crown of England'.[2]

Dorothy had other ideas, and Leicester banished her to live away from court at the home of Sir Henry Cock in Broxbourne in Hertfordshire. She was determined to marry the 30-year-old Sir Thomas Perrot, another dashing participant in the lists at court and a neighbour of the Devereux estates in South Wales. Although his father, Sir John Perrot, had served as Lord Deputy in Ireland, he was impoverished and was considered beneath her in rank. Nevertheless, in July 1583 she eloped with him, and it seems that Penelope connived in her plan and failed to warn Lettice, who strongly disapproved of Perrot. Dorothy left the house after telling Cocks she was expecting a visit from Huntingdon, who was still her guardian; instead, she went to Broxbourne Church to meet up secretly with Perrot, who arrived with a marriage licence. When the local vicar refused to marry them, Perrot produced an amenable chaplain, who officiated without a surplice and wearing riding boots and spurs. He also

27

brought five or six witnesses and two men carrying swords and daggers under their cloaks to guard the church door. When their pursuers reached the porch, they were too late to prevent the marriage ceremony. Elizabeth was furious. She banished Dorothy from court and sent Perrot and his chaplain to spend a couple of months in the Fleet prison. Being her trustee, Burghley had to intervene to gain their release and to help them in their subsequent financial difficulties, particularly because Dorothy was not entitled to a dowry, having married without her guardians' consent. They had no choice but to retire to the Perrot estates at Carew Castle in Pembrokeshire.[3]

Elizabeth did not readily forgive Dorothy. When she called on Warwick at his home at North Hall in 1587 and found Dorothy staying there, Dorothy was confined to her room. Although Essex, who was already having some success as a favourite, tried to negotiate her rehabilitation after four years of marriage, Elizabeth still would not relent.

Perrot died in 1594, and this obliged Dorothy to mend her ways. Two years later, she married Henry Percy, 9th Earl of Northumberland, this time with the queen's full blessing, but the marriage proved unhappy.

Chapter 7

Robert Devereux, 2nd Earl of Essex, 1581–85

Following his graduation from Cambridge, Essex was placed under Leicester's and Huntingdon's joint supervision. After his extravagant display at Penelope's wedding, he was encouraged to reside at Lamphey, where it was hoped that he could live within his allowance of £210 per annum. While there, he met Gelli Meyrick, a Welshman and son of the Bishop of Bangor. Although Meyrick was ten years older, Essex employed him as his steward, later involving him in his military exploits. Taking Meyrick with him, Essex spent the Christmas of 1581 with his grandfather, Sir Francis Knollys, at Grey's Court. It was no doubt hoped that Knollys would reinforce the need for his boisterous grandson to live more frugally. In February 1582, Essex and Meyrick moved on 'for service' to the Huntingdons. Although Essex may not have been an ideal influence, he was able to become better acquainted with his 12-year-old brother, Wat, who remained under their supervision.

In late 1583, now aged 18, Essex moved back with Meyrick to Lamphey. According to Henry Wotton, his secretary, he spent his time there 'largely in idleness', sheltered from affairs of state.[1] He was able to see more of Dorothy and Perrot at Carew Castle but was soon overspending his meagre allowance. He had to send a grovelling letter of apology to Burghley, saying: 'I hope your lordship in courtesy will pardon my youth, if I have, through want of experience, in some sort passed the bounds of frugality. I cannot but embrace with duty your lordship's good counsel, whose love I have effectually proved, and [of] whose care of my well doings I am thoroughly persuaded.'[2] Despite this display of penitence he did not curb his spending, and Steven Veerapen has pointed out that an 'ostentatious display of wealth' was a prerequisite for any aspiring Elizabethan courtier.[3]

Wat did not join his brother at Lamphey. In 1584, the Huntingdons saw to it that he was sent to Christ Church, Oxford, despite his bent to become a soldier. Being too young to serve in the Low Countries, he remained under their supervision. Their main ambition was to find him a wealthy wife. They looked no further than another of their wards, Margaret Dakins, who had arrived to be given a proper Puritan upbringing. She was proving a model student and was the heiress to a huge estate in Yorkshire. As she was eighteen months younger than Wat, they believed she was cut out to make him an ideally submissive spouse. It was a huge personality mismatch. Wat had all the Devereux charm and wild spirits, while Margaret was markedly plain and imbued with religious zeal (later becoming the diarist Lady Hoby, full of moral advice on the routine of Puritan observance). On their marriage in 1589, the Dakinses acquired the manor and parsonage of Hackness near Scarborough to become the couple's home.

In May 1584, Essex nonchalantly entertained Leicester at Chartley before embarking on a tour of his stepfather's extensive properties in the Midlands, Denbigh and Chester. It was shortly after this that the Noble Imp fell ill, tragically dying on 19 July. There was great sympathy for Leicester even from Elizabeth, although Lettice was still not restored to favour. Burghley made Theobalds available to the grieving couple to enable them to escape from Wanstead. Leicester now changed his will, restoring his nephew, Philip, as his heir, while training Essex to become a favourite at court to restore Dudley influence.

For nearly a year, Essex continued to enjoy his country existence at Lamphey, living in considerable style. He maintained an intimate, teasing correspondence with Penelope, always 'mutually supportive, caring and understanding'.[4] By naming her second daughter 'Essex', Penelope underlined the bond between them. In September 1585, Lettice at last asserted her authority over her son, rousing him from his reverie and hauling him back to London, so that his stepfather could advance him to royal favour.

PART II

DEVELOPMENT
OF MILITARY AND
COURTLY SKILLS

Chapter 8

Raleigh's arrival at court and his project to colonise 'Virginia', 1583–87

In 1583, when Raleigh reappeared from Ireland, he was soon accepted into a position of trust at court, exchanging verses with the queen, his goddess 'Cynthia, the moon', to celebrate her eternal power, while he played the part of her fashionably lovesick swain. Elizabeth named him, affectionately, as her 'silly pug' (but quickly realised he was far from silly). He depicted her as 'ordained by God to bring Spanish Catholicism to its knees and lead England to further Protestant greatness'.[1] Using his skills as a wordsmith, he wrote 'regularly about the arts of war, navigation and politics'.[2] It was no wonder that she later employed him to place a favourable spin on any naval or military failure, such as his turning of the disastrous capture of the *Revenge* into a story of the 'transcendent' heroism by its captain, Sir Richard Grenville.[3] He was an accomplished poet (far more so than the aristocratic Essex) and was largely responsible for creating Elizabeth's image as the omnipotent virgin queen. When Burghley, the Lord Treasurer, learned that his son-in-law, the wayward Oxford, was under house arrest after being caught in a conspiracy as a closet Catholic, he turned to Raleigh as the queen's up-and-coming favourite to make discreet enquiries on his behalf. Raleigh was soon able to advise that she intended only to provide a warning and he could negotiate Oxford's return to court.[4] For someone born without any aspiration to authority, he was doing remarkably well, but left a trail of enemies along the way. In November 1584, he was one of the stars in the Accession Day tilt, participation in which never came cheap.[5]

Unfortunately, Raleigh disturbed the somewhat cosy understanding that had existed between the Leicester faction and Elizabeth. During his absences, Leicester heard malicious rumours of Raleigh being 'an ill instrument towards her [the queen] against your lordship', an accusation which Raleigh strongly denied.[6] Raleigh was now enjoying the royal perquisites that had previously come in Leicester's direction. He was granted the use of the magnificent Durham Place, previously leased to Leicester, with its gardens running down to the Thames just below Whitehall Palace. It was here that Jane Grey had married Guildford Dudley thirty years earlier. Raleigh's increasing connoisseurship meant that it was soon lavishly furnished, positioning him to emulate Leicester in entertaining visiting delegations and to hold 'interesting and cosmopolitan gatherings' with an 'intellectual coterie' of acquaintances.[7] These included the brilliant scientist Thomas Harriot, who joined his service and went on to solve many of the navigational issues of the day.[8] He later attracted Edmund Spenser, who he had met in Ireland, and it was to 'the Right noble, and Valorous, Sir Walter Raleigh' that Spenser dedicated his *Faerie Queen.* Spenser had been Leicester's protégé until overstepping the mark with his *Mother Hubbard's Tale* to oppose Elizabeth's marriage to Anjou. This had obliged him to leave London for a career in Ireland.

With Spain being the enemy, Raleigh had an ambition to create a base in the Americas from where Spanish shipping, the lifeblood of their aggression in Europe, could more easily be intercepted. Earlier in 1584, to provide the means of challenging the Spanish, Raleigh received a six-year patent to found a colony, to be called 'Virginia' in the queen's name, on unknown lands in the New World. The objective was to send an expedition, not in conquest as the Catholic Spanish had done, but with the more laudable objective of becoming 'evangelist liberators, bringing savages to the light of [Protestant] truth'.[9] He did not go himself, but sponsored a group of explorers led by Captains Barlowe and Amadas to reconnoitre Roanoke Island off the coast of what is now North Carolina. Although it was rumoured that this was the size of England, it was in fact only eight by two miles, but protected from the Atlantic to the east by sand shoals known as the Barrier Islands. The captains reported back favourably and returned to England with two native 'Indians', who, despite their unintelligible language, were paraded in the Houses of Parliament. In January 1585 Raleigh was knighted, becoming a steward of the duchy of Cornwall and lord warden of the stanneries [tin mines], which came with their financial rewards. It was as lord warden of the stanneries that he was later able to provide Leicester with miners to support siege operations in the Low Countries.

On 9 April 1585, an expedition largely financed by Raleigh personally and led by his cousin, Sir Richard Grenville, returned to Roanoke to set up an English garrison and to return the two Indians, who had been well-treated and now spoke some English. Another passenger was Harriot, Raleigh's scientist and navigator, who hoped to master the local language. Raleigh again remained behind (and, contrary to popular legend, never visited North America nor was he the first to import the potato or tobacco to Europe). If they were to survive, the settlers would need local advice on fishing methods and on growing local produce. Although the natives thrived, the new arrivals required their help. By the end of the year, Grenville's expedition, desperate for provisions, set off back to England leaving fifteen men to maintain their claim to the island.

In 1587, a third expedition, again financed by Raleigh, set out from England led by John White, who was appointed governor of the new colony. He took with him fourteen families with building, farming and military skills, including two pregnant women. Their first objective was to establish 'the Cittie of Ralegh' next to a deep-water anchorage. On arrival, they could find no sign of the fifteen settlers who had been left behind. Furthermore, the locals were unimpressed with the heavy demands being made on them for food, and failed to provide support. In desperation, the new arrivals moved inland in search of sustenance but the locals either melted away or fired arrows at them. On 18 August, White had no choice but to return home for supplies. After a desperate journey and short of water, he reached Ireland in mid-October, but Raleigh did not receive his letters for six weeks, by which time England was braced for the imminent arrival of the Spanish Armada, and Elizabeth had embargoed the departure of any ships from English ports. When at last White returned to Roanoke, he and his party could find no colonist left alive and their fate remains unknown, despite several later attempts to trace them. This ended Raleigh's dreams of creating an empire in Virginia and the means of cutting off Spanish treasure at its source.

Despite the failure of the Virginia colonisation project, Elizabeth approved of Raleigh's philosophy to work in harmony with the locality rather than to seek its subjugation. He was now granted 42,000 acres around Youghal and Lismore in Munster to bring in settlers to populate the area and cooperate with the local Irish. In 1587, he was granted the money and estates of the traitor Anthony Babington and a monopoly over the allocation of wine licences. Although he was now sufficiently wealthy to contemplate buying Hayes Barton, the Devon farm of his father's family, his offer was unsuccessful.

Chapter 9

Essex's success at court and with Leicester in the Low Countries, 1585–88

Essex was aged 20 on his appearance at court, and his handsome looks made an immediate impression on Elizabeth when she met him at Nonsuch Palace.[1] Leicester now spent a great deal of time grooming him as his 'stalking horse'.[2] This proved hugely successful, particularly as he arrived when Raleigh was conveniently busied in Cornwall or in Ireland. Robert Lacey has explained:

> He succeeded so brilliantly not through any greater wisdom
> or effort or skill but simply through the power which his
> personal attractions exercised over one elderly, vain and
> capricious woman … He was seventeen [in fact twenty]
> when he first began seriously to attend to the work, ceremony
> and play that made up the daily routine of the royal palace
> of Whitehall, but already the ladies of the court found his
> charms irresistible.[3]

Despite his success, Essex never achieved his stepfather's dominant standing with Elizabeth and became petulant when trying to compete with both Raleigh, on his reappearance, and with a coterie of other aspiring young favourites. He threatened to duel with rivals if crossed, so that Elizabeth called him her 'wild horse'.[4] 'She no longer had youth to commend her, and she never had conventional beauty, but she did have a commanding presence and glamour.'[5] 'He wanted to be the chief man in her life', but to be left with the freedom 'to carve out his own path'.[6] His ambitious streak gained impetus when Raleigh was at court. He was cut to the quick when Raleigh suggested that his position was 'due to the good fortune of his birth and pseudo-filial link to Leicester', as was undoubtedly true.[7] Yet, Leicester and Essex had much in common. Both wanted the opportunity to prove themselves against Spain and strongly favoured providing the Dutch with support in the Low Countries. While Leicester's aim was to support the Puritan struggle against encroaching Catholicism, Essex's single-minded focus was to become a military hero.

Elizabeth was always wary of committing herself to open conflict against the might of Catholic Spain. She mistrusted the Dutch and baulked at the cost of an invasion force. In the end, she had no choice. On 10 August 1585, having realised their plight, she concluded a treaty with The States-General and sent a task force of 4,500 men under Sir John Norreys to their assistance. As a veteran of the wars in Ireland, Norreys was considered 'the finest leader in Elizabeth's army', but was up against the able Alessandro Farnese, Duke of Parma, who had taken Antwerp before Norreys's arrival.[8] With Parma demonstrating experience and cool judgement, he had the better of the early engagements, and it was clear that a larger English force would be needed.

Eventually Elizabeth agreed to send 6,000 foot and 1,000 horse, providing a loan of £125,000 for their maintenance. Even though Leicester had not served as a soldier for thirty years and his knowledge of military tactics was outmoded, he was the man she wanted in command. He gathered Essex under his wing and was joined by his steward, Christopher Blount, as master of his horse, Perrot and the young Francis Vere. On 10 December 1585, the main British force disembarked at Flushing and received a warm welcome from the beleaguered Dutch. Philip Sidney, who had been appointed Governor of Flushing, had arrived a month earlier. Even Rich considered joining with a troop of fifty lances, but this did not materialise.[9]

Elizabeth was always a reluctant participant, fearing from the outset that incursion into the Low Countries would precipitate a Spanish invasion of England. Furthermore, she did not want Leicester stealing her thunder. She forced him to retract his acceptance of the Governorship of the United Provinces, which had been offered by the Dutch, realising that their objective was to ensure England's long-term commitment. She then failed to provide him with the military resources agreed, thereby limiting him to raids and attacks on convoys. It became a war of sieges, for which Leicester was not prepared and had to send for more sappers.

Essex only wanted to win his spurs, spending £1,000 out of his parlous personal treasury to equip himself and his retainers with 'expensive armour, horses and livery'.[10] This infuriated his grandfather, Sir Francis Knollys, who complained: 'Your father hath not left you sufficient lands for to maintain the state of the poorest earl in England.'[11] This had no effect, and Leicester appointed him as 'colonel-general of the horse', a nominal, but nonetheless significant-sounding title.[12]

Even with a more sizeable English presence, fighting against Parma's battle-hardened Spanish troops proved extremely challenging, not helped by Leicester's disagreements with Norreys, who had already been in the Low Countries for a year and was infinitely the more experienced soldier (but was accused by both Leicester and Philip of profiteering).[13] Even Essex complained that 'our owne private warres ... [are] more dangerous [than] the annoyance of the enemy'.[14] Despite this and being under-provisioned, the English force acquitted itself with conspicuous bravery. Tragically, Philip's femur was shattered by a musket ball at Zutphen, where Francis Vere's life was reputedly saved by Christopher Blount. Although Philip was nursed by Frances, it was to no avail. Essex was at his bedside when he died on 17 October 1586, being left a bequest of Philip's best sword in his will as 'his beloved and much honoured lord' (and reputedly, but by no means certainly, the care of his wife).[15] This tragedy was compounded when the distraught Frances suffered a miscarriage, leaving Leicester, yet again, without the prospect of a legitimate heir.

Elizabeth was distraught at losing a person of Philip's ability. She recalled Essex, who had been made a knight banneret by Leicester after his bravery shown at Zutphen. He returned home most reluctantly. Fighting was now his bread and butter.[16] 'Not only did the cut and thrust of battle fit with his chivalric ideals, but it offered a stage on which he might be taken seriously.'[17] At the Accession Day tilt at Whitehall on 17 November, he took the place of Philip, the fallen hero, who was represented by a riderless horse caparisoned in black. Having acquired 'a surfeit of chivalrous notions honed on the battlefield', he carried a sable shield inscribed with the motto, *par nulla figura dolori* (nothing represents sorrow).[18] At New Year 1587, he provided Elizabeth with an elaborate jewel in the shape of a rainbow [Elizabeth] above two pillars, one cracked [Essex and Philip].[19] The game of courtly love was now being played with aplomb. He 'opted to pursue the lifestyle and rewards of the polished, chastely amorous, and fawning courtier'.[20] Castiglione's *The Book of the Courtier* explains that this involved 'not only moderate speech and a cool head, but wit, charm, carefully held postures and poses, elegance of manners, and a sound classical knowledge'.[21] Making the difficult 'switch to the path of the statesman' would take years of the queen's 'familiarity and affection'.[22]

When Leicester returned to England, he was unwell, probably suffering from gallstones. In 1584, he had been appointed Lord Steward of the Household, the central position at court, but to combine this with his longstanding role as Master of the Horse was proving too big a workload. He agreed to hand over the latter role to Essex. This had already been discussed before their departure for the Continent. From now on, Essex was Elizabeth's constant companion, even escorting her to the Armada thanksgiving service at St Paul's. He was called upon to sit up playing cards, 'or at one game or another with her that he cometh not to his own lodging until the birds sing in the morning'.[23] He rode with her in Windsor Great Park and 'had the virility, sophisticated wit and gallantry [she] loved'.[24] She treated him like a younger lover, but 'beneath this obscene charade [she] also felt a genuine fondness for [him]'.[25] He was now positioned to support his stepfather in discouraging her from negotiating peace with Spain.

Despite his growing standing, Essex was careful not to abuse his relationship with Leicester. When Elizabeth suggested that he should occupy his stepfather's former lodgings at court, he immediately sought his approval. Although he moved in, he found being at the 56-year-old queen's beck and call to be distasteful. (See Endnote 3)

When Leicester returned to the Low Countries in June, Essex was involved in a stormy argument with the queen when she required him to remain with her. It was really a piece of luck for Essex, and Raleigh recognised that his own absence from court left the door open for his new rival's rise in status. Such was the friction, that a duel between them had to be 'repressed' by the privy council. Elizabeth came personally from Greenwich to calm them down and cut them both out of her New Year 1588 present list!

With Burghley being in enforced absence from court for more than a year following his part in the implementation of Mary Queen of Scots' death warrant, Leicester being in the Low Countries and Raleigh supervising the West Country or his estates in Ireland, it was Essex who reaped the benefit.[26] Nevertheless, he was not made a member of the privy council and, as a mere 'decorative favourite', was not taken very seriously. He was soon portraying Elizabeth in a new persona as a warrior queen, albeit without any active participation on her part. At the same time, he accepted gifts of parsonages worth £300 per annum, and, in April 1588, was appointed a Knight of the Garter.[27] It was now that he was painted in a miniature by Hilliard as 'the young man among roses'.[28] The rose was the white eglantine – the queen's rose. This idealistic image of love showed him at what proved to be the height of his influence, and he never crossed the threshold to become a statesman, even though Leicester was soon to die.

Chapter 10

Sir Francis Vere, 1587–89

Having been appointed captain, Francis remained in the Low Countries. The first opportunity for him to make a real name for himself arose in 1587, serving under Sir Roger Williams at the heroic defence of Sluis, a fortified harbour on the mouth of the Scheldt. The town was of particular significance as the Spanish would need to use it as a port of embarkation for their proposed invasion of England. It had been garrisoned by Dutch and English troops and was protected by a system of defensive waterways. Williams was recognised as recklessly brave, having served as a mercenary for the Spanish, but his Welsh accent and satirical humour caused amusement. (He is generally reckoned to have been the model for Shakespeare's Fluellen.) With Parma being hampered by a shortage of provisions, Williams managed to fight his way into the town from Flushing with a well-provisioned detachment of allied troops. This included Francis with his company.

With the garrison strengthened to 1,600 men, Williams's defence against crack Spanish troops drew even Parma's admiration. With Francis ever at the forefront of the breach, he greatly distinguished himself despite being slightly wounded on two occasions. Although Leicester returned from England to oversee the town's relief, bringing with him a combined military and naval contingent, the Spanish had cut the bridges providing access from Ostend. It did not help that the Dutch were in no mood to take risks over what was essentially an English objective, so that, eventually, Williams was forced into surrender. This was agreed on honourable terms with the garrison permitted to leave, after which Parma offered Williams a position with Spanish forces against the Turks, which he graciously declined.

Vere continued in the Low Countries after Leicester's main force departed for England, returning to the garrison at Bergen-op-Zoom, from where Willoughby was asked to take command of the English forces still remaining in the Low Countries. He considered this a thankless task. The States-General was providing only lukewarm support. They had left his troops unpaid, forcing him to mortgage his estates to subsidise them personally. On 4 December 1587 he accepted the role only as locum tenens, while William the Silent's son, the 20-year-old Maurice of Nassau, was being established in command of the Dutch forces.

Willoughby's new appointment should have required him to resign the governorship of Bergen-op-Zoom. Although he had wanted to hand this over to Sir William Drury, Elizabeth insisted on the appointment of the older and unpopular Colonel Thomas Morgan. In light of this, Willoughby remained in situ, appointing Thomas Wilford (who had been Leicester's sergeant-major general) as lieutenant-colonel and Francis as sergeant-major. Willoughby reported that 'although young [Francis was 27], he hath experience, art, discretion and valour sufficient'.[1] The garrison also included Christopher Blount, who had remained behind following Leicester's departure and Charles Danvers who was later to become a close ally of Essex. Despite antipathy for Morgan, the garrison now bonded as a congenial and efficient unit.

With the Spanish Armada expected to arrive imminently, Francis was moved with 260 men to Flushing to pre-empt a Spanish landing in Zeeland and was responsible for destroying the Spanish *San Mateo*, which went aground between Ostend and Sluis. Parma was determined to make up for the Armada's failure by besieging Bergen-op-Zoom which commanded the strategically important entrance to the Scheldt, making it key to the protection of Zeeland. It also provided a base for Dutch cavalry to sortie out onto the roads towards Antwerp to seize valuable provisions. Willoughby immediately called up troops from Flushing to reinforce the Bergen-op-Zoom garrison, and blinds were constructed outside the gates to protect parties at the drawbridges when they sallied out.

On 7 September 1588 Parma arrived personally to supervise the siege, but his attempt to capture the adjacent island of Tholen, which would have prevented provisions reaching Bergen-op-Zoom by sea, was thwarted when Dutch fire from the parapet of a dyke caused 400 Spanish losses. When Parma surrounded the landward walls with 20,000 men, the garrison sallied out to prevent them from occupying a position threatening the Steenberg gate. This resulted in the capture of Spanish prisoners, one of whom was an Englishman serving under the

Catholic Sir William Stanley. Stanley had been particularly despised in Leicester's time for handing over Deventer to the Spanish after being left in command following its capture. The renegade prisoner took two of Willoughby's officers aside to persuade them to hand over Bergen-op-Zoom. When this was reported, Willoughby told them to play along with the plan. The prisoner was freed so that he could advise the besiegers that the northern sconce (fort) protecting the town's access to the sea was being left unmanned. Having fallen for this ruse, 3,000 Spanish troops, including Stanley's turncoats, approached the fort across marshland, timing their arrival for midnight when it was low tide. With Willoughby having hidden 2,000 men in the fort, Francis lowered its drawbridge and raised the portcullis to entice in the attackers. As soon as fifty of them had entered, he quickly closed them again. They were easily slain, and a fusillade from the walls killed a further 150 outside. Although the Spanish attacked the fort's palisades, the tide was already rising, and their remaining force was drowned as it attempted to retreat by the way that it had come. It was this Spanish disaster which, on 12 November, forced Parma to raise the siege and return to Brussels.

Even Morgan received praise, and Willoughby knighted Francis, Wilford, Christopher Blount, Charles Danvers and eight other officers. By this time, Francis was seen as 'a prudent adviser to the General [Willoughby], a cautious commander and a resourceful contriver of stratagems'.[2] Willoughby now sent him back to England after an absence of three years to report the action and to be introduced by Burghley to the queen. After spending time with his family at Kirby Hall, he returned in 1589 to the Low Countries, bringing his brother Robert with him to command a troop of cavalry.

Francis's heroism was already gaining him a reputation as one of England's most accomplished soldiers. In 1589, with many of his colleagues, including Willoughby, returning to England or to serve in France, he was appointed at the age of 29 Her Majesty's Sergeant-Major in the Field of all the English and Scottish troops remaining behind, other than those under the governors of the English garrisoned towns. With the queen's full approval, he had been appointed ahead of several more senior colleagues to command a force of close to 6,500 men. He was not about to let Elizabeth down.

Chapter 11

Sir Christopher Blount, 1584–87

Christopher Blount, like his father Sir Thomas and his elder brother Edward before him, was a long-term employee of Leicester's. It is often said that they were distant connections through Leicester's mother's family, the Guildfords, or through his own mother's family, the Poleys. No relationship has been identified and it seems unlikely, but his father was a first cousin of Henry VIII's mistress, Bessie Blount. (See Family Tree Chart 2)

Although Leicester was an ardent Puritan, Christopher, like his mother Margery Poley, was strongly Catholic, having been educated at Louvain under the Jesuit William Allen, but there is no realistic evidence to suggest this ever diminished his loyalty to either Elizabeth or Leicester. He later used his Catholic credentials to infiltrate himself into the communication network of Mary Queen of Scots, acting on both Leicester's and Walsingham's behalf. To gain credibility, he became a close associate of Thomas Morgan, who was Mary's contact at the offices of Archbishop Bethune, her ambassador, in Paris. It is never easy to be categoric about the loyalties of double agents, but Morgan, who had engineered himself into a position of complete trust with Mary, seems to have been another of Walsingham's agents. Originally he had been an employee of George Talbot, 6th Earl of Shrewsbury, but was described by Mary as 'poor Morgan' after being dismissed for providing her with assistance.[1] She gave him money and endorsed his appointment by Bethune.

Morgan was certainly mistrusted by both English Catholics and Jesuits in Paris. As early as October 1584, Mary's Jesuit priest, Samerie, had warned her against him. In March 1585, Ragazzini, the Papal Nuncio, wrote to the Cardinal of Como: 'This Morgan is considered by many here and particularly the Jesuits to be a knave; yet the Queen of

Scots relies upon him more than on her own ambassador [Bethune], as the ambassador himself has told me many times.'[2]

Although the French confined Morgan for a period in the Bastille, he was able to communicate through a window with Robert Poley, another double agent in Walsingham's employment, who may have been a connection of Christopher's mother (although Poley family records do not confirm this). He certainly acted as the conduit for a letter from Christopher to Morgan which 'ardently [confirmed] that [Christopher] would serve and honour the only saint that he knew living upon the ground, as he termed the Queen of Scots'.[3] On 20 July 1585, Morgan advised Mary at Tutbury that Christopher had been visiting Shropshire, apparently to reconnoitre a means for her escape.

With Christopher already serving with Leicester in the Low Countries, in March 1586 Morgan wrote to Mary to imply that Christopher was hoping to deliver an important town to the Spanish (as Sir William Stanley was to do). Any such disloyalty to Leicester seems unthinkable, and he proved an able and loyal cavalry officer. He later served as lieutenant to Sir Thomas Perrot and was knighted (see p.42) after the successful defence of Bergen-op-Zoom. There can be little doubt that the correspondence with Morgan was designed to provide Christopher with cover while conducting his espionage activities. Poley and Christopher are well-known for having insinuated themselves into the so-called Babington Plot, put together by Walsingham's agents to incriminate Mary in a plan for Elizabeth's assassination. This was nominally headed by the naïve Anthony Babington with a group of his friends, but they lacked any realistic means of achieving their objective. Although Poley spent a period in the Tower of London from 1586 to 1588, this was most likely for his own protection. As all the correspondence fell into English government hands and Christopher suffered no repercussions, his innocence will have been known to the authorities. (For a more detailed account of the Babington Plot, please see *The Survival of the Crown*, pp. 217-27.)

When Christopher was examined by the privy council in 1601 over his part in Essex's rebellion, he asked for a message to be taken to Elizabeth. It was reported: 'He doth also desire ... that her Majesty may be particularly informed and remembered of those great services which he did in laying the way open to the Earl of Leicester and Mr. Secretary Walsingham for the discovery of all the Queen of Scots' practices.'[4]

Chapter 12

Charles Blount's early life and military initiation, 1579–88

As the second son of a father whose financial ventures were proving unsuccessful, Charles Blount's prospects were not promising. Although he studied law, initially at Clifford's Inn, and entered the Middle Temple in 1579 when he was 16, there is no evidence that he intended to embark on a legal career. He attended Oxford University but came down 'not well grounded' without taking his degree. This did not prevent him from becoming 'a first-class theologian' and gaining his Master of Arts ten years later in 1589, when he was 26.[1] It was his good looks that came to his rescue. There is no doubting his appeal to women. He was tall, athletic and an expert horseman with the stamp of a soldier about him. He had brown curly hair, with 'a sweet face, a most neat composure'.[2] His devoted secretary Fynes Moryson later provided the following description: '[His] forehead was broad and high; his eyes great black and lovely; his nose something low and short, and a little blunt in the end; his chin round; his cheeks full, round and ruddy; his countenance cheerful.'[3] Moryson also reported his shortage of bodily hair, but what he had was blackish and thin.

We do not know when Charles first met Penelope, nor when they became lovers. Cyril Falls concluded that she shunned Philip Sidney in 1581, because she was already in love with Charles before her marriage to Rich. This cannot be correct. Other records show that Charles only saw Elizabeth for the first time in 1583, and there is no record of him having any earlier opportunity to meet Penelope. He was only 18 in 1581 and, as a younger son, did not move in Penelope's exalted circles. Falls's hypothesis is based on a claim by Archbishop Laud (who became Charles's chaplain earlier in his career) that Charles and Penelope pledged to marry before she was forced into espousing Rich, although this must be a fabrication – as will be seen.

In 1583 Charles was brought to Whitehall by his brother, William, to watch Elizabeth at dinner. While dining, she spotted his good-looking face in the crowd. Having asked who he was, it was explained that he was Lord Mountjoy's brother. On hearing his name being mentioned, Charles blushed in embarrassment. She called him over and held out her hand to be kissed, telling him that she could see his noble blood. She told him: 'Fail you not to come to the Court, and I will bethink myself how to do you good.' This was an extraordinary piece of luck for a 'bashful and poor' second son, and it greatly boosted his hopes of success as a soldier.[4] Without Elizabeth, he would have had little chance of advancement, being 'shy scholarly, modest and reserved'.[5]

Charles did not come to court immediately. In 1584, he became a member of Parliament for Bere Alston in Devon but did not take his seat. The Bere Alston estate had belonged to the Willoughby de Broke family, but on the death of Robert, 2nd Lord Willoughby in 1522, it was inherited by his daughters, Elizabeth and Anne. Elizabeth had married John Paulet, 3rd Marquess of Winchester, and Anne espoused Charles Blount, 5th Lord Mountjoy. Its parliamentary seat was now in the joint giving of the Paulet and Blount families. Joint ownership proved unworkable and, in 1598, the estate was divided with Charles receiving the manor of Bere Ferrers as his home.

Charles had a second string to his bow. Elizabeth greatly admired his skills in the tiltyard. He may not have reached the standard of George Clifford, 3rd Earl of Cumberland, but 'he was a stalwart at the sport and in demand on great occasions'.[6] Writing after Charles's death, the poet John Ford describes his facility in equestrian activities:

> Now he delights to see the falcon soar
> Above the top of heaven; than to chase
> The nimble buck, or hunt the bristled boar
> From out the sty of terror; now the race;
> Banners and sport of honourable grace,
> Not games of thriftless prodigality,
> But plots of fame and fame's eternity.

For after toys of courtship he assays
Which way to manage an untaméd horse;
When, how, to spur and rein, to stop and raise
Close sitting, voltage of a man-like force,
When in career to meet with gallant course:
As centaurs were both horse and men, so he
Seemed on the horse, nor could discernéd be.

To overcome the deficiencies in his education, he spent his time in the company of scholars. 'He read history, and made some study of philosophy, geography, and mathematics. He learned enough French and Italian to enable him to read books in those languages though he did not venture to speak them.'[7] It was a combination of these interests that cut him out to be a soldier. It may seem incongruous that a champion of the tiltyard should ponder books, but he knew that England 'had fallen behind the Continent in the art of warfare'.[8] Veterans of Continental campaigns, particularly Sir Roger Williams, the hero of the defence of Sluis, were writing on military strategy.

In August 1585, Charles joined the first wave of soldiers sent to the Low Countries under Norreys and was allocated to Ostend as captain of a company of 150 men. (He greatly respected Norreys, who remained his mentor until Norreys' death in 1597.) In October, Norreys attacked a Spanish fort on the Arnhem, but needed guns to be moved across the river within range of the walls. Determined to take his opportunity, Charles was ferried across with his pikemen. Despite his company behaving admirably, the attack was repulsed, and Charles, who was on foot, was hit in the thigh by 'chain-shot' (two cannon balls linked by a chain). Norreys praised his bravery in dispatches but, although his life was not threatened, he was invalided home and remained lame in later life.

Charles did not return to the Low Countries with Leicester's main force but, during the first part of 1586, used his convalescence to cut his teeth as a member of the House of Commons. He also visited court. With Essex being in the Low Countries, Charles had greater access to the queen and was soon well-established as one of her favourites. On 31 March 1586, Morgan reported to Mary Queen of Scots from Paris that 'either Raleigh, Elizabeth's mignon, … was weary of her or she of him since [he] had heard that she "hath now entertained one Blount, the brother of Lord Mountjoy, being a young gentleman", despite her being old enough to be his grandmother [she was 50]'.[9]

By mid-1586, Charles had sufficiently recovered from his wound to return to the Low Countries and took part in the engagement at Zutphen, during which Sidney was mortally wounded. When Leicester returned to England that November to discuss his difficulties with the queen, Essex went with him but Charles remained for more than a year on the Continent. By 11 October 1587, with Elizabeth wanting him back at her side, he was repatriated carrying letters concerning the peace negotiations being conducted with Parma. According to Sir Robert Naunton, he returned to his company in the Low Countries on several further occasions, until this was expressly forbidden. Nevertheless, before the end of hostilities, he had done enough to be knighted by Leicester.

On Charles's return to court, he was much fêted by Elizabeth. After showing off his bravado in the lists, she sent him a token of her esteem, a richly enamelled gold queen from a chess set, a gift that she reserved only for her favourites. Having fastened it to his sleeve, he proudly entered the privy chamber with his cloak under his arm, so that it could be seen. When Essex was told how the queen had acknowledged Charles's skill in the tiltyard, he retorted: 'Now I perceive every fool must have a favour.'[10] Charles could not let this go unchallenged. Despite the queen's disapproval of duelling, they met in Marylebone Fields, where Charles disarmed Essex and wounded him in the thigh. For once Elizabeth did not seem too disappointed at Essex's discomfiture, particularly as they were fighting for her affection. She swore: 'God's death, it was fit that someone or other should take [Essex] down, otherwise there would be no rule with him.'[11] Perhaps surprisingly, it was their only recorded quarrel, and they were soon firm friends again. Essex quickly realised that Charles was not challenging his exalted position with the queen, and it may have been through him that Charles met Penelope, although, in 1587 there is no evidence to suggest that it involved anything more than a casual acquaintance.

Once re-established at court, Charles, who had known Philip Sidney in the Low Countries, became a close friend of his brother Robert. Another ally was Shakespeare's patron, Henry Wriothesley, 3rd Earl of Southampton, 'cultivated and popular but reckless and unbalanced'. Charles also became friendly with Sir Christopher Blount, who was seven years older and a remote relation (a 6th half-cousin of Charles's father).[12] He also befriended his 5th cousin, another Charles Blount, born in 1568, the son of Sir Michael Blount of Mapledurham, with whom he is sometimes confused. This Charles was on Essex's Cádiz expedition in 1596, when he was knighted, and later served under Essex in Ireland.

Charles never flattered and was 'a listener rather than a talker'. 'He loved private retiredness with good fare and some few choice friends.'[13] His focus was on military matters and on the Spanish Armada approaching the English Channel. Its imminent arrival on its cumbersome journey from Lisbon seems to have deterred him from standing for Parliament in 1588.

PART III

THE ARMADA AND ITS AFTERMATH

Chapter 13

The Spanish Armada, 1588–89

Three factors triggered the Spanish Armada: English piracy of Spanish vessels returning laden with bullion and other valuable cargoes from their outposts in the third world; English support for the Dutch in the Low Countries; and Mary Queen of Scots' execution. The Spanish were not seeking to avenge Mary's death, but her execution removed England's dynastic heir with her inconvenient French affiliation. Her demise left the Spanish free to promote their Infanta Isabella, a descendant of John of Gaunt, to replace the 'illegitimate' English queen.

Invading England was a logistical nightmare, and the huge Spanish fleet would lose any element of surprise. Despite being made up of 130 vessels, it was unable to transport the 55,000 men considered by Parma to be the minimum acceptable number for his invasion force. For this reason, the force was to be manned by battle-hardened troops already stationed in Flanders. There were to be three distinct phases: the first was to deliver a fleet in sufficient strength to defeat or at least neutralise English sea-power, and to deliver 18,000 military personnel from Spain to the Low Countries (being the maximum that could be accommodated on board); the second was to land a sufficient force in England to act as a bridgehead for the invasion force arriving from Flanders; and the third was to transport the invasion force across the Channel. Given the shoals in Dutch and Flemish harbours, this was to be shipped in 200 flat-bottomed boats, which would require the fleet's protection while crossing the Channel, to prevent them becoming easy pickings for English shipping.

The story of the Spanish fleet's difficulties against more manoeuvrable English vessels with superior firepower is well-known, but the Spanish ships were so strongly built that English guns needed to come within 100 yards to have any chance of a broadside penetrating their hulls. This put the English ships at risk of being rammed for grapple-boarding. The Armada's 130 vessels included twenty-eight purpose-built men-of-war, but were outnumbered by the English, who had 197 smaller but more nimble ships, all in good condition. Elizabeth's well-known parsimony did not extend to stinting on her navy, and Effingham wrote to Cecil: 'I do thank God that they be in the state that they be in: there is never one of them that knows what a leak means.'[1] The English tactic was to avoid challenging the might of the Armada full on, but to provoke it into firing from out of range, to pick off stragglers and to prevent any of its fleet from making landfall on English soil (although the Spanish had planned to revictual on the Isle of Wight). Effingham also wanted to push the Armada eastward up the Channel to allow additional English warships, which had been stationed further along the coast to deter a Spanish landing, to be brought into play with his main fleet.

The Spanish had a second problem that Parma could provide only 16,000 able-bodied men from Flanders to join his invasion force. Although he was instructed to pick a further 6,000 from those arriving with the Armada, he still had only 40 per cent of the personnel that he deemed necessary, and he prophesied disaster. The remaining 12,000 new arrivals were to be retained in Flanders to maintain control. With the Dutch blockading the shallows round their coastal ports, he also had a problem of embarking and disembarking his men and reprovisioning the fleet.

The English had retained a flotilla of thirteen ships under Lord Henry Seymour, Admiral of the Narrow Seas (next to Dover) to protect the expected Spanish landing area on the Kent coastline. Young men like Charles, detained at court by their demanding queen, saw Seymour's vessels as their final opportunity to join the action. Having made their way to Dover, Charles and three others were chosen. Seymour reported to Walsingham that he had placed these 'worthy gentlemen' on his flagship the *Rainbow* of 364 tons. After being launched only in the previous year, she sailed 'low and snug in the water, like a galleasse'.[2] She was one of three 'good ships' in Seymour's fleet, each with a complement of 250 men including gunners and soldiers. Another was the *Vanguard*, with the experienced Rear Admiral Sir William Wynter in command. There were also six 'medium ships' and four pinnaces.

Although Seymour feared that they would miss the action taking place on the other side of the channel, on 27 July his flotilla was summoned to join Effingham outside Calais. On arrival at about 8.00 pm, they found both the Spanish and English at anchor. On the following day, Effingham called a council of war aboard his flagship, the *Ark,* to develop a plan for dislodging the Spanish, who were anchored in close formation near the shore. A decision was taken to launch eight fire ships down wind and tide at midnight. As the burning ships approached, the Spanish gave orders to weigh anchor but, in their haste, many had to cut or slip their cables, leaving them unable to re-anchor. Although the fireships burnt out harmlessly, the Spanish were left spread out in open water. At 9.00 am on 29 July, The English closed near Gravelines with Drake attacking from the landward side, Howard in the centre and Seymour to seaward, driving the Spanish back into each other. It had always been the Spanish tactic to fire a devastating broadside and then use their gun crews to man the shrouds for grapple-boarding. With their equipment stored on the gundecks, reloading would be difficult. The English continued to provoke Spanish fire while staying out of range. They then employed their superior gunnery skills to fire repeated salvoes into the Spanish hulls as they closed. Charles was in the thick of it; the *Rainbow* and *Vanguard* 'struck some of the deadliest blows that day', maiming the *San Juan de Sicilia,* which eventually sank.[3] Wynter recorded that he fired 500 shots over nine hours. Two other Spanish ships were so damaged that they were later captured by the Dutch.

The outcome was decisive. While the Spanish lost 2,000 men, the English had only fifty casualties. Although very few Spanish ships sank, many were out of ammunition, 'spoiled and unable to resist longer'.[4] Those without anchors were ill-prepared for the journey home around northern Scotland and Ireland. When a violent squall caused the English to abandon their pursuit up the North Sea, the Spanish were able to restore their formation as they headed on. Effingham now resumed his more careful policy of preventing their return south. It was not an annihilation, but the effect was overwhelming.[5] In its journey in battle-damaged vessels round Scotland and the west coast of Ireland, often without anchors, the Armada lost half the ships with which it had left Lisbon with such high hopes in the previous spring.

Even now, it was feared that Parma had some trick up his sleeve for moving his invasion force across the Channel. On 30 July, Seymour was ordered back to guard the Thames estuary, but entered Harwich with the *Rainbow* on 1 August to end Charles's involvement in an experience he would never forget. He returned to court on a military captain's full pay, and Elizabeth provided him with salaried employment to keep him out of the firing line. By the end of 1589, he had been appointed keeper of the New Forest, despite the competing hopes of the Earl of Pembroke, and became one of the 'gentleman pensioners', providing her bodyguard. Elizabeth rated Charles's charm most highly and seems to have turned a blind eye to his later extra-marital affair. Being a favourite had its rewards.

Chapter 14

Leicester's last hurrah! 1588–89

When it came to the defence of England's shoreline, Elizabeth would always turn to Leicester to lead her forces. This was a huge challenge without a standing army. Unlike the English navy, it would be a massive task to bring England's land-based forces up to military readiness. During the winter of 1587–88, Leicester was in frequent attendance at council meetings to discuss the imminent Spanish threat, but faced the perennial problem of Elizabeth's ambivalence and an empty Exchequer. Even before his official appointment, he was 'issuing commands, ordering supplies and enquiring into the state of coastal defences'. A great chain of beacons was established on headlands and hills along the south coast to bring news of sightings of the Armada and to summon the militia to their posts. His main concern was the lack of any civilian enthusiasm to take up arms and the delay in recruitment. When Rich was tasked with raising the militia in Essex, Leicester wrote: 'Though he be no man of war, I find the country [the county of Essex] doth much respect and love him, especially that he is a true, faithful subject to her majesty and known to be jealous in religion.' (This does not imply that he was by then at daggers drawn with Penelope.)

As it was recognised that Parma's first objective would be to gain control of London, Leicester took personal responsibility for the defence of the Thames estuary, focusing his attention on entrenching the camp at Tilbury, which guarded the north bank of the Thames, opposite Gravesend on the south side.[6] He considered Tilbury an entirely suitable location to station the main English force for London's protection, but on 22 July, five days before the Armada's arrival at Calais to embark troops, he was still doubting whether either location could be made impregnable in time. It was a further two days before he was formally appointed Lieutenant and Captain General of the queen's armies and companies, the position he had held in the Low Countries. Although he supervised the construction of a boom across the Thames, he worried whether it was adequate. He complained that most men of substance were taking their retainers to serve under Hunsdon, who was in command of the bodyguard protecting the queen and the capital. The men of Essex were trickling slowly towards Tilbury, but by 25 July only 4,000 of them had reached the camp. Although, on paper, local musters raised 50,000 foot and 10,000 horse, those reporting for duty fell far short of this and even the trained bands from London were not readied. A shortage of victuals forced Leicester to stay 1,000 men in London until they could transport their own provisions. He ordered beer at his own expense and had to send town criers into the surrounding area to appeal for food from local farmers.[7]

Veterans of the Irish and Dutch campaigns were engaged in training new recruits, and, by 27 July, some semblance of order had been established at Tilbury. Leicester immediately urged Elizabeth to make a personal appearance. On 8 August, she was rowed down the Thames by forty men in her barge to review her troops, now numbering 11,500 men. In a piece of masterful stage management, Leicester created an illusion of military might with tents and pavilions in orderly rows and breastplates gleaming. Elizabeth knew exactly how to react, dressed all in white, and, according to legend, wearing a polished steel cuirass and mounted on a grey gelding with a page bearing her white-plumed helmet on a cushion. Leicester was mounted on her right, Essex on her left, and Norreys behind. When she reached the cheering soldiers, she shouted out that she came among them as:

> Your general, judge and rewarder, [ready to] lay down for my God and my Kingdom and for my people, my honour and my blood. I know I have but the body of a weak, feeble woman, but I have the heart and stomach of a King – and a King of England too – and think foul scorn that Parma, or Spain, or any Prince of Europe should dare to invade the borders of my realm.[8]

This was stirring stuff, worthy of Shakespeare. After dining with Leicester and his officers, she slept at Ardern Hall, one of the Rich family homes nearby. During dinner, she received news that the Armada had been driven by storms up the east coast to Scotland. Despite this, there were still fears that Parma might yet launch an invasion force, and, with the Dutch refusing to challenge him further, there were persistent rumours that he was ready to cross the Channel. This persuaded Elizabeth most reluctantly to return to London.

By mid-August, the danger was past. Leicester was required by his money-conscious colleagues on the council to break up the camp at Tilbury. He must have been thankful. He had been considerably weakened by his efforts, with discomfort from the pain in his stomach and continuing malaria. Despite his ailments, he made a triumphant entry back into London with an escort of gentlemen and 'a picked contingent of soldiers'.[9] None of them had fired a shot, but, in the prevailing euphoria, they were welcomed as heroes.[10] While Leicester watched with the queen from a window, Essex staged a troop review in the tiltyard at Whitehall and took part in two jousts against Cumberland, 'two of the best horsemen in the country'.[11] Leicester's continuing malaria prevented his attendance at any further celebrations and, after providing him with medicine prescribed by her own physicians, Elizabeth readily agreed that he should return to Buxton.

On 26 August, Leicester and Lettice set out by easy stages for the Midlands spa from Wanstead. He was 56, feverish and very ill, but managed, over several days, to reach his lodge at Cornbury in Oxfordshire. On arrival, he took to his bed and died there on 4 September. On 10 October, he was buried in the Beauchamp Chapel at Warwick with Charles as one of his six pallbearers.

Elizabeth promoted Essex to Leicester's former role as her lord steward. He now acted as the host for visiting dignitaries, allocating apartments for them at court. In January 1589, she helped to defray some of his expenditure by granting him a licence 'for the farm of sweet wines', previously held by Leicester. This 'hugely lucrative monopoly' was a boon to his depleted finances but was a drop in the ocean, and much of its future income had to be used as security for a debt of £4,000 to the jeweller, Vanlore. Furthermore, he was soon complaining to Burghley over irregularities in its collection.[12]

Christopher Blount only returned from the Low Countries in January 1589, four months after Leicester's death, but he rejoined Lettice's service. She needed help to sort out Leicester's voluminous debts. Richard Bagot, the Devereux agent at Chartley, was called upon to evict the tenant at Drayton Bassett, who was 'squatting' without paying rent. Leicester's agent, Thomas Fowler, having collected £8,000 from Leicester's debtors, absconded with the money to Edinburgh.[13]

By this time, Christopher's Catholic faith seems to have wavered. In June 1588, he had written to Walsingham from Utrecht: 'God hath altered me for my opinion in religion, and I not altered it to please any man, but to save my soul.'[14] (This change of heart does not seem to have endured. According to Thomas Jones, Bishop of Meath, while serving with Essex in Ireland in 1599, Christopher was reconciled to the Church of Rome by two Irish priests.)

In April 1589, eyebrows were raised when Christopher married Lettice, despite being twelve years her junior, 'relatively poor and without a position at court'.[15] There were immediate rumours that she had poisoned Leicester, so that she could marry her lover. This is unthinkable, and she later chose to be buried next to Leicester at Warwick.

Chapter 15

Raleigh's waning standing at court, 1588–94

In 1588, as the Spanish Armada loomed, Raleigh did not join the English fleet. With Devon and Cornwall seemingly in the front line for a Spanish attack, he was confirmed as Lord Lieutenant of Cornwall and entrusted with its defence. This was a key role, as the area was known to have Catholic sympathies. He positioned men and weapons along the Cornish coastline from Land's End to Plymouth. Guns were mounted on wheels to enable them to be moved as required. Of course, not all the promised reinforcements for such 'a long and thin' county were delivered by his parsimonious monarch and he worried about its security.[1]

In the summer of 1589, Raleigh was required by the queen to focus on his Irish plantation project. (At this time, Essex was involved in a hair-brained expedition in support of the attempt by the Portuguese pretender, Dom Antonio, to recover his homeland from the Spanish, as will be seen.) Knowing that the main issue was to import sufficient English settlers, he persuaded both Harriot and White, who had both been on the expedition to Roanoke Island, of the opportunities on offer. Nevertheless, prospective arrivals were gripped with anti-Catholic hysteria and, despite every effort being made to dispel their anxieties, they worried that their future on Irish soil was just as unpromising as in 'Virginia'. Raleigh's remedy was to restore dispossessed Irish lords back to their confiscated estates. As Burghley put it, 'to avoid the stirring up of rebellion in Ireland', Raleigh had to win the hearts and minds 'of all the nobility [who had] of late [been] greatly grieved by very hard dealings, and to permit them to continue their ancient greatness, strength, honour and surety'.[2] This gained him local cooperation. By 1602 when he sold his interests to Sir Richard Boyle, later Earl of Cork, he was passing on information gained from his Irish tenants about Spanish plans for colonisation. They had by then concluded that Spanish methods would be more threatening than his own. (Boyle followed Raleigh's philosophy, and Oliver Cromwell later stated that if his methods had been adopted all over Ireland, there would be no unrest.)

Inevitably, Elizabeth's continuing generosity to him did much to inflate Raleigh's growing self-importance. He was always immaculately dressed in the finest silks and acquired two pearls the size of quails' eggs, which he wore in one ear only.[3] This did nothing to improve his flagging popularity despite his eloquent attempts 'to set out his parts to the best advantage'.[4] In 1591, when appointed captain of the guard, he insisted on his men cutting a dash by wearing 'spangles' on their coats.[5] Elizabeth loved his 'swashbuckling style' but kept him away from government policy and real power.

With men and ladies of the court promoting sexual appeal in their court finery, Raleigh's flamboyance endeared him to Bess, the daughter of Sir Nicholas Throckmorton, who had been Leicester's close ally. With Sir Nicholas having died in 1571, his widow, Anne née Carew, was determined to achieve a good marriage for her only daughter. In November 1584, after various suitors had been rejected, the 19-year-old Bess was appointed a gentlewoman of Elizabeth's privy chamber, among whom extra-marital affairs were heavily frowned upon.[6] 'Illicit sex and unauthorised marriage were threats to the social hierarchy ... Lax morals among [Elizabeth's] attendants was a stain on her princely image.'[7] This did not prevent Bess, in 1591, becoming pregnant by the wealthy and irresistibly good-looking Raleigh. (He already had an illegitimate daughter, born while he was in Ireland. The child's mother, Alice Gould was left £333 in his will.) The erotic nature of his relationship with the attractive Bess is not in doubt. He wrote of her:

> Nature that washed her hands in milk,
> And had forgot to dry them,
> Instead of earth took snow and silk,
> At love's request to try them,
> If she a mistress could compose
> To please love's fancy out of those.
>
> Her eyes he would should be of light,
> A violet breath and lips of jelly

> Her hair not black, nor over-bright
> And of the softest down her belly;
> As for her inside he'd have it
> Only of wantonness and wit.[8]

By this time, Raleigh's standing with the queen was beginning to plateau. He wrote that the court shone 'like rotten wood', despite him continuing to benefit from royal perquisites.[9] His favour was declining because Essex was successfully combatting his near monopoly of Elizabeth's attention, but he was not ignored completely. In 1592, he was granted the crumbling Sherborne Castle in Dorset and, by 1594, had sufficient wealth to build a new modern residence in the French style with huge windows and magnificent plasterwork on the site of its former hunting lodge. 'Sherborne Lodge', now more generally known as 'Sherborne New Castle', is still standing.

Although the Devereux family mistrusted Raleigh, Penelope was an acquaintance of Bess, and Essex needed his backing for a campaign he was planning in support of the French Huguenots. With Essex cultivating him, Penelope renewed her friendship with Bess and soon learned that she was expecting Raleigh's child and in need of help. Elizabeth would certainly not approve, but Penelope, who was in a similar condition with Charles Blount's child, was present when Raleigh secretly married Bess in the fourth month of her pregnancy on 19 November 1591. After Bess's son, Damerei (from Raleigh's ancestor, John de Amerie, a Plantagenet connection) was born on 29 March 1592 at her brother Arthur Throckmorton's house at Mile End, he was moved with a wet nurse to Leicester House. On 10 April, Essex was a godfather when Damerei was baptised at St Clement Danes.

Ever the consummate dissembler, Raleigh hotly denied his marriage when challenged by Robert Cecil, but Cecil already knew he was lying. Raleigh had by then been appointed admiral and was in the middle of planning and provisioning an expedition, which he had financed, to challenge Spanish settlements in Panama. As soon as Damerei was born, he sailed from Chatham, reaching Portland two days later to load supplies before moving on. Up to then he had rarely gone to sea and, by his own admission, never slept well onboard ship. It was not until 27 April that a favourable wind enabled him to depart, and, on the same date, Bess returned to court.

With Cecil watching Raleigh's every move, he sent Sir Martin Frobisher to catch up with his fleet carrying a demand from Elizabeth to recall him to court. With his fleet continuing on its way, he returned to Plymouth on 16 May and set out for London. Cecil and Elizabeth did not pounce immediately. With Raleigh having joined Bess, he arranged for her to return with Damerei and a wet nurse to her brother at Mile End and belatedly provided her with a marriage settlement. Then the questioning began. By June, the couple were under house arrest at Durham Place accused of offending their queen with a demonstrable lack of loyalty, and Bess was dismissed from court.

Even now, Elizabeth seemed to mellow, and, on 27 June, confirmed the transfer of the Sherborne estate to Raleigh. Nevertheless, he remained frustrated at his continued detention and told Howard of Effingham that he would benefit the queen very much better by rejoining his expedition. Despite writing sycophantic letters to his 'goddess', they carried no weight and he failed to acknowledge his wrongdoing. It was probably on Cecil's instigation that on 27 August, Raleigh and Bess, who was unwell, were moved with Damerei to the Tower, which became more fearful because the plague had again broken out in London.

Raleigh's fleet, over which he remained technically in command, had sailed on to the Caribbean. Although it failed in its objective of looting Panama City, as it returned it had the good luck to intercept and capture the *Madre de Dios,* a Spanish treasure ship containing a cargo worth £500,000. Without Raleigh in control, his crews were soon dissipating their captured booty, leaving only £150,000 worth of cargo on board. Cecil was horrified. When the ship was brought into Dartmouth, there were sailors 'bedecked in diamonds'.[10] Sir John Hawkins immediately called for Raleigh to be permitted to assist in protecting what was left of the cargo. When Raleigh promised Elizabeth and her council £80,000 if she would release him from his 'unsavoury dungeon' in the Tower, she signed the order. Although he remained banned from court and from his position as captain of the guard, he retained the Sherborne estate and his appointments in the West Country. Not wanting to confuse things, he did not seek Bess's release from the Tower. With London being hot, the plague remained virulent causing the new law term to be brought to an end. The playhouses remained closed and the queen stayed at Hampton Court. In October, Damerei, who was aged 6 months, died of the plague. It was mid-winter before Bess was released, but she went straight to

Sherborne, while Raleigh returned from the West Country to Durham Place, still dealing with the booty he had been able to recover.[11]

With his 'ransom' paid, Raleigh was freed. Although he attempted to return to favour, Elizabeth clipped his wings by playing him off against Essex, just as Hatton had been used as a means of reining in Leicester.[12] Raleigh was still seen as an unpopular 'upstart' and became arrogant when faced with opposition. When Elizabeth stood up for him, Essex revealed all his immaturity by exploding 'into a barrage of character assassination against his hated rival'.[13] He was soon complaining that Raleigh was 'economical with the truth', condemning what he said as 'so rawe a lye' and playing on his nickname of 'Water', as a pejorative reference to his Devon burr. Raleigh, who was already in his forties and eleven years the elder, could no longer withstand this challenge for the queen's favour.[14]

On his release, Raleigh found himself outcast from political and courtly manoeuvring and was forced to remain away from the limelight. Even in his absence, the knives were out. In 1594, he was forced to deny accusations of atheism before The Court of High Commission arising out of his scientific meetings at Durham Place. Nevertheless, he remained extremely wealthy with his fortune enhanced by the surplus booty recovered from the *Madre de Dios*. He became a member of parliament and attended to his military and business commitments in the West Country, where he was financing privateers for overseas expeditions.

Raleigh was soon back with Bess but, by remaining away from court, was hopeful of his ultimate restoration to Elizabeth's favour. It was great compensation for them both when, in the autumn of 1593, Bess gave birth to a second son, who was baptised Walter (later shortened to Wat) on 1 November at Lillington, near Sherborne. Mother and son both endured an outbreak of the plague nearby and were temporarily separated, but both survived. Wat remained the apple of his father's eye and was the principal beneficiary of his will made in 1597, while Bess was granted a somewhat meagre £200 per annum with no further interest in his property. This lack of generosity has caused debate, but their mutual devotion cannot be doubted. Anna Beer has suggested that 'Bess Throckmorton had allied herself to one of the most visionary, mercurial men of her generation. It might be difficult to be relaxed in the company of a man who lived so intensely but it may well have been very exciting.'[15]

Chapter 16

The expedition to Portugal, 1589–91

With England having demonstrated its naval superiority during the Armada, Essex's continuing ambition was to distinguish himself militarily, seeing this as his route to political authority. The war against the Spanish was far from won, but with Armada vessels scattered round the Scottish and Irish coasts, there seemed to be a window of opportunity to take the battle to Spanish soil.[1] The Armada's defeat had been a Spanish setback but was not a killer blow.[2] Philip II was determined to take his revenge. If anything, its failure made the Spanish more resilient and they were soon wise to attacks by privateers on their shipping along the Iberian coastline. Many galleons returned unscathed from the Armada (it was its armed merchantmen that suffered worst) and were soon refitted to return to the fray. Their fleet became far more effective after the building of twelve massive new warships, 'the Twelve Apostles', designed along English lines for improved speed. By developing better navigational skills with more accurate cartography and cosmography, they could now provide their treasure fleets with an escort of warships. They also strengthened their fortifications in the Azores.

One promising English means of challenging the Spanish in Portugal was to support the claim of Dom António, Prior of Crato, to the Portuguese throne. Dom António was a grandson of the former King Manuel I, as an illegitimate son of the deceased Prince Louis, Duke of Beja. Nevertheless, he had been defeated by the Spanish in 1580 at the battle of Alcântara and was not a charismatic leader. He later made an unsuccessful attempt to form a Portuguese government in the Azores, before fleeing with the Portuguese Crown jewels to France, where he made an offer to hand over Brazil to the French if they would support him. In July 1582, despite receiving help from French, Portuguese and even English adventurers, their combined fleet was defeated by the Spanish at Ponta Delgada in the Azores. Although he returned to France, he was now in fear of being assassinated by Philip II's agents and turned to England for assistance.

In April 1589, Elizabeth agreed to send an Anglo-Dutch expedition to support Dom António in return for his promise of a permanent military base in the Azores from where Spanish shipping could be intercepted. By supporting him, she legitimised the use of English privateers in what would otherwise have been acts of piracy. The expedition was led by Drake, as Admiral, and Norreys, as General, financed with £80,000 raised by a joint stock company, to which Elizabeth contributed £20,000 and the Dutch £10,000. Essex's steward Gelli Meyrick believed that Essex provided £10,500. As usual, the funding was insufficient, but there were three objectives: to destroy the Spanish Atlantic fleet in harbour at Corunna, San Sebastian and Santander; to free Portugal from Spanish domination by placing Dom António on the Portuguese throne; and to set up a permanent base in the Azores, from where Spanish treasure fleets returning from America to Cádiz could be waylaid.

Despite contravening Elizabeth's express orders, Essex was determined to join the expedition and 'seemed hell bent on ruining his favoured position'.[3] Without telling even his closest confidants or servants, he crept away from court with his secretary to join the fleet, reaching Plymouth in a day and a half, ready to face any danger for the opportunity of capturing Spanish treasure. He had already recruited his younger brother, Wat, who was looking for a respite from the Puritan devotion of his tiresome wife. On arrival, he sent his groom back to London to provide Rich with the keys to his desk. This contained letters addressed to the queen and government members setting out his plans. His letter to Knollys, his grandfather, explained his financial predicament:

> What my courses have been I need not repeat, for no man knoweth them better than yourself. What my state is now, I will tell you: my revenue no greater than when I sued my livery; my debts at least two or three and twenty thousand pounds; her Majesty's goodness hath been so great as I could not ask more of her; no way left to repair myself but mine own adventure, which I had much rather undertake than to offend her Majesty with suits, as I have done heretofore. If I should speed well, I will adventure to be rich; if not I will

never live to see the end of my poverty. And so, wishing that this letter, which I have left for you, may come into your hands, I commit you to God's good protection. From my study some few days before my departure.[4]

Although Elizabeth sent messengers to recall him, he was determined to shake himself loose from dependence on her, seeing 'it as his duty to defy her when her demands failed to live up to his expectations on how a monarch should act'.[5] He now joined Wat on the *Swiftsure* under the captaincy of Sir Roger Williams. (In the previous year, Wat had served under Williams to support the Huguenots in Navarre.)[6] Although Knollys and Huntingdon chased after Essex, on their arrival in Plymouth on 5 April, the *Swiftsure,* with Essex on board, had already sailed for Falmouth hoping to join up with Drake's fleet, in which Williams was to command one of its five squadrons. With Drake and Norreys having already sailed, the *Swiftsure* did not catch up with them until after the main fleet's attack on Corunna.

From the outset, the Anglo-Dutch expedition was disorganised. It comprised six naval galleons, sixty armed merchantmen, sixty Dutch flyboats and twenty pinnaces. It was delayed at Falmouth when the Dutch failed to provide their promised ships on time (but not long enough to await the *Swiftsure*'s arrival). This resulted in one-third of the victuals on board being consumed before their departure.[7] Although the expedition had amassed 19,000 volunteers, only 1,800 were veterans, and a lack of siege guns and cavalry compromised its objectives. Drake did not attack Santander, where many Spanish ships were 'unrigged upon the shore', as the unfavourable wind made it an extremely difficult target by sea. He thus focused on Corunna, which contained only one galleon, two galleys and a few lesser vessels, making it almost defenceless. Norreys's troops inflicted 500 casualties in taking the lower town with its wine cellars, while Drake destroyed thirteen merchant ships. Nevertheless, the fortified upper town was vigorously defended and, being without siege guns, Norreys lost 1,500 men when three major assaults were repulsed. They also lost four captains and three ships, which resulted in twenty-four transports, carrying 3,000 mainly Dutch personnel, retiring back to England or to La Rochelle.

The next step (and the most important in terms of potential reward) was to stir up a Portuguese uprising in support of Dom António's claim to the Portuguese Crown, which had been held by Philip II since 1580. Only a few days out from Corunna, the fleet was at last joined by the *Swiftsure*. While this was welcome, Drake and Norreys had received orders to send Essex back to England, which he was determined to ignore. Luckily, adverse winds made his return impossible and Essex was one of the first ashore when they landed at Peniche in Portugal on 6 May, 'wading through the water up to the shoulders'.[8] When Williams and Essex took the castle, they left the town in the hands of Dom António's supporters, while the Portuguese pretender headed overland for Lisbon, expecting to gather support as he went. Norreys and Essex went with him taking 11,000 men, while Drake moved his 110 ships along the coast to Cascais at the entrance to the Tagus. Support from the Portuguese failed to gather momentum, and only forty local horsemen rallied to Dom António's call. Norreys's troops were forced to plunder for food as they went and arrived outside Lisbon at the end of May exhausted and ineffective, having been continuously harried by Spanish cavalry. With the Archduke Albert (a younger son of Maximilian II, the Holy Roman Emperor) now being the Portuguese Viceroy, he had garrisoned Lisbon with 7,000 Portuguese and Spanish troops. Although Essex attacked grain stores outside the walls and embedded his lance in the city gates, this was to little effect in the face of continuing lightning cavalry attacks. With the archduke having forty ships positioned to protect the Tagus, Drake held back and, although he seized the cargoes of sixty Baltic merchantmen, these provided small recompense. With Norreys being without guns, he sent to Elizabeth for reinforcements or a siege train, but she was reluctant to embark on a land war. This left him with no choice but to abandon the attack on Lisbon.

By this time supply ships had arrived from England, bringing a letter to Essex from the queen reiterating her call for his return. This continued:

> Your sudden and undutiful departure from our presence and your place of attendance you may easily conceive how offensive it is, and ought to be, unto us. Our great favours bestowed on you without deserts have drawn you thus to neglect and forget your duty: for other constructions we cannot make of those your strange actions.[9]

Although Essex was furious at being treated as her poodle, he obeyed her instructions and, in June, left for England with Norreys, who brought the sick and wounded with him onboard the main fleet. They now hit adverse weather and lost more men after facing opposition when landing at Vigo for repairs.

Drake, who had fallen out with Norreys, continued the expedition's plan by sailing on to the Azores, determined to salvage a positive outcome. He took twenty ships and his pick of the remaining 2,000 men fit for service, hoping to hunt down a Spanish treasure fleet. With disease reducing his available manpower, the Spanish got the better of skirmishes at sea and, after encountering a heavy storm while plundering Porto Santo in Madeira, he could no longer continue, particularly as his flagship, the *Revenge,* sprang a leak (and nearly foundered as he returned to Plymouth). It was a disaster. The expedition's investors had lost forty ships, many of them on the return journey to England, in addition to eighteen launches lost at Corunna and Lisbon. Dom António received no further English support and died penniless in 1595 in exile in France.

Although Rich and Penelope tried to soften Elizabeth's wrath, Essex found himself shouldering the blame, and her fury threatened to end his career. Williams was so scared that he made a will, leaving 'my great ruby unto my Lady Rich'.[10] Even now, Essex remained popular after his much-vaunted heroism in taking Peniche and at Lisbon. Such was Elizabeth's indulgence when she saw him that he was soon back getting his own way, but was forced to sell his manor house at Keyston, being 'so far in debt, and so weary of owing'.[11]

It was not all doom and gloom. In the three years following the Spanish Armada, English privateers, financed by the likes of Raleigh, Cumberland and Martin Frobisher, had some notable successes, particularly in capturing the Portuguese treasure ship, the *Madre de Dios*. They accumulated a haul of more than 300 prizes with a declared value of more than £400,000. The London merchant John Watts financed several expeditions, particularly those led by Christopher Newport, who raided the West Indies in 1590 and, despite the loss of an arm, blockaded Cuba in 1591.

By 1591 the Spanish had become better able to retaliate. On a major expedition to the Azores, Lord Thomas Howard with a squadron intent on waylaying Spanish treasure ships was attacked at Flores by a much larger Spanish fleet of fifty-five vessels. Despite being heavily outnumbered, he slipped away to safety. This left Sir Richard Grenville, his Vice Admiral on the *Revenge*, who had been left while transferring crew members back on board recuperating from a fever epidemic. He now found himself confronting the Spanish on his own in what proved a suicide mission against overwhelming odds. He fought for twelve hours, heavily damaging fifteen galleons, but when he was mortally wounded his crew, who were out of powder, surrendered. By this time, according to Raleigh, the *Revenge* was 'marvellous unsaverie, filled with bloud and bodies of deade and wounded men like a slaughter house'.[12]

PART IV

HONING DEVEREUX AMBITIONS

Chapter 17

Building bridges with James VI, 1589–90

It was Leicester who had been determined to cultivate all the potential heirs to the English throne to ensure that he was favourably positioned when Elizabeth died. He maintained a warm correspondence with Mary Queen of Scots, assuring her that he would support her claim on Elizabeth's death. He had also remained on friendly terms with both Catherine Grey (the sister of Jane) and Margaret, Countess of Lennox, who, as descendants of Henry VII, also had a claim. Margaret infuriated Elizabeth when her surviving son, Charles Stuart, secretly married Elizabeth Cavendish, the daughter of Bess 'of Hardwick', Countess of Shrewsbury. When their daughter Arbella was born, Leicester arranged her betrothal to his illegitimate son, Robert Sheffield, later substituting 'the Noble Imp'. Despite having made these overtures, he paid even more attention to James VI, and it has already been seen that Dorothy Devereux eloped with Thomas Perrot, following her stepfather's proposal that she should marry the Scottish king.

With James being brought up as a confirmed Protestant, he never veered from his adherence to the reformed faith and his claim to rule by divine right. His views were criticised by the Scottish Government, led by John Maitland of Thirlestane, who argued that he ruled by the will of the people. Both at home and in his aspirations to become the English king, James began to soften the edges of his religious affiliation to attract a broader church of supporters, despite remaining politically Protestant to appeal to the English government's Puritan bias.

James found the structure of the Church of England with its hierarchy of bishops much more appealing than that of the Scottish Kirk. To weaken the Scottish government's authority, he turned to a group of dissident Scottish Catholic earls led by the Earl of Huntly to undermine Thirlestane's 'overweening' authority. This opened him to accusations of being in sympathy with Catholic views. With no obvious Catholic pretender having a reasonable dynastic claim to compete with him, James promoted the notion among European Catholic powers that he would make a more tolerant Protestant monarch of England than Elizabeth, hoping they would recognise that if either France or Spain should gain control of England, the delicate European balance of power would be lost. At the same time, he cultivated the Dutch rebels in their stance against the Spanish, hoping to demonstrate a greater commitment to their cause than the ever-cautious Elizabeth. As a by-product of this policy, he greatly enhanced Scottish trade in northern Europe.

Even the Spanish saw James as a more appropriate claimant than his mother with her close French ties. He thus carefully represented himself as 'well-disposed' to the European Catholic world and built bridges with Henri IV, who pragmatically became Catholic to retain the French throne. To avoid the opprobrium of papal excommunication suffered by Elizabeth, James permeated his tolerant views in a secret correspondence with Pope Clement VIII and cultivated 'the civil friendship of Roman Catholic governments'. Although the Pope never endorsed James's claim to the English throne, he never denounced it, but rumours of James's negotiations were mistrusted and misinterpreted in Scotland.

It was Penelope who took up her brother's cause against what the Devereuxes saw as the younger Cecil's seemingly corrupt Puritan government. She rekindled Leicester's former friendship with the Scottish king as the means of promoting their interests. She was able to recommend the poet, Henry Constable, to act as James's go-between with the papacy.[1] With the Cecils firmly in authority in English government, Essex's hopes of advancement lay in the expectation that James would succeed Elizabeth. James had always favoured those of noble blood and saw the Cecils as political upstarts. He knew that Essex was his leading English supporter and recognised their need for each other.[2] James's demonstration of sympathy for Catholics fitted well with Catholic support for the Devereux faction in London. Following Leicester's death, James wrote to Essex to commiserate, and Essex confirmed that he would support him as Elizabeth's likely heir, just as other courtiers were doing.[3] With Burghley making overtures for peace with the Spanish, the Devereuxes hinted to James that the Cecils preferred the Infanta's rival claim to his own (although this was never the case).

Constable, who dedicated about thirty of his sonnet-sequence on *Diana* to Penelope, became one of her couriers. He delivered a gold-cased portrait miniature of her by Nicholas Hilliard with a poem written in her praise as a gift for the Scottish king. James was impressed by the portrait (and the 'fineness of her wit') but her mild effort at flirtation ended abruptly on his betrothal to Anne of Denmark.[4] Later in the year, Essex and Penelope wrote joint letters to James delivered by Richard Douglas, a nephew of Archibald Douglas, the Scottish ambassador in London. (Archibald is better known for being the likely murderer of James's father, Lord Darnley, at Kirk o' Field.)[5] With Jean Hotman having handled Leicester's earlier negotiations with James, Penelope also took him into her employment, providing him with lodgings in London. Although Jeanne's growing family now prevented her from working for Penelope, she continued to make her headdresses. Rich, who had not been consulted about Hotman's appointment, objected to the expenditure, but Penelope wrote to Jeanne on 11 September 1589 that she had had it out with him and they could remain for the time being. The letter also contained a one-line instruction for Hotman to act as her go-between delivering a message to James.[6] Unfortunately, Burghley received a tip off from Edinburgh about Penelope's correspondence from the same Fowler who had absconded with £8,000 collected from Leicester's debtors. As Burghley had signed the warrant for Fowler's house to be searched, he was clearly not too particular from where he sourced sensitive information.

In July 1589, Jean Hotman delivered a first consignment of letters to his contact at the Scottish court, who turned out to be in Fowler's pay. Fowler reported back that the Essex faction was telling James of its distaste for Burghley's government.[7] He also reported that James was receiving friendly overtures from 'Rialta, Ernestus and Richardo'. He had seen 'a long scroll' which divulged that Rialta was Penelope, Ernestus was Essex and Richardo was Rich, while James was codenamed Victor. Burghley was shown messages, which explained that, with Elizabeth unlikely to live more than a year or two, James could count on their support for him rather than for Arbella Stuart. This was dangerous, as the Treason Act of 1571 made it a crime to assert someone's succession rights.[8] Had he wished, Burghley could have proceeded against them, but did not do so, perhaps fearing the likely repercussions when Elizabeth died.[9]

Essex was now the Scottish king's most trusted English ally, but with Hotman's delivery system having been infiltrated, he was no longer useful. In the autumn of 1590, after the birth of Penelope's son Henry, the Hotmans returned to the more palatable religious regime developing in France.

Chapter 18

Devereux romances and unrest in France, 1589–93

Following the failure of the Portuguese expedition, Essex managed to return to favour with Elizabeth with help from both Leicester's sister-in-law, the Countess of Warwick, who was a lady-in-waiting, and from his mother's uncle, Hunsdon, assisted by the likes of Burghley, Hatton and Walsingham. It was clear that they did not see his negotiations with James VI as a political threat. He was also championed by Leicester's former Puritan allies, who needed a friend at court. Having no equivalent backing, Raleigh retired to Ireland. Even now, Elizabeth remained unrelenting in her hatred of Lettice. She told Essex to persuade his mother to hand Wanstead over to him, arguing that it would make a fitting country estate for a queen's favourite to entertain official visitors. Lettice preferred Benington and had not spent much time at Wanstead since the death of the Noble Imp. Even so, Essex was reluctant to approach her on so delicate a subject and, in March 1590, wrote to assure her that he did not want her to 'lose one penny profit or one hour of pleasure that you may have there'.[1] With Elizabeth continuing to apply pressure, she asked him to entertain her there on May Day 1590, but refused to allow him to visit his mother to discuss it. The negotiations took months, and Wanstead was not formally transferred to him until 1593. Elizabeth did not stop there. She seized Leicester House, selling most of its contents to pay off Leicester's debts due to the Crown before returning it denuded of furniture. Lettice refurbished it from Wanstead, but later handed it over to her son, who renamed it Essex House.

Essex was enjoying an on-again, off-again sexual relationship with Walsingham's daughter, Frances, Philip Sidney's widow.[2] This had continued in secrecy for some time, although it is not clear when it was first consummated. In December 1589, Walsingham, who had suffered

75

for years with urinary problems, made a will and died in the following April at his house in Seething Lane. Elizabeth had rather feared her 'moor', but greatly respected him for having outlaid vast sums from his personal fortune in maintaining his spy network. She forgave his debts and provided Frances with an annuity of £300.

Although it is romantic to believe that Philip Sidney had asked Essex to look after his wife and infant daughter, this is by no means certain. (Sir Roy Strong claimed that she went through some form of betrothal ceremony six months *after her husband's death*, but Steven Veerapen has questioned whether he intended to say *after her father's death* more than three years later.) By 1590, she was indisputably sleeping with him, and their eldest son was born in January 1591. She was an attractive widow and may have set her cap at the handsome beau, but even with £300 per annum, she was in no position to rescue his parlous finances.[3] As a narcissistic favourite surrounded by ladies seeking his favours at court, their marriage has been seen as a social obligation to the wife of his dead colleague, even though it took him more than three years to come round to it. Meanwhile, he continued to enjoy the company of other court ladies, and he married Frances only after she became pregnant. It was never a great romance; he found her 'submissive, obedient and pleading', and lacking the Devereux sparkle of his mother and sisters.[4] When Elizabeth learned of the marriage, she 'raged volubly' at Frances's lack of fortune and nobility, considering her inappropriate as an earl's spouse. Furthermore, she did not approve of her favourites marrying without her consent, believing that it made her look a laughing stock.[5] Raleigh took advantage of Essex's discomfiture with acrimonious verses to demean him, but Elizabeth recognised the 'necessary evil' for a favourite to beget children, so that, within a fortnight, he was restored to her side.[6]

Following the assassination of Henry III of France in August 1589, the Guises had formed a Catholic League with the Spanish to challenge the accession of the Huguenot Henry of Navarre, now Henry IV. Essex now saw France as 'the theatre and stage whereon the greatest actions are acted'.[7] Through his childhood acquaintance, Gabriel Montgomery, he asserted his credentials by writing a personal letter to the French king and had been courting his ambassador, Jean de la Fin, Sieur de Beauvoir La Nocle since his return from the Portugal expedition.

In October 1590, the Spanish sent an expedition of 4,500 men under Don Juan de Àguila (who was to cross swords with Charles Blount in

Ireland ten years later) to Saint-Nazaire in support of Philippe Emmanuel of Lorraine, Duke of Mercoeur, commanding the Catholic League. With the Spanish needing harbours to resupply their troops and fortresses to maintain control, Mercoeur captured Blavet (later Port Louis) on the south Brittany coast. From here the Spanish could threaten shipping and harbours along the south coast of England and support the rebels in Ireland.

With the Dutch having prevented the use of the Low Countries as a prospective base for Spanish attacks on Dutch and English shipping, the Spanish occupied Dunkirk from where Spanish privateers under the much-feared Admiral Antoine de Bourgogne, Seigneur de Wäcken, were able to challenge local shipping. Although the Dutch tried to keep the 'Dunkirkers' holed up, their blockade was frequently broken. With Henry IV having his hands full, Elizabeth offered her assistance if he would provide her with Calais as a secure base.

Despite being heavily pregnant, Penelope cultivated Huguenot friendships through the Hotmans, sending another portrait miniature by Hilliard to the new ambassador, Aymar Chaste. Her son was born on 9 August 1590 at her mother-in-law's house at Stepney, and on 6 September she was 'churched' there after his safe delivery. With Rich having helped in her attempts to improve her brother's standing with Elizabeth, Essex approached Henry of Navarre, newly enthroned as Henry IV of France, with an invitation to become a godfather for the new arrival, who was named Henry in his honour.[8]

Although the baby Henry joined his siblings in the nursery at Leighs, Penelope did not return there immediately, but wrote that she had spent the next month 'a hundred miles from my house'.[9] She is known to have been with Frances in the latter stages of Frances's pregnancy, visiting her during her lying in at Walsingham House in Seething Lane. Despite believing that her brother could have chosen better, Penelope remained on friendly terms with her sister-in-law. It is not clear what else she was up to. She had no need to support Essex, who was at the height of his power, but her actions seemed to be motivated by her having a new love.

On 17 November 1590, Essex stage-managed the Accession Day tilt hoping to upstage the other challengers at the joust.[10] Its timing signalled Elizabeth's return to London to be seen by the people after her progresses around the country to avoid the prevalence of the plague and to be seen by her subjects. With church bells being rung and cannons fired, the streets were thronged with people enjoying the festivities. Penelope knew all the participants at the tilt, many of whom were family members, but Essex stole the show dressed in black armour and driving a black chariot drawn by 'coal black steeds'.[11] Was this his way of mourning Philip Sidney, whose wife he had recently married? He certainly rode more recklessly and shattered more lances than the other competitors.

Another participant who stood out from the crowd was the less well-known but equally flamboyant Sir Charles Blount, dressed in armour in the Sidney colours of gold and blue. With Sidney's admiration for Penelope being well-known, this may have been a gesture that she was now Charles's Stella. This analogy was not lost on George Peele, who recorded the joust in a poem:

> Comes Sir Charles Blount, in or and azure dight:
> Rich in his colours, richer in his thoughts,
> Rich in his fortune, honour, arms and art.

This echoed Philip's lines in sonnet 37 of Astrophil and Stella, mentioned earlier:

> Towards Aurora's Court a Nymph doth dwell,
> Rich in all beauties which man's eye can see:
> Beauties so far from reach of worlds, that we
> Abase her praise, saying she doth excel
> Rich in the treasure of deserv'd renown,
> Rich in the riches of a royal heart,
> Rich in those gifts which give th'eternal crown:

Early in the New Year of 1591, Frances was safely delivered of a son, who, on 22 January, was baptised Robert at St Olave's, Seething Lane, with Lettice as godmother and Sir Francis Knollys and Rich as godfathers. While still in London, Penelope enjoyed the company of her old friend Anne Bagot, now married to Richard Broughton, the steward at Chartley. Although her relationship with Charles may not, by then, have been consummated, the rumourmongers were busy. Broughton wrote to Anne's father 'that she does not greatly care how extraordinarily she be used'.[12] It is not known when the relationship began. Certainly, she did not become pregnant with Charles's child until about June 1591 and he was occupied in military matters during much of the intervening period. With no satisfactory form of contraception and her undoubted fecundity, it is reasonable to assume that, at the time of the joust, their romance was 'chivalrous and platonic'. It is sometimes said that she had children by Rich even when her affair with Blount was in full swing. This is probably because her earlier children by Charles all took her married surname of Rich. It seems more likely that her conjugal relationship with Rich ended after Henry's birth, and only afterwards did she begin an affair with Charles. The couple went to great lengths to maintain secrecy, 'preserving the semblance of Penelope's marriage' to Rich, not knowing how he would react. Both before and after becoming pregnant by Charles, she spent extended periods with her children at Leighs, even taking her mother and Dorothy with her. Rich placed no bar on her visits and seems to have condoned her affair, perhaps hoping it would blow over. He wanted to maintain his close association with Essex, benefiting as he did from his powerful position at court. Penelope continued to support him in public life and even returned to nurse him when he fell ill. There is no evidence that he treated her badly, despite Charles's later claims, but he wanted to avoid appearing as a cuckold.

Following the Accession Day tilt, Essex pressurised Elizabeth to send a force to support the Huguenots in protecting the strategically important port of Brest. Despite pleading on bended knee to be given command, she turned him down, probably to punish him for going to Portugal and for his secret marriage, appointing the far more experienced Norreys in his stead. In the spring of 1591, Norreys set out for Brittany.

If a romance between Charles and Penelope did begin in the latter part of 1590, it was threatened by Charles's determination to gain more military experience. 'He was grown by reading (whereunto he is much addicted) to the theory of a soldier; so was he strongly invited by his genius to the acquaintance of the practique of war.'[13] In early 1591, he 'stole' away to Dover to join up with Norreys at Brest. He arrived in Brittany with his company but, having been promoted colonel, hoped to command a regiment. When Elizabeth heard of his departure without her consent she was furious and recalled him immediately. She told him: 'You will never leave it until you are knocked on the head, as that inconsiderate fellow Sidney was. You shall go where I send you. In the meanwhile, see that you lodge in the Court, where you may follow your book, [and] read and discourse of the wars.'[14] Despite him being over

30, she was treating him as an 'irresponsible youngster and an arm-chair soldier'.[15] Penelope must have been greatly relieved.

It was some compensation for Charles that he remained on full pay, receiving £400 for his military services in 1591 and 1592 by special warrant of Her Majesty.

> In June 1593, Elizabeth wrote that Sir Charles Blount, having been kept in attendance on her, had been forced to absent himself from his charge in Brittany. She therefore directed that he should be paid £200 (per annum), with the usual allowance for servants, from April 1593, during her pleasure. [He] was being paid a fighting officer's wages for lodging in the Court.[16]

If she had any inkling of his romance with Penelope, she ignored it.

Charles was lucky not to be in France. The campaign in Brittany went badly. On 10 May 1592, Àguila and Mercoeur routed a Huguenot and English force (much reduced by sickness) besieging Craon. Although Huguenot lives were spared, the Spanish massacred any remaining English to avenge the slaughter of Armada refugees in Ireland. In 1593, with France remaining irretrievably split, Henry IV shocked his Huguenot allies by becoming Catholic, famously concluding that 'Paris is worth a Mass'. This did not end the hostilities. In a later action, Norreys supported Royalists under Marshal d'Aumont attempting to regain control of Fort Crozon commanding the entrance to Brest. 'On 10 November 1594, after a month's siege, during which three assaults had been bloodily repulsed, the attackers burst through the breaches and put the remnant of the garrison to the sword.'[17] Its 300 Spanish defenders under Àguila had caused the deaths of 3,000 attackers, either killed or from sickness. Cyril Falls claims that this loss of life influenced Charles's later decision in Ireland to allow Àguila's garrison at Kinsale to surrender on generous terms.

Chapter 19

Essex's support for Henry IV, 1591–92

By mid-July 1591, Elizabeth had been encouraged by Burghley to send a second expedition to support Henry IV and the Huguenots. Essex was given command, even though he was not yet 25, but his earldom made him of appropriate rank and his appointment was supported by Burghley, Hatton and even Henry IV. In all probability, Burghley, who doubted Essex's ability, may have seen it as a way to demonstrate his shortcomings to Elizabeth. It also provided an opportunity, in Essex's absence, to promote his son to the position of Elizabeth's secretary, which Essex was opposing. This role had remained vacant since William Davison, the previous secretary, was thrown in the Tower after implementing Mary Queen of Scots' death warrant. (The newly knighted Robert Cecil did not receive the job at this stage but was appointed to the privy council.)

'On 22 July [Elizabeth] signed Essex's commission as "Captain General of the English forces sent into Normandy" and he set off [taking] his brother Wat with him.'[1] Following his return from Drake's expedition to the Azores, Wat had retired back home to await another opportunity for military action with his marriage already in trouble. His 'high spirits' in the company of Yorkshire squires 'didn't square with Margaret's piety'.[2] Huntingdon had 'to lecture him for not spending more time with his wife'.[3] After receiving his brother's call, Wat came at once, and Essex departed without a word being said to Frances, who was again pregnant and deeply hurt at 'your going away without taking leave of me'.[4] When she eventually received a letter, she meekly promised to 'strive to overcome those extreme passions which my affection hath brought me to, and I will have the more care of myself for your little one's sake'.[5]

Henry IV gained Elizabeth's trust with a sycophantic letter asking to 'spend two hours with you so that at least once in my life I may have the honour of seeing her to whom I have dedicated my time and my life and whom I love and revere more than anything in the world'.[6] She travelled to Portsmouth to meet him, but he did not show up. Although she had been taken in, Essex continued his extravagant plans, spending £14,000 beyond Elizabeth's allowance to outfit his troops in his distinctive orange and white livery. In July, she inspected them at Covent Garden before their departure.[7] In an effort to curb him, she provided a 'royal commission' to delineate his actions.[8]

The campaign went badly from the outset. On arrival at Dieppe, Henry had not signed the treaty underpinning English support, and Essex was not permitted to join up with him until he did. Henry also failed to live up to his ambassadors' undertaking to pay the English troops on arrival. At last, Williams, who had arrived with an advance party, brought an invitation for Essex to meet Henry at Compiègne, north of Paris, but this involved a journey through Catholic territory. On arrival with his escort of 200 cavalry, Essex was greeted and feasted in style by Henry. Although Essex had understood that his role would be to assist him in taking Rouen, he soon learned that Rouen was of little interest to Henry, who merely wanted the English to deter its Catholic garrison from sallying out elsewhere. Meanwhile, Henry went off to attract support from German Protestant princes, but promised to join the siege once Essex had prepared the ground.

Essex now had to lead his escort in its very distinctive livery back to his main force which had marched to Pavilly, fifteen miles from Rouen. As he went, members of his escort were picked off by raiding parties sent out from Rouen, and he reached Pavilly to find that his main force (many of whom were his tenants from home) was being decimated by disease.

Fully expecting that Henry IV would send troops to join him, Essex disobeyed Elizabeth's orders and commenced the siege. On 8 September, Wat was killed after being shot in the head by a sniper. Essex was devastated and kept to his tent in a state of depression and suffering from fever. Although Elizabeth sent a message recalling him, he captured the town of Gournay, from where Rouen was being provisioned, and pleaded to be allowed to continue. She fumed over what she saw as his costly failure, although it was she and Burghley who had been duped by the French king. Although he made 'two brief trips to court to keep her informed, [he] ignored her advice to call off the campaign'.[9] She was incensed and sent him an order 'upon the sight hereof, to make your speedy return'.[10] She then changed her mind. With his bravado being generally admired, she countermanded her instruction and authorised him to stay, citing his success in taking Gournay. She was still complaining at the bad influences surrounding him, blaming Williams's 'rashness' for the loss of Wat. Essex did not receive her second message before setting out back to England. He was furious at being recalled and wrote: 'I see your Majesty is constant to ruin me; I do humbly and patiently yield to your Majesty's will.'[11]

In reality, Elizabeth held him in 'deep affection' and her mood softened when she saw him.[12] With Henry IV at last focused on Rouen, Essex returned to Normandy only to find half of his force dead or dying of plague, malaria and dysentery. After sending Elizabeth an expression of loyalty, she sent him 1,000 men from the Low Countries, and he bolstered morale outside Rouen by knighting twenty-four of his officers and inspecting his troops. Even now, Henry IV was dragging his feet and only arrived in November. In December, Essex had time to return to England with Wat's body. Although he was back at Rouen in mid-month, the winter was upon them and his men were deserting. In a final throw of the dice, he sent troops to scale the walls, but the ladders borrowed from Henry's troops were 8ft too short. He then offered to fight the Catholic League general in single combat, but his proposal was turned down. On Christmas Eve, Elizabeth ordered him to call off the siege and to return to England. With Hatton having died suddenly, she wanted him at her side, and he was home in the following month.

The tragedy of losing Wat hit Lettice hard, but it was less of a disappointment to his wife, Margaret. Even before his body was repatriated for burial, the Huntingdons were seeking a new husband for her, and she joined them in London with her mother. Being a wealthy widow, she was courted by Sir Thomas Posthumous Hoby, the son of the English ambassador to France, and by another Huntingdon ward, Sir Thomas Sidney, Philip's youngest brother. On 22 December, three months after Wat's death and before his burial at Carmarthen on 19 February 1592, she married Sidney; when he too died in 1595, Hoby took his opportunity and they were married on 9 August 1596. She continued living at Hackness, but none of her marriages provided her with children.

Chapter 20

Devereux marriage difficulties, 1591–92

It was not just Penelope's marriage which was facing difficulty. Essex became very rapidly bored with Frances. Following the birth of his heir, she did not involve herself in official entertaining. After his restoration to favour, she had the good sense to keep away from court and 'live very retired in her mother's house', leaving Elizabeth free rein to be with her favourite.[1]

There was a second problem; Frances was not following her father's Protestant path after having developed a close friendship with Marie Bochetel, the Catholic wife of the French ambassador, Michel de Castelnau, Sieur de Mauvissière. It was through Marie that she developed Catholic sympathies and ultimately converted. Their friendship was unwise as Castelnau's embassy had been infiltrated by a clerk in English government pay. As the embassy had provided a delivery service for Mary Queen of Scots' correspondence, it had all been read by the English government, which established that Castelnau was at the heart of the plotting against Elizabeth. He was soon recalled after being discredited in both England and France.

It was Penelope who became Essex's political hostess. In April 1591, he entertained the new French ambassador with his entourage at Wanstead after their arrival to seek help against Spanish incursions in western France. The visitors were sumptuously entertained in its forty acres of walled gardens surrounded by deer forests. Catering for them at short notice stretched the limits of Essex's steward, but bread flour was sent from 'Lady Rich's bakers at Leighs'.[2] Penelope was perfect in her role, speaking fluent French, buck-hunting with the best of them and, in the evening, singing to her lute or dancing to pieces written especially for her.[3] In May, she again returned to Wanstead for hunting parties. Shortly afterwards, she was pregnant with Charles's child, so he was probably there with her. Giving birth to an illegitimate child was a threat to her future with Elizabeth at court, but she and Charles were soon being entertained together by friends.

During the winter of 1591/92, with the plague failing to peter out as expected, Elizabeth disrupted court life by moving to Nonsuch Palace. Early in the new year, Frances gave birth to a second son at Walsingham House. On 21 January, he was baptised Walter after her deceased brother-in-law, with Sir Thomas Perrot, Sir William Knollys and Lady Walsingham as godparents, but sadly the child died within a month and was buried on 19 February. Frances may not have known that Essex's mistress, Elizabeth Southwell (one of Elizabeth's maids-of-honour) gave birth to a child, another Walter, at Lamphey only weeks earlier. It was common knowledge that Essex had been conducting affairs at court with four maids-of-honour simultaneously while married to Frances. He faced a dressing down from Lady Bacon, Burghley's sister-in-law (the mother of Anthony and Francis), who told him that he had made his wife's 'heart sorrowful to the hindrance of her young fruit within her'.[4] Although he hotly denied any wrongdoing, the knives were out for him. Even Penelope and Dorothy were shocked. Dorothy wrote: 'I infinitely long to hear that you are freed of your ill companion which is unworthy to be entertained by you.'[5] He managed to avoid censure from the queen for his indiscretion over 'Mistress Southwell's lameness' by 'persuading' Thomas Vavasour to accept the blame. Poor Vavasour faced a term of imprisonment in the Tower, and Elizabeth did not learn of the child's true paternity for years. When the boy was born, he was placed in Lettice's care and Elizabeth Southwell was later forgiven. At the age of 30 she married Sir Barentine Moleyns, who suffered an unfortunate nasal condition giving him an unsightly appearance, but she later provided him with a son and heir.[6]

Penelope's first child by Charles was a daughter born on 30 March 1592, the day following the arrival of Bess Thockmorton's son, Damerei. They could not break cover, and the child was immediately baptised Penelope 'Rich' at St Clement Danes in the Strand, before being moved to Leighs. Charles must have found this galling, but to live in open adultery was unacceptable and, having yet to inherit as Lord Mountjoy, he had no suitable establishment of his own.[7] So long as Essex remained alive, Rich did not wholly disassociate himself from Penelope, although they spent much time apart. She now lived mainly at Essex House, Wanstead and Chartley as her brother's guest, but frequently visited her grandfather at Grey's Court. She still made occasional visits to Leighs with lady friends, including Lettice, Dorothy and Anne Broughton, to see her children, and she nursed Rich there when he became ill. Frances, who was soon pregnant again, gave birth to a daughter at the end of 1592, named Penelope after her aunt, who became a godmother.

Chapter 21

Essex's attempts to develop his political standing, 1592–95

Essex's main objective after his trips to Portugal and Rouen was to restore his personal standing with Elizabeth, still hoping to outdo the Cecils and Raleigh. After successfully defending Lisbon, the Archduke Albert had been appointed Governor of the Low Countries. With Essex looking for an opportunity to restore his flagging military standing, he was determined to counter Spanish aggression caused by the archduke's arrival. He was not alone in feeling threatened by Burghley, who was progressively handing over authority to his son Robert. Anthony and Francis Bacon, the nephews of Burghley's wife, were bitter at finding their careers blocked to make way for their cousin. They sided with Essex, who found Francis Bacon's legal expertise invaluable despite his overt homosexuality. Anthony explained that although 'the bright beams of [Essex's] valour and virtue [had] scattered the clouds … malicious envy had stirred up against his matchless merit, [which] made the Old Fox [Cecil] to crouch and whine'.[1]

Although Essex continued to dream of military glory, the Bacons warned him that this was not the way to rise to supreme heights in government, as courting popularity made Elizabeth feel threatened.[2] They explained that she had never viewed him as a politician and retained him at her side only to amuse her, write sonnets and dance with her. They encouraged him to develop a political rather than a military persona. This was a bitter pill for him to swallow, but he tried to follow their advice while continuing to lean Elizabeth towards a more militant foreign policy.

Essex launched a charm-offensive and it was even suggested that he had turned over a new leaf. Anthony Bagot wrote to his father that he was 'a new man, clean forsaking all his former youthful tricks, carrying himself with honourable gravity'.[3] By the end of 1592, he was back at Elizabeth's beck and call. He spent Christmas with her at Hampton Court, where she granted him lands to help pay off his debts. By showing maturity and contrition, on Shrove Tuesday 1593 he was at last invited to join the privy council. Elizabeth always wanted to balance its opposing interests, and his appointment can be seen as an attempt by her to provide a counterweight to the overly mighty Cecils. He was expected to support Howard of Effingham over England's defensive arrangements and to consider the state of governance in Ireland.[4]

On 21 and 22 May 1593, Essex again hosted a party for French diplomats at Wanstead. This continued on a grand scale for several days. Penelope again acted as hostess, speaking both French and Spanish, as they also entertained Philip II's former Spanish secretary, Antonio Pérez. Having fallen foul of the inquisition and becoming a target for assassins, Pérez had fled to France in November 1591. He was a devious double-dealer, 'wanted for every crime from sodomy to seducing the king's mistress'.[5] After attaching himself to Henry IV's staff, he had arrived in England in the previous month, serving in the official envoy's train. He enjoyed the Wanstead hospitality and, despite being aged 59, was fascinated by Penelope. When the French delegation left in October, he remained behind and was employed at Essex House to provide information from both Paris and Madrid. Penelope found him intellectually stimulating. He shared her love of literature and her family's humanist philosophies. Like herself, he was an expert linguist but was a superficial rogue. He showered her with flowery compliments in Spanish, full of sexual wordplay, knowing that she was the only member of the household who would understand their meaning. She enjoyed his company and reciprocated with flowery responses of her own. He was also a hypochondriac, recommending the potions that he carried with him to her friends.

On the Bacons' advice, Essex concluded that he could develop his political authority by building up a spy network as Leicester and Walsingham had done. This would position him to shape England's foreign policy. Despite being crippled by gout, Anthony Bacon was now employed at Essex House as the backbone of an intelligence-gathering service. He had spent twelve years spying on Walsingham's behalf in France until forced to return after having to be rescued by the future Henry IV from legal proceedings over accusations of homosexuality with a page. Back in England, he retained a network of Continental connections, particularly with the Catholic double agent, Anthony Standen, who now returned from Spain to work for Essex in London. Another to join them was Thomas Phelippes, who had deciphered Mary Queen of Scots' correspondence during the Babington plot. They soon gathered up Walsingham's motley collection of agents and informants in need of a paymaster, and, with access to others through Pérez, were able to develop a clear lead over the Cecils in intelligence gathering.

Penelope became a key component in the espionage activities, often dining at Essex House to exchange information. She diffused any suspicion of underhand activity with displays of great courtesy when writing to Robert Cecil. Although Rich remained in the Devereux circle and visited Essex House, Penelope often dined with the secretariat without him and organised meetings as her brother's private secretary. Essex seems to have worried that she was moving about London too independently and asked Pérez to act as her escort. This concerned the Bacons, who found Pérez an uncomfortable colleague.

Although Henry IV called for Pérez, who remained in his employment, to return to France, Essex took him to court to gain Elizabeth's support for him to stay. When she agreed to delay his departure for the time being, Essex, Bacon, Pérez and Penelope dined at Walsingham House to celebrate. After spending more time in Pérez's company, Penelope became concerned for his health and safety. When he later fell ill at Essex House, there was concern that he had been poisoned on Philip II's instructions. Essex heard that Philip was employing the services of Dr Roderigo Lopez, Elizabeth's physician, for this purpose. Essex summoned Roger Giffard, another royal physician to investigate. Lopez was a Portuguese of Jewish extraction, who had been raised as a Christian and served at the Royal Court in Spain until pressure from the Inquisition had forced him to leave. On arrival in England, he had developed a successful medical practice in London and, in 1581, became Elizabeth's physician-in-chief. He also provided medical advice to Burghley and Robert Cecil and was reported, probably scurrilously, to have treated Essex for venereal disease. Unknown to Essex, Walsingham had previously employed him as an undercover agent, and he maintained contacts in Portugal and with Spanish officials, even acting as Elizabeth's intermediary with Dom António.

In 1593, Anthony Bacon learned that the Portuguese Stephano Ferreira da Gama, who was lodging with Lopez in London, was in secret communication with Spanish officials in Flanders. Bacon's investigations revealed that several Portuguese were associated in a spy ring with Lopez, apparently having worked on Walsingham's behalf. Further investigation showed that in 1591, Burghley was aware that another Portuguese, Manuel Andrada, had travelled to Spain using Lopez's name, hoping to trick Philip II into providing him with money and jewels to assassinate Elizabeth. Burghley was not clear whether Andrada was trying to extort money from the Spanish on false pretences, or whether Lopez was involved in a genuine plan for Elizabeth's murder, but Andrada had travelled without English government knowledge. Although Burghley tried to arrange Andrada's arrest on his return, he escaped abroad, but Lopez remained in England. After investigating Lopez, Burghley had concluded that he was not involved.

It would of course be a huge coup for Essex's new spy network if he could establish that Lopez was, after all, involved in a plot to poison Elizabeth. Despite having stumbled on the Portuguese spy ring's renewed communication with the Spanish, Essex remained unaware of Burghley's earlier investigation. He burst into Elizabeth to reveal his concerns that Lopez was a traitor. With Elizabeth being aware of Burghley's conclusion that Lopez was innocent, she refused to believe Essex, mocking him for trying to get even with Lopez for revealing his treatment for venereal disease. This made Essex even more determined, but, as Burghley was too unwell to be involved in investigating Lopez, it was left to Essex and Robert Cecil. They interrogated Manuel Luis Tinoco, another Portuguese spy, who arrived from Flanders with a promise of safe conduct. Under threat of torture, he admitted being tasked with co-opting Lopez into the murder plan. Furthermore, Tinoco was carrying letters instructing Ferreira to assume Andrada's role in the original murder plot. Although this demonstrated that a plot to entice Lopez into murdering Elizabeth existed, Lopez hotly denied involvement except for having retained some unwise contacts and having received a ring for his daughter from the Spanish. When Essex threatened Lopez with the rack, he admitted having tried to extort money from Philip by undertaking to poison the queen, but had no intention of doing so. With anti-Semitic feeling running high, Lopez, Tinoco and Ferreira were now doomed and were hanged, drawn and quartered. Elizabeth only reluctantly signed Lopez's death warrant and later contributed to the cost of his son's education. It is generally reckoned that Lopez had had no intention of poisoning her, but had been extremely foolish.

Essex House was not just the hub of the spy network. It had been used by Leicester as a centre for a cultivated circle of writers, artists and thinkers, including Philip Sidney, Edmund Spenser and Nicholas Hilliard, bent on shaping opinion on topical issues. 'Culture and politics went hand in hand and manipulating public opinion was an art form.'[6] Essex continued his stepfather's policy, providing magnificent displays of hospitality including revels, music and laughter in its riverside gardens.[7] With the cognoscenti congregating there, the court was in bleak contrast. With the aging queen increasingly withdrawn, its glamour was a thing of the past.

In 1596, Spenser returned to Essex House to write *Prothalamion* in celebration of the marriages of Elizabeth and Lucy Somerset, the sisters of Essex's ally, the Catholic Edward, 4th Earl of Worcester, Huntingdon's brother-in-law. Each verse ends with the refrain:

Sweet Thames, run softly, till I end my song.[8]

Shakespeare, with his focus on 'topical dramas with political bite', naturally gravitated towards the intellectual stimulus offered by this 'most exciting and avant-garde group of intellectuals and aristocrats in London'.[9] *Love's Labour Lost* 'recreated the diplomatic deer hunts at Wanstead' with Don Armado representing Pérez.[10] *Henry V* makes a reference to Essex's return from Ireland. With Shakespeare's first patron, Southampton, being an Essex ally, Shakespeare lampooned the Cecil faction, depicting William Brooke, 10th Lord Cobham, as Sir John Falstaff (despite hotly denying it!).[11] Furthermore, his sonnets contain puns on the name 'Rich'.[12] In late 1594, Southampton needed Essex's help to resolve a problem. His close associates, Charles and Harry Danvers had committed murder and needed to 'disappear' abroad. When Essex spirited them to France, they became his lifelong allies.

Penelope was the life and soul of the party. Richard Barnfield's *The Affectionate Shepheard* was dedicated to 'the right excellent and most beautiful lady, The Lady Penelope Rich'. There were countless allusions to *Astrophil and Stella,* the first unauthorised published version of which became available in 1591. (It was subsequently withdrawn, but the full sonnet sequence was printed in 1598.) The Catholic William Byrd, 'the finest composer of the Tudor age', set parts of *Astrophil and Stella* to music and wrote other songs about her.[13] His pupil, Thomas Morley, is said to have used her as the model for Diana in his *Oriana* songs. John Dowland made frequent mention, particularly in *Lady Rich's Galliard,* and an unknown composer wrote *Corranto Lady Rich.*[14] The French lutenist, Charles Tessier, dedicated his *Premier Livre de Chansons et Airs* to her, and two of its thirty-five songs were written for her to perform. One of these, *Câche toi, céleste soleil!,* compares her to Apollo, with the words:

> Your fine golden hair is not as rich
> As that of the lovely Rich
>
> And Europe does not deserve
> As much as our Penelope.[15]

Constable became 'spellbound' by her singing and beauty:

> Seeing and hearing thee we see and hear
> Such voice such light as never sung nor shone...

Penelope loved the adulation but was more than a beautiful adornment to the Essex House circle. She was one of its most accomplished performers with a 'magnificent mind'.[16] Her correspondence involved multi-layered wordplay, much admired by James VI. Her linguistic skills were undoubtedly honed with Pérez, but she may also have learned from the language tutor, John Florio, another member of the Devereux/Sidney circle, who dedicated works to her.[17] Florio was employed by Frances's friend, Marie Bochetel, to teach her daughter. Praise for Penelope benefited, of course, from the respect in which her brother was held, but she retained a cult following his downfall. (She was still dancing and singing into her forties despite having produced ten children.)

In February 1595, Essex visited Cambridge in a public relations exercise to promote his patronage and interest in learning. He was accompanied by Rich, Charles Blount, Pérez and Sir Robert Sidney,

Philip's brother. He chose the Accession Day celebration in November 1595 to demonstrate once more his prowess in the tiltyard. To maintain his standing as the most chivalrous knight and the crowd's hero, he took on fifteen challengers and shattered fifty-seven lances.[18] He also prepared a pageant, depicting himself as Elizabeth's official favourite.[19] This backfired when she thought he was trying to outshine her on what should have been her day.

Chapter 22

The Devereux flirtation with Catholicism, 1594–95

In May 1594, when Penelope was pregnant with Charles's second child, she developed a friendship with a charismatic Jesuit priest, John Gerard, son of Sir Thomas Gerard, Sheriff of Lancashire. Gerard had been secreted with the Wiseman family at Broadoaks (or Braddocks) Manor near Thaxted, about fifteen miles from Leighs. Despite regular searches, his priest hole remained undiscovered, but the Wisemans became concerned for his safety. With the Wisemans being the Riches' relations by marriage, Penelope agreed to harbour him in the relative security of the Puritan household at Leighs, and he arrived under the guise of delivering a message from Dorothy. He and Penelope had much in common. He was well-to-do, spoke several languages and was 'happy to indulge in hunting, hawking, cards and gambling' as a cover for his Jesuit activities.[1]

There was much about Gerard's quiet bookishness that reminded Penelope of Charles Blount. After dining with her with her household, she took him aside to discuss her religious doubts with him, while he tried 'to stir her into becoming a Catholic'. Before he left, she asked him 'how to prepare for confession'.[2] Sally Varlow argues that she was contrite about her long-running affair with Charles, despite her enduring love for him, so that she contemplated renouncing him. Conversing with a known Jesuit was not an action to be undertaken lightly, and Penelope will have been deadly serious. Before taking confession, she wrote to Charles to explain her plans. He dropped everything and came immediately to Leighs to dissuade her. Rather than challenge Gerard on the merits of Catholicism, he adopted subterfuge by providing Gerard with a series of questions to imply his own religious doubts. As an 'inveterate [and somewhat pedantic] student of theology', he listened to Gerard's answers and proceeded to wear down his arguments. Penelope now realised that if she took confession, he would cease to be her lover.[3]

By the end of April, Gerard had been arrested in London after a member of the Wisemans' staff informed on his whereabouts. Penelope never saw him again. He spent three years facing intermittent torture at the Tower, suspended by his wrists for hours at a time. In October 1597, he managed to escape by climbing over a roof and down a rope to a waiting boat on the Thames, from where he was spirited away.

Despite Charles remaining stalwartly Protestant, both he and Penelope had genuine sympathy for Catholics, employing them among their servants. They are known to have helped other Jesuits and to have associated with Catholic families such as the Digbys and her stepfather, Sir Christopher Blount. Essex was always supportive of Sir Christopher. In 1593 and again in 1597, Sir Christopher was granted a seat in Essex's giving in the House of Commons.

Dorothy also developed Catholic affiliations. In early 1594, Thomas Perrot died. Although they had a daughter, Penelope, their son, Robert, born two years earlier, did not survive. After the general disapproval of her marriage to Perrot, she was determined to redeem her standing with Elizabeth by opting for a glittering match with Henry Percy, 9th Earl of Northumberland, the only problem being that he was considered 'the white hope of Catholic resistance'.[4] He was also known as 'the Wizard Earl' in view of his interests in science, astronomy and mathematics.[5]

Marriage into the Percy family positioned the Devereuxes at the height of their influence. Essex hosted the wedding reception at Essex House, employing professional players at a cost of £10 to entertain the guests. The couple moved to live at Syon House on the Thames, which they leased from the Knollys family. In 1560, Sir Francis Knollys had been appointed Keeper of Syon for life, and, in 1577, the reversion had passed to his son, Robert. Neither father nor son considered Syon as their home, and it was used by the Exchequer during the plague in 1563. Having moved in, Northumberland almost immediately acquired the freehold, which has remained in Percy family ownership ever since. Northumberland was an anti-social and difficult husband (perhaps because he was deaf), and it proved a stormy marriage. Nevertheless, when Frances gave birth to Essex's third child, a son, in the spring of 1595, Northumberland stood as godfather, with the boy being named Henry after him. The baptism took place on 14 April at St Olave, Seething Lane, with Essex's ally, Sir Thomas, 5th Lord Burgh of Gainsborough (who later became Lord Deputy of Ireland) as the other godparent. Sadly, yet again, the child died the following year.

Catholicism became widespread among Essex's allies. Many of those supporting his rebellion were later involved in the Catholic-inspired Gunpowder Plot in 1605. With Essex calling for religious toleration, he faced serious embarrassment when a book by the Jesuit Robert Persons, under the pseudonym R. Doleman appeared from Antwerp entitled: *A Conference about the next Succession to the Throne of England*. This was not a subject that Elizabeth would discuss. She was determined to avoid naming a successor, fearing that any nominee would act as a catalyst for opposition to her rule. Anyone who was heard discussing the succession faced imprisonment or worse. To his great discomfort, Essex found that Persons had dedicated his book to him, mockingly claiming that 'no man is more high and eminent in place or dignity at this day in our realm than yourself'. Elizabeth found its content an anathema. It dismissed all the Protestant Tudor claimants, including James VI and Arbella Stuart, rejecting the Tudor belief in their divine right to rule. It argued that the Infanta Isabella of Spain (a descendant of John of Gaunt) was the preferred alternative. It then claimed that no one would 'have a greater part or sway in the deciding of this affair than the Earl of Essex'.[6] Although Essex's royal blood was not alluded to, it was well-known that he was descended from four of John of Gaunt's sons, (see Family Tree 1) and there were, of course, rumours that he was Henry VIII's great-grandson, albeit illegitimate. (See Endnote 1) The book only added to Elizabeth's paranoia. To avoid showing James VI undue favour, she ignored his invitation to stand as godmother to his son, Prince Henry, born in 1594. Nevertheless, she mollified Anglo-Scottish relations by embarking on correspondence with his queen, Anne of Denmark, while Essex continued to correspond with James.

With Elizabeth blaming Essex for Persons's book, he retired to his rooms for a few days until she visited him as the 'concerned lover' to accept his assurance that he was unaware of its origin. Even now, he was losing his powers over her. Another problem was his desperate financial situation. By 1598, he owed £30,000.[7] He had always enjoyed gambling and spent money extravagantly on his own and his family's behalf. On ceremonial occasions, he appeared with an entourage of a hundred or more supporters rigged out in his livery. The cost of subsidising his spy ring exceeded £400 per month. In July 1595, Pérez had finally been recalled to France by Henry IV, and no further effort was made to retain him. Even now, Essex provided him with a pension despite suspicions about his loyalty, and Penelope also remained in contact.

Chapter 23

Essex's efforts to focus attention on the growing Spanish threat, 1595–96

During 1593, the worst outbreak of plague for twenty years had forced Elizabeth to celebrate her Accession Day in November at Windsor rather than Whitehall. Successive wet summers from 1594 to 1597 caused failed harvests and skyrocketing prices. London was an uncomfortable place to live, and the poor were worse off than for 250 years. When rioting broke out in Southwark, its playhouses remained closed for months, forcing watermen, who carried passengers across the Thames, out of business.

Criticisms of government failure were compounded by fears of another Spanish invasion attempt. These were proved right when, on 27 July 1595, a landing party from Blavet, in Brittany, burned Mousehole, Newlyn and Penzance in Cornwall, while in Ireland Tyrone's rebels began to receive Spanish support.[1] Essex concluded that the only way to counter the Spanish was to renew an alliance with Henry IV, who was finding himself placed under similar pressure. Anti-Spanish concerns caused sufficient alarm for Essex's Francophile foreign policy to gain support. Although Essex hoped to be offered the use of Calais as a Continental base, Archduke Albert seized one of the forts overlooking its harbour and installed Spanish guns to deter English and Dutch ships from using it to resupply Henry IV. Essex called on Elizabeth to launch an expedition to restore the situation, but, as so often, she dithered, and he despaired at her lack of understanding of the military imperative. By 7 April 1596, the Spanish had broken into Calais, although the French continued to hold its citadel. Essex still believed that prompt action might have recovered the town, but Elizabeth's indecisiveness forced the French garrison into surrender, so that a relief expedition, which was to have included Charles, had to be abandoned. Spain now occupied Calais as a deep-water port on England's doorstep.

Despite the archduke's success, Essex returned to Plymouth determined to try once more but was again frustrated by Elizabeth. She ignored Pérez's reports that a massive fleet was being readied in Spain for a fresh invasion attempt.[2] 'Roberto il Diavolo', as Essex named Cecil, advised her to pay no attention, arguing that the Spanish ships were needed as escorts for their treasure fleets. Essex concluded that it would be 'against her will' to give him the opportunity to demonstrate his military prowess.[3] Further warnings arrived from as far away as the English ambassador in Turkey that Spain was not just building ships but was mobilising a mighty army. While this might be allocated to support Spanish troops at Calais, Brittany, or the increasingly militant Irish rebels, England was the more likely target.

Meanwhile, Essex was locked in a power struggle with Robert Cecil. With his network of agents having protected the queen, he was proving more than just a 'decorative' favourite.[4] He wanted Burghley's role as Elizabeth's chief political adviser, seeing himself as Leicester's natural successor to promote a hawkish foreign policy. Burghley was nervous of his alliance with the Bacons, fearing that their combined standing might outshine his son. He had even arranged for Robert Cecil to be knighted in 1591 to make him more appealing as his successor, and chose the timing of Essex's absence on the Cádiz expedition the following year to confirm with Elizabeth his formal appointment as Secretary of State (although he had been doing the job for seven years – but without the title or pay).

The Essex faction believed that Burghley wanted a seamless handover to his son to avoid his government's corrupt practices being revealed. Like his father, Robert Cecil wanted to prevent a war which might reveal the English exchequer's parlous state. While Essex and Penelope continued to respect Burghley as their former guardian, they had nothing but disdain for his son. This split the Council into opposing camps. If Essex dared to turn his back, he knew that the Cecils would pounce.

It was not just a matter of power. The role of Secretary of State generated substantial income. Burghley had amassed a huge fortune, building fabulous properties at Burghley in Northamptonshire and Theobalds near Enfield after holding the two most lucrative posts in government as Lord Treasurer and Master of the Wards.[5] Father and son also benefited from the plight of the Catholics. After Elizabeth's excommunication in

1571, although most papists remained continuously loyal, Burghley's agents had initiated a series of apparently Catholic plots designed to tarnish the image of Mary Queen of Scots as England's prospective heir. Robert Cecil had expanded his father's practice of pocketing fines from Catholic recusants to condone their non-attendance at Church of England services. This enabled Essex to appeal for Catholic support by promoting religious toleration, as Elizabeth had done at the beginning of her reign.

Despite the development of the Essex faction's espionage ring, Robert Cecil's relationship with Elizabeth went from strength to strength.[6] The Cecils' great advantage was that they could sit quietly beside her, while others destroyed themselves physically and financially on military campaigns, as Essex's father and Leicester had done, leaving the Cecils to promote 'their unspoken pact with the Queen'.[7] 'She would not investigate too closely and would support them down to the line, so long as they delivered her safely and took on jobs she did not like.'[8]

Waste and corruption were on a massive scale in England and even more so in Ireland. Elizabeth took no notice and was pleased to visit Theobalds for the hunting. The Cecils' grasping nature was not lost on the Essex faction. William Knollys saw Robert Cecil as thoroughly devious, writing to Essex:

> If we lived not in a cunning world, I should assure myself that Mr Secretary were wholly [your ally. He seems] to rejoice at everything that may succeed well with you, and to be grieved at the contrary … I pray God it have a good foundation. Yet will I observe him as narrowly as I can, but your lordship knoweth best the humour both of the time and the person and so I leave him to your better judgement.[9]

PART V

FURTHER CAMPAIGNS AGAINST THE SPANISH

Chapter 24

The continuing campaign in the Low Countries, 1589–95

Beginning in 1589, Francis Vere's new role in the Low Countries had brought him into close contact with Maurice of Nassau, now aged 23. He reported:

> His Excellency is worthy to be esteemed, for I hold him to be as rare a young gentleman as is in Europe, and one that may prove a good and able servant to her Majesty and the States ... He is very likely to grow great. He useth me well, and I am persuaded he desireth much to be well thought of in England.[1]

Maurice was to become heavily reliant on Francis's skill and judgement, generally giving him command of the combined English and Dutch forces. In turn, Francis took guidance from Sir Thomas Bodley, the queen's envoy in the Hague, who sat on the States-General Council. Bodley was a friend of Burghley and greatly respected Francis.

The English and Dutch allies were nothing if not creative. In March, in a plan developed by Maurice redolent of the wooden horse of Troy, seventy Dutch troops entered Breda hidden in a compartment constructed in a peat barge before overpowering the guard and opening the gates to the attackers. To take the forts protecting Zutphen in May 1591, soldiers quickly gained control after entering dressed as countryfolk carrying baskets of eggs and vegetables, in which their weapons were hidden.

Francis's first action in command was at the Bommel-waart, an island between the Maas and the Waal, where, in July 1589, he had advanced with 1,140 English and Dutch. His objective was to watch the movements of Count Charles Mansfelt, who was planning to cross the Maas with

12,000 men in flat-bottomed boats to support the Burgundian Marquis of Warrenbon in his siege of the strategically important Rheinburg. When Maurice and Count Hohenlohe advised Francis to abandon his position in the face of this overwhelming force, Francis dissuaded them, fearing that, without orders from the States-General, it would signal weakness in the new command. He undertook to hold the island until orders arrived and continued building entrenchments and positioning artillery. In August, when Mansfelt embarked his Walloon and German forces to cross the river, his unpaid Spanish troops mutinied. This forced him to abandon the plan.

With the immediate danger averted, the States called on Count Meurs, the Governor of Gelderland to deliver provisions to Rheinberg with support from Francis and 900 English troops. Two days after his arrival, Francis found himself in command after Meurs was killed in an accidental explosion. On 3 October, having crossed the Rhine sixteen miles further north at Rees, to pick up provisions previously loaded into wagons, he marched straight to Rheinberg, where he surprised the besiegers who were isolated in their entrenchments allowing him to deliver provisions into the town in the enemy's full view, before returning the way he had come.

With Mansfelt having regrouped his troops to support Warrenbon, Francis was asked to make a second trip to provision Rheinburg, this time with 2,600 men and four fieldpieces. With his route from Rees passing through a dense wood near the castle of Loo, five miles from the town, Warrenbon positioned men in its impenetrable undergrowth. On reaching the wood, Francis sent his Dutch troops to follow the narrow track leading through it as quickly as possible, with orders to turn into line of battle on the other side. Meanwhile he reserved his English contingent at the rear with fifty horse. When further enemy troops sallied out from the castle, his rear-guard drove them back, enabling him to lead them through the wood to join into line with the Dutch. Although the enemy charged before his line was fully positioned, he advanced against them with 450 English pike and shot, leaving the Dutch in reserve. Although the thrust of a pike killed his horse, pinning him down, his men pressed on with 'resolute tenacity' and he was rescued with no more than a bruised leg and several pike thrusts through his clothing.[2] With English 'shotmen' having skirted the wood, they used flanking fire to force the enemy back, while his pikemen continued their advance 'in a serried unbroken line'. Enemy cavalry caught up in the dense undergrowth were forced to leave their horses and flee on foot. Even Warrenbon's horse was captured and was sent by Francis as a present to Walsingham.

Leaving the Dutch to protect their rear, Francis now marched on to Rheinberg, entering the town with the same 450 men two hours after sunset having easily put twenty-four companies of Neapolitan infantry to flight.[3] Although Mansfelt sent reinforcements from Brabant, they were routed as they approached the wood at Loo by the main body of English and Dutch troops left on the plain. At break of day on the following morning, Francis left Rheinberg in fog, reaching the fort opposite Rees by evening. His achievement enabled Rheinberg to hold out until January, but then the garrison had no choice but to surrender.

Francis now made his headquarters at Utrecht, from where he could oppose the enemy at river crossings, before over-wintering at the Hague. During the break from hostilities, he created a depot at Utrecht to improve supply lines. He also ensured that his men were paid on time and he put in place a proper system of discipline. His brother Robert was sent to England to visit his mother and to collect Horace, his youngest sibling, to serve in his infantry. This allowed the three to be together.

In late March 1590, the allied army of 2,800 men moved into the Betuwe, the land between the Waal and the Rhine, intent on challenging Nymegen, whose Catholic townspeople supported the Spanish. With Francis commanding the nine English companies, his first task was to construct a fort, named Knodsenburg, on the opposite bank of the Waal to Nymegen, while the States-General constructed a dyke across the Betuwe to provide protection from flooding. Despite being wounded, Francis played his full part in the building works. When finished in July, it was garrisoned with 600 men under the able Dutchman, Gerart de Jonge, and provisioned for six months.

Francis, with 800 English infantry and 500 cavalry (serving under his brother, Robert), was now tasked with the relief of Recklinghausen, where States-General troops were under siege from the Duke of Cleves. Despite making a rapid approach hoping to surprise the besiegers, he arrived to find that they had constructed a fort with bastions at each angle opposite the west gate. Being without artillery or scaling ladders, he divided his troops into eight detachments, sending four of them to attack each bastion simultaneously, while holding the remaining four in reserve. In the face of strong resistance, the first four detachments made little progress, but as soon as Francis judged that the garrison was short of ammunition, he sent the four held in reserve to scale the walls, at which the garrison fled. Despite having eighty men killed or wounded, he returned towards Wesel, where he forced a fort protecting one of the Rhine crossings into surrender.

In January 1591, Maurice developed a plan to take Dunkirk, hoping to surprise its garrison by sending a force in the dead of winter by sea. Despite the English privy council being sceptical of the scheme, Francis landed his men nearby. While reconnoitring a position where he could plant scaling ladders undiscovered, he was seen by a sentry and shot in the leg. His incapacity caused the mission to be abandoned and he returned to the Hague to recuperate. While there, he was visited by Norreys with a message from the queen offering him, if he wished, a command in Brittany, but he was too injured to move immediately and preferred to remain in the Low Countries. With Parma being called away with a large body of his troops to challenge Henry IV in France, the allies now saw an opportunity to make progress. By 14 May, with Maurice already at Arnhem, Francis arrived at Doesburg hoping to take Zutphen and Deventer.

With Francis having captured the fort outside Zutphen by subterfuge (see p.102), he called for Maurice's assistance in besieging the town. On 20 May, after Maurice's arrival with eleven companies and boats to cross the river, Zutphen surrendered. With attention now turned to Deventer, Maurice managed to deliver siege guns down the river by boat. After spending eight days entrenching an approach, his guns managed to breach the walls in a ten-hour bombardment launched from across the river. Although the bridge of boats which they constructed initially proved too short, they resumed the attack on the following morning. Again the garrison capitulated and was permitted to leave.

With Parma still in France, the allies' next targets were the northern provinces of Drenthe, Groningen and Friesland. The key was to capture Groningen, Steenwyck and Coevorden, which were under the command of the able Spanish general, Francisco Verdugo. Although Maurice had intended to besiege Groningen, he found it too well defended, but Delfziel surrendered as soon as Francis manoeuvred his guns into position.

News then arrived that Parma had returned from France and was marching with all his forces bent on taking Knodsenburg, but the States-General considered its retention imperative. Although it had strong defences and was well provisioned, the allied forces were greatly outnumbered. With Spanish cavalry patrolling the nearby countryside hoping to pick off allied scouts, Francis asked for 1,200 foot and 500 horse to provide a 'bait' to attract a Spanish patrol. With the opposing armies about five miles apart, Francis sent forward 200 light horse to 'beat in the enemy's outposts and then retreat' in a leisurely fashion, hoping to pull the enemy's cavalry after them. He then positioned his infantry in ambush with Maurice's larger force hidden in trees further back. Although the light horse acted as planned, the enemy cavalry failed to follow them. When scouts at last brought a message that the enemy was moving forward, Maurice's cavalry jumped the gun and galloped into attack without orders. They soon retreated with the enemy following them in force. Although this obliged Francis to bring his men into action earlier than intended, he was well positioned to challenge the enemy flank with shot and pike. As soon as the enemy stalled, Francis sent in his cavalry. It was a rout, with many prisoners, including officers of rank, and 500 horses being taken. In the light of this setback and Knodsenburg's stubborn defence, Parma raised his siege on the following day and retreated across the Waal. With Nymegen left unprotected, it surrendered without a shot being fired, although its mainly Catholic citizens remained hostile.

By 1592, with Spain focusing on hostilities in France, there was a lull in military activity in the Low Countries. With Parma having returned to France, Mansfelt remained to command the Spanish forces in the Low Countries, while Verdugo supervised Friesland. Francis now had the unpalatable task of having to release some of his better companies to serve in France and Ireland. Although he was given the opportunity to move with them, he preferred to remain where he was, building on his close cooperation with the States-General and Maurice.

The allies now focused on removing the Spanish from northern Holland. They began by besieging Steenwyck, midway between Deventer and Groningen. On 7 May, Maurice and Francis encamped before the town and brought in a siege train with fifty pieces of artillery by barge. They also built a 'lymstande', a tower on wheels with canvas sides, so that they could fire at soldiers on the ramparts or walking in the town's streets. With entrenchments having been prepared, on 13 June they began battering the walls on the south side but achieved no practicable breach.[4] The attackers now ran two mines under the defences. At dawn on 23 June, these were exploded in a cloud of dust, allowing William-Louis of Nassau-Dillenburg to carry the ruined bastion, while Francis and his English troops gained the parapet. The Governor immediately called for terms, and, on 5 July, the garrison marched out, but Maurice had lost 600 men and was slightly wounded, as were Francis, Horace and Robert Sidney (who had joined them from Flushing).

Maurice soon moved on to besiege Coevorden, despite Verdugo being in the neighbourhood. Although Francis had received orders from England to retire to Doesburg, on hearing that Verdugo was threatening Maurice's trenches, he flew to his rescue. After marching through the night, he arrived on 28 August to find battle commenced, but, on his appearance, the enemy was forced to retire, and, on 3 September, Coevorden surrendered.

During the winter of 1592/93, Francis was obliged to write lengthy reports on the conduct of campaigns (resulting in justifiable complaints about his handwriting!) and was involved with Maurice in improving their forces' administration. He criticised Burghley when he granted leave to some of his officers without consulting him. He was again involved in shipping trained soldiers to France and Ireland, but was blamed by both Burghley and Elizabeth when the regiments he delivered were not up to full strength, despite inevitable losses from having served in the Low Countries. There was a further problem that several of his men had married Dutch wives and were reluctant to leave. Although Maurice complained personally to Elizabeth at 3,600 trained English troops being sent to Brittany and Normandy, there were still 4,000 in the Low Countries (although a considerable proportion were in the garrison towns of Flushing and The Brill). Acting as the point of contact between the English Government and the States-General, Francis needed to show diplomacy, but the removal of English forces was unhelpful.

On 3 December 1592, Parma died at Arras aged 46. He had undoubtedly been the most able general of his day. This left Mansfelt in command of the Spanish troops with Verugo placed at Groningen and Cristóbal de Mondragón y Mercado, now aged 88, at Antwerp. With the Netherlanders' wealth having burgeoned from their growing trading activities, the Spanish were no longer the formidable enemy of the past, and their men's grievances over pay were still undermining Spanish discipline.

There were two key strongholds still in Spanish hands, Gertruydenburg in Brabant and Groningen in the north. The approach to Gertruydenburg involved traversing a network of ditches and canals and the besiegers needed to fortify their positions from a challenge by Mansfelt's army. Access to the town was blocked from all directions, and 100 ships had been positioned to prevent an approach up the Maas. Francis spent the whole of March fortifying his camp from external attack while leaving it still able to receive local produce. Although Mansfelt appeared in May with 7,000 foot and 2,000 horse, he was forced to retire, after being unable to access provisions. With this external danger removed, Francis attacked the garrison with 1,600 men, repulsing its infantry so that on 26 June 1593 the town surrendered.

Meanwhile, William-Louis of Nassau-Dillenburg was having difficulty in holding Friesland against Verdugo, whose troops had been reinforced. In July, Francis again commanded an allied force to assist him if he should be forced back. Even then, their combined force was insufficient to attack Groningen. With their desperate need for more men, the States-General gained Elizabeth's consent to recruit in England. To retain Francis's services, and with her approval, they offered him the rank of general in command of all English recruits in Dutch pay, in addition to his existing role as sergeant-major of the queen's forces. This came with a handsome salary of 800 florins per month and he personally sourced 400 English recruits on the States-General's behalf.

In October, Francis moved his men back to winter quarters at the Hague, from where the States-General focused all their resources on capturing Groningen. On 20 May 1594, Francis arrived outside the town leading Maurice's army of 125 companies of foot and twenty cornets of horse, having again transported artillery on barges. The plan was to build trenches for an attack on the south wall. Although William-Louis of Nassau-Dillenburg succeeded in capturing the outlying fort of Auwerderzyl, and the artillery inflicted much damage to the town's walls, the defence remained stubborn, despite its shortage of provisions, and caused considerable English losses during a sortie from the town. This resulted in Horace being promoted captain in command of an infantry company, while his brother, Robert, continued to lead a cavalry company.

On 5 July, 200 defenders were killed when a mine was exploded under the ravelin at the Ooster Poort. The principal citizens now sought terms for surrender with the 400 remaining Spaniards from its original garrison of 900 being permitted to leave. On 15 July, Maurice made a triumphal entry before returning by way of Amsterdam to the Hague.

With his English troops being distributed between various garrisons, Francis, with a Dutch contingent of twenty-six cornets of horse and 5,000 foot, was asked to escort Philip of Nassau through enemy territory to join the Duke of Bouillon at Sedan in France and then to return with all speed. Philip of Nassau crossed the Rhine on 22 October, followed by Francis the next day. On reaching Treves, they had to change their route after learning that the enemy was waiting for them near Maastricht with 5,000 men and 1,800 horse. They hurriedly crossed the Moselle and joined Bouillon at Metz on 7 November. On his return, Francis kept to the right bank of the Rhine, crossing only on 19 November to reach Gelderland without losing a man.[5] This was a huge relief to Maurice as Francis had the 'flower' of the Dutch cavalry with him. Nevertheless, he received a reprimand from Elizabeth for his 'want of prudence', but was soon forgiven.[6]

In July 1595, Maurice and Francis again took to the field, this time to attack Grolle. With Verdugo having died, the Spanish were under the command of the able Mondragon, still the Governor of Antwerp, despite being aged 91. Although the entrenchment for the siege was expeditiously begun, the States-General ordered its abandonment when Mondragon appeared in superior numbers. Although Maurice entrenched his army at Bislich on the Rhine below Wesel, Mondragon was watching his movements from further upriver at Orsay, with an outpost on the Tester-berge hills, east of Wesel and to the south of the river Lippe. Philip of Nassau now developed a daring plan to cut off the outpost by swimming the Lippe with 500 cavalry, including Robert Vere's English contingent. This was particularly reckless, as Mondragon, having realised their intent, sent his forces forward from Orsay during the night. This left the allies' 500 cavalry having to face half the Spanish army without support. Faced with the option of a hasty retreat or a glorious death, the cavalry did not hesitate.[7] Robert was killed by the thrust of a lance in his face and Philip of Nassau was taken prisoner when his horse was killed under him, but died later of his wounds. Although Maurice's covering fire enabled many to make it back across the river, Mondragon ravaged the surrounding countryside, forcing both sides back into winter quarters.

Francis and Horace were distraught at Robert's death and returned temporarily to Kirby Hall to break the news to their grieving mother. During this visit, Francis also called on Elizabeth, who offered him a command in an expedition which would require Dutch support to take the war to the enemy by attacking Cádiz.

Chapter 25

Charles's appointment as governor of Portsmouth, 1592–95

With the Spanish becoming continually more aggressive, Parliament's focus was on raising money to combat the threat of a second Spanish invasion. In February 1593, with Burghley being ill, it was Robert Cecil who shouldered the task of steering a bill through the Commons to raise taxes. To Elizabeth's annoyance, this was opposed by his cousin Francis Bacon, who, as a member of the Essex camp, seemed to be acting on entirely political motives. Francis was warned that he would not be appointed to the role of Attorney General to which he aspired. Although Essex thought he could persuade Elizabeth to approve Bacon's appointment, Burghley's nominee, Sir Edward Coke, was granted the role and Elizabeth was disappointed in Essex for attempting to use his position on the privy council to gain political advantage.

Following the birth of his daughter by Penelope in March 1592, Charles had returned to a more mundane life of politics, again sitting for Bere Alston. Nevertheless, increasing aggression on the Continent meant that a military role would soon become available. Following the death of Henry Radcliffe, 4th Earl of Sussex, in December 1593, Charles was nominated to succeed him as Captain of the Town and Island of Portsmouth. With the Spanish threatening England's south coast, and Portsmouth being England's largest naval base, this was an important appointment. In his dotage, Sussex had not acted effectively, and, despite the town being a prime target for the Spanish, its fortifications were in need of modernisation. His lieutenant, John Munns, was 'always ready to do nothing in an orderly way and to avoid giving trouble'.[1] With Elizabeth anxious about its security and Sussex gravely ill, she sent Charles to assess the means of securing it against a Spanish incursion. Sir George Carew, Lieutenant of the Ordnance, went with him to provide an inventory of its stores. He was soon under Charles's spell, providing him with thorough support.

Charles considered the prospect of an appointment at Portsmouth the opportunity he had been waiting for but was initially concerned that his depleted finances would debar him from the role. Nevertheless, he made clear that he would be more effective than Munns, who had been in post for nearly twenty years. Although he became anxious for the queen to remove him from his uncertainty, his eagerness eventually won the day, and the patent appointing him was issued on 26 January 1594. He later told Cecil that he had little time to write reports as he was continually coercing Munns into action. Carew reported to Cecil:

> As touching the new Governor, I protest to your Honour without affectation or flattery I do think the Queen could not have made choice of a more worthy man as well for her service as for his sweet and noble demeanour to the townsmen and garrison, who are so well pleased with the same as they think his coming amongst them to be their year of jubilee, having now some hope to grow rich, which heretofore was impossible by reason of the great dislike between them and the late Earl.[2]

Carew's comments had been endorsed by the town's citizens even before his confirmation as Governor. On the previous 26 December, Charles had been appointed as one of its burgesses (as, confusingly, was his distant cousin, Charles Blount of Mapledurham, then aged 25, who was to serve under him).

Charles's standing was greatly enhanced in July when he succeeded as 8th Lord Mountjoy on the death of his 33-year-old brother, William. William had dissipated much of what remained of the Mountjoy patrimony in a long-running legal dispute with Huntingdon, who claimed to hold mineral rights on his Dorset estates. Charles inherited an income depleted to 1,000 marks (£666) per annum and needed his Portsmouth salary to keep up appearances at court. On 3 September, his political influence was greatly enhanced when he was unanimously elected High Steward of Portsmouth, a position previously held by Sussex. This gave him the right to nominate one of the borough's two Parliamentary members.

Charles had greater difficulty in gaining approval for his ambitious plans to improve Portsmouth's defences. On 12 February 1595, he was still seeking a meeting with Burghley, Howard of Effingham and Essex to consider his proposal to spend £7,354 but, with Elizabeth continuing to cut corners, he was limited to £3,000. When payment was offered in instalments as the work proceeded, he complained that the money for the stone and implements was needed in advance.

In March 1596, Charles reported that he had made the money granted go as far as possible by deepening the moats and using the spoil to strengthen the walls' bulwarks. He had also improved the ramparts, providing a covered way within the outer wall, and extending the defences on the town's north-west side to protect against an incursion into the harbour. He wanted privy council representatives to review his progress as he still did not consider Portsmouth secure and would have preferred to follow his original plan.

With the Spanish navy now more powerful than at the Armada, rumours that an invasion force was being readied in Spain were to cause great anxiety during the remainder of Elizabeth's reign.[3] By the end of 1596, with Charles believing that its arrival was imminent, England's lack of preparedness was confirmed when the privy council had to instruct the Lord Lieutenant of Hampshire to arm the militia with pikes rather than bills, and with muskets and calivers rather than bows.[4]

Charles did not remain continuously in Portsmouth but was recalled to London by Elizabeth to advise on other military matters. Although it was rumoured that she would appoint him as a privy councillor, this did not happen. As she was probably aware of his relationship with Penelope, which was well-known to an inner circle at court, she may have feared unbalancing the council with another Devereux ally. Nevertheless, he was growing in her esteem as a military adviser.

Charles stayed in London over the New Year revels in 1595, attending the Inns of Court to see Shakespeare's popular *The Comedy of Errors*. This enabled him to be present during January, when Penelope gave birth to his second daughter at Essex House. As before, the child was baptised Isabella 'Rich' at St Clement Danes on 30 January before joining the nursery at Leighs. The long-suffering Rich never complained, despite believing that Charles was communicating with his wife through the sealed correspondence she received from Essex.

One of Charles's and Penelope's close friends was Sir Robert Sidney who was still based in Flushing with his wealthy wife Barbara Gamage, after having succeeded his brother Philip as Governor in 1587. By the beginning of 1595, he had been in post for eight years, and was anxious to return home. After giving birth to two children, Barbara had returned to lie in for a third at Baynards Castle, the London home of Robert's sister, Mary, while Robert remained in post. In the following year, with Barbara pregnant once more, she again returned for her child's birth, attending court on 24 November 1595 with her three elder children, Mary, William and Catherine, to lobby for her husband's repatriation. There was much sympathy for her, and Elizabeth provided her with a private chamber to dine with her children, who proved a great success. Mary was told that she was 'already a fit maid for the queen', but Barbara's efforts to gain her husband's recall were to no avail.[5] Robert Sidney wrote to her that both 'Lady Rich and Lord Mountjoy' should be the new arrival's godparents, with the third to be chosen depending on its sex. Before the birth, the elder Sidney children contracted measles and passed it on to their mother. When her 'goodly fat boy' arrived on 1 December, he was 'as full of measles in the face as can be'.[6] This did not prevent Penelope from agreeing to officiate at the baptism, although it had to be postponed because a pimple on her skin was enough to prevent such a beautiful face from appearing in public.

Although Penelope spent Christmas with Rich and her children at Leighs, she returned to London on the following day. Meanwhile, Barbara and her family stayed with Frances and her children. With Robert Sidney remaining in Flushing, he sent boar pies (including one for Robert Cecil, in the hope that this might jog him into arranging his recall). At last Penelope named New Year's Eve as the day that she could attend the baptism, arriving with Charles and the third godfather, William, 2nd Lord Compton. It was worth the wait. Her presence turned it into a social gathering of Essex allies.

One advantage of having Robert Sidney in Flushing was his usefulness to the family for arranging purchases from the Continent. Rich needed new tapestries, and, despite their estrangement, Penelope still seems to have remained as the mistress of Leighs and was involved in choosing them. When Robert sent samples, she confirmed that she was happy with them, but that Rich would want to see them, and Lettice thought them expensive. When Rich objected to the depth of their borders, it was Penelope who explained the changes required, while repeating her mother's concern at their expense.

It was Huntingdon's sudden death on 14 December 1595 which at last triggered Robert Sidney's recall. Being his heir, he needed to sort out his uncle's debt-ridden estate, and Elizabeth invited him to comfort his grieving aunt Catherine. Catherine remained one of her oldest companions at court, living there while Huntingdon stayed at York as president of the Council of the North. As one of Essex's most senior allies, his death lessened support for him on the council. Although Charles was considered as a replacement, his affair with Penelope made this unacceptable to Elizabeth.

Chapter 26

Raleigh's first expedition to 'Guiana', 1594–96

In the hope of achieving his rehabilitation by making a direct challenge against Spain, and despite Bess's misgivings, in December 1594 Raleigh persuaded Elizabeth to permit him to lead an expedition to 'Guiana', an area surrounding the Orinoco delta in present day Venezuela, to search for the fabled El Dorado, 'the great and golden city of Manoa'. This was a place of 'great plenty of gold, pearl and precious stones', and would gain an empire and untold wealth for the queen.[1] Earlier in the year, Leicester's son Robert Sheffield, now aged 20, had nearly stolen a march on him while exploring the area, and he too reported on the potential for gold. Raleigh's plan was received with scepticism. He was in his early forties and was not a 'first-rate seaman'. With Elizabeth already fully committed against both Irish rebels and the Spanish, she was unlikely to contribute to the voyage's cost, and even Bess demanded a bond so that those funding it could not resort to her for repayment.

Although the Spanish had sent numerous unsuccessful expeditions, Raleigh was confident of finding workable gold mines. As in Virginia and Ireland, his objective was colonisation. It was to be 'a conquest without blood', avoiding the Spanish practice of trade and plunder, in the hope of gaining 'the willing acceptance of the legitimacy of English supremacy by the indigenous people'.[2] He would become king of 'Raleghana' as a loyal servant of the English queen.[3] Captain Jacob Whiddon was sent to reconnoitre, and he returned with two South American Indians.[4]

Raleigh eventually sailed in early January 1595, reaching Trinidad on 22 March. He brought back the two Indians, who had now learned some English, to use as interpreters. He told the Spanish Governor Berrio that he had been blown off course while heading for Virginia, but had circumnavigated the island noting its fertility and abundant produce.

He met natives, who complained at the cruelty and torture meted out to them by the Spanish. They warned him that Berrio was highly suspicious of him and had sent for reinforcements. Raleigh took no chances. He overpowered the Spanish guard, taking Berrio and the Portuguese Captain, Alvaro Jorge, on board. Berrio behaved as a 'gentleman' and told him much about 'Guiana', explaining that the Orinoco region was supervised by a second Spanish governor, Vides, who was much hated locally after having brutally 'stolen' 300 Indians for sale as slaves. When Raleigh admitted that he was searching for gold, Berrio became unhelpful. He warned that the delta was too shallow for navigation by ship or even pinnace, that small boats would be unable to make against the current, and that the local Indians would remain out of sight and refuse to trade.

Raleigh was undaunted. His narrative turns the venture into a 'gripping yarn'.[5] Despite the difficulty of finding his way through the shallows of the Orinoco delta, his men eventually found their way in open wherries, but were bitten by mosquitoes while sitting on hard boards in the burning sun. Although they had plentiful bread, the smell of pestered victuals and wet clothing meant that 'there was never any prison in England that could be found more unsavoury and loathsome'.[6] Despite all these challenges, the party was buoyed up by the thrill of it all. On climbing a nearby hill, they could see the river stretching ahead, with 'overfalls' the height of a church tower in the distance. At first, they thought the spray was smoke from a distant town. Later, a boat went hard aground, and it took a lot of 'tugging and hauling' after removing its ballast to refloat it.

Everyone took turns rowing against the 'violent current'. With increasing heat 'breeding great faintness' and their bread running low, they were saved from starvation by the 'fruits, flowers, fowl, fish and trees' and saw 'birds of all colours'.[7] As the river narrowed, they had to cut their way through overhanging trees with their swords. Eventually they saw lights from a village through the darkness where Indians provided a 'good store of bread, fish, hens and Indian drink'.[8] In the morning they woke to find themselves in a plain 'twenty miles in length, the grass short and green' with deer coming down to the river to drink. Raleigh eulogised over a female Indian:

> In all my life I have seldom seen a better favoured woman,
> she was of good nature, with black eyes, fat of body, of an

excellent countenance, her hair almost as long as herself, tied up again in pretty knots, and it seemed she stood not in that awe of her husband, as the rest, for she spoke and discoursed, and drank among the gentlemen and captains, and was very pleasant, knowing her own comeliness, and taking great pride therein. I have seen a lady in England so like her, as but for the difference of colour I would have sworn might have been the same.[9]

He insisted that the women should not be molested, despite them being 'stark naked' and he provided small presents, so that they realised that they had none of 'the deceit and purpose of the Spaniards', who 'used them for the satisfying of their own lusts, especially such as they took in this manner by strength'.[10] (As Anna Beer points out, the Portuguese and Spanish had already been visiting 'Guiana' for one hundred years.)

Although Raleigh's crew gathered rock samples, there was little more to be done and, having promised to return on a future trip to assist the villagers against the Spanish and local foes, Raleigh set off back to the sea, saying farewell as 'a foreigner, whose friendship was worth cultivating'.[11] On reaching the open sea, they faced a 'mighty storm' and 'the river's mouth was at least a league broad'. With their boats drawing five feet, they were in danger of grounding, but, on the following night, they found Raleigh's barge and set out, with a faint cheer for encouragement, to cross to Trinidad and rejoin the anchored fleet.

Although Raleigh made a parting attack on the Spanish on the mainland, he admitted little about it, except that their local guide did not prove as reliable as hoped and 'led them by a devilish road overlooked by two forts'.[12] Nevertheless, they were entertained by the Lieutenant-Governor who negotiated the release of Berrio and Jorge.

By the end of September, Raleigh was back in England without losing a man, and reached London a few days later. Apart from a few rock samples, which he claimed to be 'like gold ore', and a few natives, who returned with him as servants, he came empty-handed. He had taken no 'refiner and trier of metals' with him but continued to promise that gold and other metals were there to be found, undertaking 'to load 1,000 ships with the ore' when able to return. Unfortunately, his audience at court remained unconvinced, but he wrote an embellished and sanitised account of his voyage in the hope of attracting funding for a further voyage in search of gold. This narrative makes 'glorious travel writing' and his fascination with the Indians and how they lived has been 'judged a profoundly valuable ethnological text ... during a period of almost first contact'.[13] Nevertheless, it is often 'hard to tell where truth ends and fiction begins'.[14] Despite its three editions, it was considered a 'pleasing dream of golden fancy' and, despite his continuing pleas, he gained no support for a second expedition.[15] The timing was unfortunate as another Spanish invasion of England was threatened.

In the following year Raleigh funded a second small expedition personally. This was led by a member of his household, his old university friend, Lawrence Keymis, who had been on the first voyage. It set out in January 1596 but, on arrival on 14 March, Keymis found that Berrio had established a small garrison close to the Orinoco delta to protect the route leading to the supposed goldmines where the white stones had been found in the previous year. Although he bypassed the Spanish and was able to meet some of the Indians seen previously, he returned empty-handed after failing to reach the mines. Bess admitted that nothing had been achieved of 'much worth: for that the Spaniards are already possessed in Guiana'.[16] Keymis's account now confirmed Guiana's bountiful prospects more in terms of farming and trade than in gold. With the dream of Raleghana receding, Raleigh was bitter at Elizabeth's lack of support, and found himself standing 'alone, forsaken, friendless, on the shore'.[17]

Chapter 27

Drake's expedition to Puerto Rico, 1595–96

During mid-1595, with Raleigh still in South America, Drake and Sir John Hawkins were busied in Plymouth fitting out an expedition 'to strike a blow against the source of Spanish silver' in Puerto Rico.[1] There were already rumours of a significant invasion fleet being readied in Spanish ports, but this was unlikely to reach England before June 1596 when the weather was expected to be milder. Elizabeth initially thought that the Puerto Rico voyage should be deferred, but later insisted on it returning by the following May to provide time for their ships to be refitted before facing the expected Spanish onslaught.

Drake and Hawkins left Plymouth on 28 August 1595 with 2,500 men in a fleet of twenty-seven ships, but Essex was not permitted to go with them. By this time, Spanish treasure fleets returning from the Americas were enjoying powerful escorts. Although this progressively stacked the odds for success against English adventurers, sailors remained attracted by the lure of gold and preferred serving on privateers.

A convoy of treasure ships had left Havana for Spain on the previous 10 March, carrying 2 million pesos of gold and silver, but a storm in the Bermuda Channel had forced it back to Puerto Rico, where it arrived on 9 April to make repairs. The treasure was unloaded and moved to La Fortaleza for safekeeping while the work was undertaken. Meanwhile, Admiral Pedro Tello de Guzmán had been sent with five frigates to retrieve the cargo. By complete chance, he encountered Drake's fleet near Guadeloupe and, after capturing an English ship, learned Drake's destination. This lost the expedition its element of surprise. Guzmán hastened to Puerto Rico to prepare its defence, sinking two ships at the entrance to the harbour at San Juan to impede Drake's access. Being supplemented by the addition of the crews from Tello's frigates, the

Spanish had 1,500 personnel and seventy land-based cannon, in addition to those on the frigates.

Drake's journey was delayed by an outbreak of fever on board, and on 12 November Hawkins succumbed to it. On the expedition's eventual arrival at Puerto Rico on 22 November, Drake anchored off the Boquerón Inlet outside San Juan, but the Spanish brought up cannon, which scored a hit on his flagship, the *Defiance,* killing two of his officers. This forced him to retire out of range to the Isla de Cabras. At 10.00 pm the same evening, Drake launched an attack with twenty-five well-armed boats, each carrying fifty to sixty men, to set fire to the Spanish frigates in the harbour at San Juan. Although four of the frigates were set alight, their crews extinguished three of them, but the fourth illuminated the bay. This made Drake's boats easy pickings for the shore batteries, which sank ten of them, killing or wounding 400 of his men. Drake had no choice but to leave three days later. Apart from one burnt-out frigate, the Spanish had suffered little corresponding loss, and their treasure fleet departed for Spain on 20 December.

To compound this disaster, Drake moved on to attack the port of Panama, where he developed dysentery. He died on 28 January 1596 and was buried at sea. Sir Henry Newbolt's ballad, written in 1897, records:

> Drake he's in his hammock an' a thousand miles away,
> (Capten art tha sleepin' there below?)
> Slung atween the roundshot in Nombre Dios Bay,
> An' dreamin' arl the time o' Plymouth Hoe.

From *Drake's Drum*

The remainder of his battered fleet made its way back to England but was in no condition to regroup to provide protection against a Spanish invasion fleet.

Chapter 28

The attack on Cádiz, 1596–97

With Spanish plans to invade England inexplicably delayed, Essex and Raleigh persuaded Elizabeth to carry the fight to Spain before they set out. To defray some of the cost, Elizabeth hoped to involve the Dutch. It was for this reason that she had offered Francis Vere a command with instructions for him to negotiate with them. On 1 March 1596, he travelled to the Hague and persuaded the States-General to support an expedition to attack Cádiz, 'a city at once rich, vulnerable and strategic', as the principal point of departure for treasure ships to the Americas.[1] The Dutch agreed to provide twenty-two ships, manned with 2,000 men under Admiral John de Duyvenvoorde, Lord of Warmond (Markham says incorrectly that they were commanded by William-Louis of Nassau-Dillenburg). They also agreed that Francis should take 1,000 Low Country veterans, including his brother Horace and Maurice's brother, the young Louis of Nassau. On 22 April, the Dutch force set out from Flushing to join the English fleet at Plymouth.

Elizabeth appointed the 60-year-old Howard of Effingham as Lord Admiral in command of the expedition, although controlling his hot-headed subordinates would be a challenge. The fleet was divided into four squadrons headed by Effingham on the *Ark Royal*, Essex on the *Repulse*, who at the age of 28 was appointed Lord General, the experienced Lord Thomas Howard (later Earl of Suffolk), aged 35, as Vice-Admiral on the *Mere-honour*, and Raleigh, aged 44, as Rear-Admiral on the *Warspite*. Francis, now aged 36, was appointed Lieutenant General and Lord Marshal on the *Rainbow* and was to be Essex's chief adviser in control of all shore operations. He spent the whole of May at Plymouth while the ships were being equipped, drilling and training 6,360 troops, 1,000 volunteers and 6,772 sailors (despite a difficulty in recruiting naval personnel).

Essex divided the military personnel into four squads headed by Francis, Raleigh, Lord Thomas Howard and himself. 'With a high idea of his own importance', Raleigh saw his involvement as the means of clawing 'his way back to something like his former glory'.[2] He considered himself senior in rank to Francis, but Francis argued that it was critical that he should report directly to Essex as general. To prevent a falling out, Essex devised that Francis was of superior rank on shore, with Raleigh senior at sea.

With the fleet being gathered at Plymouth, Raleigh set out down the Thames from Blackwall bringing Rich, who had contributed £1,000 towards the expedition's cost. Extremely rough weather delayed them in the Thames estuary and on reaching the Goodwin Sands, they had to slip anchor to protect their vessels from running aground. With the anchors being marked with buoys, they were later recovered and transported to Plymouth by sea. On reaching Plymouth on 26 May, Rich was prostrated with seasickness and was obliged to return home. This was to the disdain of Sir Christopher Blount, who had hoped to see him as 'a partaker in the glory'.[3] Charles also remained behind, fully occupied in strengthening Portsmouth's defences.

Essex had ambitions to establish a permanent base on Spanish soil for the future disruption of its shipping, but this was opposed by Elizabeth. On his departure, he left a message asking his fellow councillors to lobby to gain her agreement, but Burghley, who was in no mood to enhance Essex's standing, kept the expedition short of funds.

At last, on 13 June, Effingham left Plymouth hoping to emulate Drake, who in 1587 had 'singed the King of Spain's beard'. He had 150 ships, of which seventeen were Royal Navy vessels, and twenty-two were Dutch. To maintain secrecy, the fleet sailed well offshore, but he sent three faster vessels ahead to intercept any local shipping, which might divulge their presence. On arrival at Cádiz at 2.00 am on 30 June, after three weeks at sea, the city had received no warning.

Cádiz is positioned at the northern end of a narrow spit of land, guarding the entrance to a bay, which is very shallow apart from a channel to Puerto Real on its inward side. On their arrival, there were four large warships stationed to protect forty richly laden merchantmen anchored outside the entrance awaiting departure to Mexico. With bad weather inhibiting night-time access though the narrow entrance, Effingham anchored off the fort of San Sebastian at the end of a narrow promontory to seaward. Despite the bad weather, he had contemplated landing troops at La Caleta, a bay immediately north of San Sebastian.

Elizabeth I ("Ditchley Portrait")
Her 'eroticised political relationship' with her favourites enabled her to play one off against the other.

Geeraerts, Marcus the Younger (c.1561-1635) / National Portrait Gallery, London / Photo © Stephano Baldini / Bridgeman Images SBL868237

Charles Blount, 8th Lord Mountjoy, later Earl of Devonshire
Despite being the second son of an impoverished father, he rose to become England's finest general, succeeding in Ireland where Essex ignominiously failed. He became the lover of Essex's sister, Penelope Rich, by whom he had five children.

Oil on Panel, English School, 1594, Private Collection, courtesy of the The Weiss Gallery, London

Sir Francis Vere
The battle-scarred hero of the wars in the Low Countries, was never the personality to be a favourite but was key to the Anglo-Dutch successes against the Spanish.

The Portland Collection, Harley Gallery, Welbeck Estate, Nottinghamshire / Bridgeman Images 7072129

Sir Walter Raleigh
His good looks helped him to succeed the Earl of Leicester, as Elizabeth's favourite, but he embellished his successes as a soldier, colonist and explorer with his writing and poetry.

French School (16th century) / Kunsthistorisches Museum, Vienna / Bridgeman Images XAM68919

Robert Devereux, 2nd Earl of Essex

Although extraordinarily attractive to women, recklessly brave and popular, his lack of judgement and stability under pressure made him totally unsuited to high command.

Oil on panel, Gheeraerts, Marcus, the Younger (c.1561-1635) / Private Collection / Photo © Philip Mould Ltd., London, Bridgeman Images MOU1262567

Dorothy (l) and Penelope (r) Devereux

The talented and beautiful sisters of the Earl of Essex. Dorothy married Sir Thomas Perrot and later Henry, 9th Earl of Northumberland ("the Wizard Earl"). Penelope was eulogised by Sir Philip Sidney in *Astrophil and Stella*. She married Robert, 3rd Lord Rich and later became the mistress of Charles Blount 8th Lord Mountjoy.

©Reproduced by permission of the Marquess of Bath, Longleat House, Warminster, Wiltshire

Sir Philip Sidney
Extraordinarily talented as a diplomat, soldier, and in the lists. Recognised as the greatest poet of his age having written *The Countess of Pembroke's Arcadia* and *Astrophil and Stella,* but was mortally wounded a Zutphen in 1586

English School (17th century / Blickling Hall, Norfolk / National Trust Photographic Library / Bridgeman Images USB1160876

Frances Walsingham with her son Robert Devereux later 3rd Earl of Essex
Daughter of Sir Francis Walsingham, married first to Sir Philip Sidney, then to Robert Devereux 2nd Earl of Essex and later to Richard Burke, 4th Earl of Clanricarde.

Peake, Robert, the Elder, 1594 / Photograph by courtesy of Sotheby's

Bess Throckmorton, Lady Raleigh
The daughter of Sir Nicholas Throckmorton, and Lady-in-Waiting to Elizabeth, but became the mistress and then the wife of Sir Francis Raleigh, with whom she was besotted.

Segar, William, 1595/ Bridgeman Images

Above left: **William Cecil, Lord Burghley**

Elizabeth's much respected Secretary of State, who dominated political affairs until his death in 1598.

    English School (16th century) Burghley House Collection, Lincolnshire / Bridgeman Images BH26901

Above right: **Charles, Lord Howard of Effingham, later 1st Earl of Nottingham**

Lord Admiral in command of the English fleet during the Armada in 1588, and of the English invasion force at Cadiz in 1596, after which he was created Earl of Nottingham.

    Mytens, Daniel (1590 -c. 1648) / His Grace the Duke of Norfolk, Arundel, West Sussex / Bridgeman DON279020

Sir Francis Drake

The leading privateer of the Elizabethan period and a noted navigator and scourge of Spanish treasure fleets. Died at sea, while contemplating an attack on Panama in 1596.

    Oil on canvas, English school c.1580 / National Portrait Gallery, London / Photo © Stephano Baldini / Bridgeman Images SBL2562091

Henry Wriothesley, 3rd Earl of Southampton
Close ally of the Earl of Essex and happily married to his cousin Elizabeth Vernon, despite his bisexual inclinations. He was the first patron of William Shakespeare and probably his lover.

English School (17th century) / National Portrait Gallery, London / Photo © Stefano Baldini / Bridgeman Images SBL2562090

Elizabeth Vernon, Countess of Southampton
Lady-in-Waiting to Elizabeth and a confidante of her cousin Penelope Rich. Was dismissed from Elizabeth's service after becoming pregnant with Southampton's child.

English School (17th century) / Fitzwilliam Museum, Cambridge © Fitzwilliam Museum / Bridgeman Images FIT63104

Above left: **William Shakespeare**
Transformed drama and poetic writing for the
cultivated court society which surrounded both
Elizabeth and James I.
  *Taylor, John (d. 1651) (attr. to) / National
Portrait Gallery, London / Bridgeman Images
XCF266086*

Above right: **James I**
Was a close ally of the Essex faction while still
in Scotland and rehabilitated them on his arrival
in London, but developed strongly anti-Catholic
views after the Gunpowder Plot in 1605, and
later supported Robert Cecil against his enemies
to the detriment of both the Essex faction and
Sir Walter Raleigh.
  *Somer, Paul van, (c.1576-1621), Prado,
Madrid / Bridgeman Images SCP 36893*

Right: **Anne of Denmark**
On arrival from Scotland with James I, she
transformed the genre of the masque into an art
form, lavishing money on court entertainments.
  *Gheeraerts, Marcus, the Younger
(c.1561-1635) / Woburn Abbey, Bedfordshire /
Bridgeman Images BAL72695*

***Above left*: Sir Robert Cecil, later Earl of Salisbury**
Despite being a hunchback and only 5 ft. tall, he took over his father's role as Elizabeth's principal advisor and engineered James VI of Scotland's succession to the English throne without mishap. He was probably the nemesis for the remaining members of the Essex faction by turning James against them.

Critz, John de, (c.1555-c.1641) / Private Collection / Photo © Bonhams, London / Bridgeman Images PFA73332

***Above right*: Henry Danvers, 1st Earl of Danby**
With his brother Charles, he was a close ally of Essex. Although Charles was executed for his part in Essex's rebellion, Henry survived and was much admired by James I for his military accomplishments.

Dyck, Anthony van, (1599-1641) / Dunham Massey, Cheshire / National Trust Photographic Library / Bridgeman Images USB1162566

Sir Francis Bacon
With his brother Anthony, he joined forces with the Essex faction by setting up a spy network to challenge the Cecils' political dominance. When Essex came to trial, Francis found himself forced to give evidence against him but ultimately became Lord Chancellor.

Oil on Canvas / Somer, Paul van (c.1576-1621) / Private Collection / Bridgeman Images GRH320999

When Raleigh arrived later than the rest, he strongly opposed this plan, warning Effingham and Essex that until the Spanish fleet round the town was dislodged, a landing would be doomed. He proposed that they should fight their way through the bay's entrance to approach Cádiz from the east. With this plan agreed, the landing parties were brought back on board, although some of the boats were swamped. It took until the next evening for the fleet to anchor at the bay's entrance ready to attack on the following morning, but by then the heavily laden merchantmen had retired to Puerto Real, leaving the four Spanish warships lined out broadside-on to protect the entrance.

Having called a council meeting on the *Ark Royal*, Effingham gave instructions for Raleigh to lead the attack on the following morning's incoming tide, 'but the eagerness to be first outweighed all other considerations' and rival officers 'were all behaving like a pack of schoolboys'.[4] Lord Thomas Howard switched to the shallower drafted *Nonpareil* and took Effingham on board. The engagement with the four Spanish warships (and several smaller vessels close to Cadiz) lasted for eight hours. By evening, two of them, the *San Mateo* and *San Andres*, had been captured and the Spanish set the other two alight, causing many of their crew to be drowned. During the action, Dutch ships under young Louis of Nassau captured merchantmen carrying heavy ordnance being used as ballast, but Raleigh was severely wounded in the leg by a splinter, which put him out of action in the subsequent proceedings and he walked with a stick for an extended period afterwards.

Having passed through the narrows, Francis took charge of a landing party at a point between the city and the fort of El Puntal protecting Cádiz from the south. He took with him 2,000 men (including volunteers) from regiments led by Essex, Sir Christopher Blount, Sir John Wingfield, himself and several others. The garrison was completely unprepared, with its artillery in a poor state of readiness and short of ammunition. Although 5,000 Spanish personnel from two of the galleons arrived at midday, no chain of command was put in place, and the landing party faced no opposition.

On its landward side, Cádiz was protected by a wall across the narrow spit of land with a central gate and bastions at each angle. The initial plan had been to fortify an encampment as a bridgehead for landing heavy guns, but Francis developed a more adventurous ploy, which would always appeal to Essex. Having sent half his men south to a narrow point in the spit beyond El Puntal to provide protection from their rear, he proposed using his remaining 1,000 men to attack Spanish troops drawn up with some light horse under the walls. With the spit being half a mile across, he could see enemy cavalry and foot hurrying back into the town behind low hills on its western side. He thus moved half of his remaining men forward behind these hills hidden from the view of the troops at the walls. He then sent Sir John Wingfield forward with 200 picked men to drive in any skirmishers, with his remaining 300 men ready to follow. If the Spanish force advanced, Wingfield was to make a hasty retreat to join the supporting force and then turn in a furious attack on the enemy, while the troops behind the low hill, including Essex, Louis of Nassau and himself would appear on their flank. Everything went to plan, and the Spanish fled back over the walls or through the gates, which were rapidly closed, leaving their cavalry horses abandoned.

With all the landing party having been brought forward, Essex gallantly led 200 of Francis's veterans to scale both the outer and inner walls, while other troops entered through lightly protected gates on the town's east side. When Francis climbed the ramparts to direct operations, he could see Essex rushing recklessly through the streets. He eventually forced open the main gates to provide access to his reserve force which marched in in good order to join Essex in the market place. Having retreated into the town hall, most of the citizens surrendered, allowing the streets to be scoured, with the remaining inhabitants being driven into the castle of San Felipe or the convent of San Francisco from where they too surrendered. The whole attack was over in an hour. Although losses were not great, Sir John Wingfield was mortally wounded in the marketplace just as resistance was coming to an end.

When Effingham landed more troops, discipline was lost, and the town was ransacked. Fifty-one English prisoners captured in earlier campaigns were freed. When the citizens agreed to pay a ransom of 520,000 ducats, 5,000 of them were permitted to leave, but several of the more prominent ones were retained as hostages for its payment. The success was not complete. Thirty-two of the Spanish ships now at Puerto Real were burned and scuttled to prevent their capture on orders from the Duke of Medina-Sidonia.

Although Essex, Francis and the Dutch commanders were in favour of retaining Cádiz as a base for future operations, this would have contravened Elizabeth's orders and was vetoed by Effingham, who feared a Spanish counterattack. Before setting sail with the hostages on 14 July, Cádiz was set ablaze, as was Faro in southern Portugal on their return journey. When Essex learned that a Spanish treasure fleet was approaching the Azores, he tried unsuccessfully to persuade Raleigh to join him in challenging it, but this was again vetoed by Effingham, and the fleet sailed on to Plymouth. The great majority of those on board had supported Effingham's decision, wanting to return home with the booty from Cádiz already amassed.

To Raleigh's chagrin, Essex engineered the Cádiz expedition as a personal triumph, writing to Burghley to list its successes. He made the most of his perceived bravado in scaling the walls but ignored the failure to maintain discipline. He was seen as the hero of the hour and even Effingham admitted to Burghley: 'There is not a braver man in the world than the Earl is; and I protest, in my poor judgment, a great soldier, for what he doth is in great order and discipline performed.'[5] (Effingham had not, of course, seen what had happened.)

On arriving in London, Essex was greeted as a hero and tried to breed 'war-fever'.[6] Spenser described him as:

> Great England's glory and the world's wide wonder,
> Whose dreadful name, late through all Spain did thunder.

This cut little ice with Elizabeth. His courting of popularity continued to make her feel threatened and she wanted him brought down to earth. It was Effingham who was rewarded. He was created Earl of Nottingham and Francis was invited to remain at court for the winter of 1596/97.

By now, support for Essex in the privy council had been diminished by the deaths of his 80-year-old grandfather, Sir Francis Knollys, on 19 July 1596, his great uncle Hunsdon (see Endnote 1) and his guardian Huntingdon. His old comrade Sir Roger Williams was also dead. The loss of the old guard was a blow to the whole family, only made worse when Hunsdon's position as Lord Chamberlain was granted to Cecil's ally, Cobham, rather than to Hunsdon's son, George Carey. Elizabeth also confirmed Robert Cecil as secretary of state and called for an investigation into Essex's conduct of the campaign.[7] He responded by embarking with a second fleet to southern Portugal, which gained no more than the content of the local bishop's library.

The Cecils took their opportunity to criticise the mission's failure to capture more of the Spanish fleet. Elizabeth also complained that much of the treasure taken was secreted by the crews and failed to come her way. With her Exchequer under great pressure, she instructed Charles at Portsmouth to impound any booty being offloaded. She particularly wanted two bronze cannons, being shipped on the *Swan of London*. Furthermore, she had been made to look like an aggressor and felt obliged to publish a justification for sending the expedition in the first place.

Everyone was anxious to see how Philip II would react. In September 1596, Gilbert Talbot, 7th Earl of Shrewsbury, led a diplomatic mission, which included Rich, to the French king at Rouen hoping to goad him into expelling the Spanish from Calais. Having embarked on the *Antelope* on 12 September, the mission's members were kept at sea for several days by storms. Shrewsbury reported to Cecil: 'All our gallants have been notably sick and some of them ready to make their will but that they wanted a scrivener.'[8] On arrival in France, Henry again strung them along, wining and dining them for a fortnight with his aging mistress, Gabrielle d'Estrées, while they awaited his triumphal entry into Rouen. Meanwhile, Rich met up with Pérez, who entrusted him with a letter 'of great secrecy' to give to Essex.

With Rich speaking only limited French, Essex wrote to recommend a French secretary; but Rich declined the offer as, after being so seasick, he had no desire to repeat his 'French experience'. Penelope was amused at her husband's lack of sea legs and tampered with his reply to imply that his reluctance to repeat his French experience was occasioned by a dose of the 'French disease' (syphilis)! She suggested that a language secretary might enable him to communicate better with his mistress to overcome his sexual shortcomings. Essex had no such difficulty. He was again seeing a former mistress, thought to be Elizabeth Vere, Burghley's granddaughter and Robert Cecil's niece, who, in 1594, had married William Stanley, 6th Earl of Derby.

Philip II had been indignant at the Cádiz attack. He was forced to dishonour the archduke's bills in the Spanish Netherlands, thereby bankrupting the Spanish economy. Despite the retention of hostages, payment of their ransom was left unresolved until James I's accession in 1603. It was a psychological blow from which Philip never fully recovered, but the arrival of more treasure from the Americas soon restored his financial position, and he was determined to teach the English a lesson. In October, his second Armada was at last ready to set out for England, where the situation was grave. His timing had left the country completely unprepared. Most of its troops were in the Low Countries or Ireland and the fleet, which had returned from Cádiz, was at Chatham being refitted.[9] Elizabeth's calls for London merchants to build a new naval squadron were being strongly resisted. It was only a fortuitous storm in the Bay of Biscay that forced the Spanish fleet to limp home with the loss of seven galleons and several smaller ships. Philip's admirals had been sent to sea far too late in the year, but Spain now had a base at Calais in addition to Brittany. Both were to remain threats until the Treaty of Vervins in 1598, when the Catholic League at last came to terms.

Being stationed at Portsmouth, Charles had remained extremely concerned. He warned Cecil that it would be hard to combat a landing on the Isle of Wight, and his small garrison could not resist an attack on Portsmouth, which might occur before reinforcements were mustered. Despite being promised 2,000 militia, they were widely dispersed and, if needed in short order, he doubted if 600 could be put together.[10] He also lacked experienced officers, knowing that to serve any useful purpose, militia would depend on leadership by example. To protect the Isle of Wight, he wanted Portsmouth 'held in a special state of readiness' with cavalry available to strike a strong blow at the moment of a landing.[11] He also called for 'good marksmen and hardy fellows' among the town's poor to be provided with weapons.[12]

As it so happened, the government recognised the Isle of Wight's vulnerability. Charles's letter crossed with one to Sir William Paulet, 3rd Marquess of Winchester, and to himself, as joint Lords Lieutenant of Hampshire, requiring them to send 450 men, with a warrant to the justices in Wiltshire to send a similar number. On hearing that Philip's expedition had set out, Charles immediately went to Plymouth, hoping to establish its whereabouts, reporting to Essex that he had learned nothing, but hoped the recent storms might have forced it back. He was now concerned that the ships available in Plymouth were too few and ill-prepared to mount a challenge, declaring: 'This country must be presently [immediately] ordered for a war.'[13]

Penelope realised that she needed to support her brother, but she had developed smallpox and there were great fears that the rash would disfigure her perfect complexion but, miraculously, she recovered without ill effect. To avoid spreading the infection, she retired to Rich's house at St Bartholomew's, where, very decently, he remained with her. With Essex having taken to his rooms, her absence offered the Cecils an advantage. Although he needed her at court, she became stuck at Leighs, pregnant with Charles's third child. Although she had heard that Pérez was back in England as part of a mission from Henry IV seeking support to end Spanish incursions into France, he failed to contact her despite learning of her pregnancy. In late 1576, she gave birth to a son, who was baptised Mountjoy Rich. (For full details of Penelope's children by Charles, see Endnote 4.) Being illegitimate, he could not inherit the Mountjoy title, but to Elizabeth's relief his paternity was not raised.

At last Penelope was able to return to court as Essex's go-between. He did not reappear there over Christmas, and Elizabeth did not visit him at Wanstead. On Twelfth Night 1597, Penelope attended the revels in the Middle Temple, during which theatricals, music and banqueting continued into the small hours.[14] Sadly, the festivities were brought to an abrupt end on 24 January with the death of Cecil's wife, Elizabeth Brooke, after a miscarriage.

Although Essex remained in a depressed state, he grudgingly visited Elizabeth when called to her chamber at court. She was still emotionally dependent on him and turned down his request to retire to Lamphey until after Easter. Following Cobham's unexpected death on 5 March, Essex was reinvigorated when Cobham's role as Lord Chamberlain at last passed to George Carey, now Lord Hunsdon. With Cobham having also been Lord Warden of the Cinque Ports, Robert Sidney approached Penelope, hoping to gain that position to enable him to return from Flushing with his growing family. Penelope delivered Robert's letter to Elizabeth personally, confident of gaining her agreement to Robert's appointment. To her consternation, it was granted to Cobham's son Henry, now the 11th Lord, who was Cecil's brother-in-law and Essex's political foe. 'There was little that could dishearten loyal supporters more than being unable to gain them favours.'[15] With Cecil being too cunning to be drawn into continuing spats, Essex had no choice but to patch up their working relationship.[16]

Chapter 29

The 'Island Voyage' to the Azores, 1597–98

Essex now hoped to improve his standing by making another incursion onto Spanish territory, and he brokered a rapprochement with Cecil and Raleigh to gain their support for another full-scale attack. The three of them were even to be seen riding to Essex House together, united in their fear of a Spanish fleet being readied at Ferrol and Corunna.[1] Although Essex was increasingly branded as overly militant, he convinced Cecil that Spain was planning another invasion of England. His objective was to disable the Spanish fleet with a pre-emptive strike before its departure, hoping to replenish the English Exchequer by capturing any treasure ship in his path. In early 1597, to his great delight, his 'bountiful' queen placed him in overall command of an expedition, despite her knowing that he was unreliable under pressure. Although he had hoped to be appointed Earl Marshal, on 10 March 1597 he was granted the less prestigious title of Master of the Ordnance. With Nottingham having retired, the experienced Lord Thomas Howard was given naval command of Essex's fleet. Raleigh, who was back at court after five years of disgrace following his marriage to Bess Throckmorton, was appointed Rear Admiral.

Essex's friends, including his stepfather, Sir Christopher Blount, who joined the military contingent as First Colonel, advised him to watch his political back as, if he were not careful, the knives would be out both for him and those surrounding him. As overwork always caused him headaches before an expedition, they advised him to appoint a deputy to enable him to stand back from the detail. Both Charles and Peregrine Bertie, 13th Lord Willoughby de Eresby, were suggested. Although Willoughby was an experienced soldier, having fought as a mercenary for the Huguenots under Henry of Navarre, it was probably on Elizabeth's instruction that Charles was appointed lieutenant-general and second-in-command of the military contingent. She was in no doubt of his worth after his success as Governor of Portsmouth, describing him as 'a noble and wise man', and insisted on him joining the council of war to provide Essex with guidance.[2] She also seems to have respected his discreet handling of his relationship with Penelope. She later wrote to Essex: 'Forget not to salute with my great favour good Thomas [Howard] and faithful Mountjoy.'[3]

It is very difficult to understand why Francis did not come into the reckoning to be appointed second-in-command, as he was always expected to join the expedition. His long record of success in the Low Countries made him far the most experienced English general. He had been second-in-command of the military contingent at Cádiz, masterminding the attack on the town, and probably saving Essex's shaky reputation in the process. Although he retained the rank of marshal, he was now downgraded from his former role as Essex's aide. With Charles, who was three years, younger, having little comparable experience of high command, Francis was understandably extremely hurt to find him being brought in over his head.[4] After returning from Cádiz, he had resumed command in the Low Countries with instructions to induce the States-General to release 1,000 English troops in their pay to join the expedition and to provide more ships.

On arriving back in England, Francis visited Essex at Sandwich to tackle him over what he saw as his demotion, only to find him still in bed. Essex claimed that Charles's appointment was not at his choice, and Francis would report directly to him. Leaving Charles with a title but no specific role did not placate Francis.[5] He confirmed that he would serve under Charles, whom he had always respected, but believed Essex could have prevented having him foisted on them against his will. He concluded that he had lost Essex's favour and asked him not to seek his employment in future.[6] Perhaps it was the penalty of not being a favourite. Remarkably, there was no hint of ill-will between Francis and Charles during the voyage, although on their return it was reported at court that Charles would not speak to him.[7]

The queen's instructions were for Essex to sail to Ferrol and Corunna where the main Spanish squadrons were reported to be based. It was unclear whether these were being readied for an invasion of England or to defend the returning treasure fleets, but he had orders to engage the enemy by land and sea. If the fleet had already sailed, he was to seek it out and to defeat it.[8] With that accomplished, he was to intercept a returning treasure fleet at the Azores. Her fear was that the lure of gold would attract him to the Azores before dealing with the fleet at Ferrol and Corunna.

The English fleet consisted of 120 vessels, about half of which were men-of-war. Seventeen were from the Royal Navy, including the *San Mateo* and *San Andres* captured at Cádiz the previous year.[9] The remainder were privateers equipped for war, together with a Dutch squadron, transports, pinnaces and supply ships; 6,000 troops were to be spread across the fleet to avoid over-crowding, with two companies on board the Spanish prizes, which had particularly good accommodation.[10] After leaving Chatham, troops were embarked at Dover and Weymouth, but the provisions on board were depleted when the fleet was delayed by contrary winds. On 6 July, Essex held a 'council of war' with Howard, Charles, Sir Christopher Blount, Carew, and Fulke Greville, after which Greville was sent to requisition a further month's supply of victuals. The queen and council acted promptly, employing the trustworthy Marmaduke Darrell's supply ships to deliver ample good quality provisions. Meanwhile, the fleet made its way through poor weather to Plymouth, but on arrival several vessels had sprung leaks and many of the pressed sailors were proving 'useless land-lubbers'.[11]

With autumn approaching, Essex could wait no longer, and, on 10 July, he set out from Plymouth without being reprovisioned, in expectation that Darrell would revictual them at sea. The fleet was divided into four squadrons, under Essex, Howard, Raleigh and the Dutch Admiral Duyvenvoorde, who had been on the Cádiz expedition. Charles on the *Defiance* and Southampton on the *Garland* joined Essex's squadron. Despite being prone to seasickness, Rich loyally joined Essex. Their plan was to rendezvous at Cape Ortegal, some forty miles north-east of Ferrol. Only a day out from Plymouth, the fleet hit another violent storm with gale force winds. When Essex's flagship sprang a leak, he struggled back to Falmouth, arriving on 19 July; Raleigh, having lost sight of 'my lord General' Essex, returned to Plymouth after only eight days at sea. The two Spanish prizes, the *San Mateo* and *San Andres,* which were in Raleigh's squadron, had proved unmanageable and impossible to sail in poor weather. After travelling overland to Falmouth, Raleigh found that three-quarters of the fleet had returned, many in desperate condition with ill or dying crews. Being prostrate with seasickness again, Rich was sent home. Essex told Elizabeth: 'If I had carried him to sea, [he] would have been dead in a week.'[12] Although Howard was their most experienced naval commander, his flagship had been leaking even before leaving Plymouth, but his squadron, which was probably better prepared, remained at sea, gaining vessels from other groups. These included Southampton on the *Garland* and Charles on the *Defiance*, despite the *Defiance* being damaged in a collision while leaving Plymouth Sound.

On 20 July, the storm had sufficiently abated for Charles and Southampton to confer with Howard on his flagship. They agreed to sail for the rendezvous at Cape Ortegal, hoping that the other squadrons would catch up with them. They sent the *Tramontana* back to Plymouth to report their intention. Although Essex responded that they were to await his arrival but avoid action, his message was never received. On reaching the Spanish coast on 25 July, Howard placed his squadron in full view of the Spanish, but no vessels appeared from either Ferrol or Corunna to challenge him, and he turned back to Plymouth.

Despite the unseaworthy state of Essex's ships and his touchy relationship with Raleigh, they worked effectively together making a commendably quick job of repairing the damage. By 29 July, they were awaiting a favourable wind when Howard reappeared. Despite their impatience to be going, many troops in Howard's squadron had fallen ill. When Howard reported the lack of any challenge from Ferrol and Corunna, Essex and Raleigh surmised that the Spanish fleets were not ready to sail and little purpose would be served by returning there. They contemplated taking their better ships to intercept the treasure fleet at Havana in Cuba, but when this was discussed at their council meeting Francis argued that they were inadequately provisioned, and their absence in the Caribbean would leave the Channel open to a Spanish attack. Essex and Howard rode to London to discuss the options with Elizabeth.[13] Her answer is not known, but Francis was relieved that the plan to sail to Havana was dropped.[14]

With the fleet remaining locked into Plymouth by unfavourable winds, Essex decided to leave behind the unserviceable transports and any other vessels unfit for an Atlantic buffeting. He discharged all his recently pressed seamen, retaining only those with experience, who could be spared from other ships. He also dismissed those military personnel who, like Rich, could not handle bad weather, but he retained Francis's 1,000 veterans. With fewer men, the victuals would go further but he was now less able to challenge opposition and would need to rely on fireships if he went to Ferrol. Although Elizabeth approved this revised plan, he left Plymouth Sound on 14 August – before receiving her confirmation – to take advantage of a fair wind. Howard, Charles, Francis, Raleigh, Duyvenvoorde, Southampton, Carew and Sir Christopher Blount came with him. Even now a southerly wind impeded headway, but this enabled Darrell's ten supply ships to revictual them at sea. With the wind at last veering north, they ran before it with the supply ships following.

Cecil, who was aware of the debilitating rivalry between Essex and Raleigh, was pessimistic about the venture. On 21 August, he wrote to Thomas, Lord Burgh, the Irish Lord Deputy, that the fleet was victualled for ten weeks but had sailed without its land army. He concluded that Essex would avoid any attempt to set fire to the Spanish fleet at Ferrol, that the attempt to capture the Azores would fail and carracks from the East Indies were probably already back in Spanish ports. The 'spirits of the noble earl' were reduced to 'weak, watery, hopes'.[15] Penelope did what she could to contain Cecil's criticisms. On 24 September, she asked him to provide her with any news when received but had to reassure him of her loyalty after rumours from 'another lady' that she had criticised him.

Essex had agreed to rendezvous at Cape Finisterre off north-west Spain, but a strong westerly drove the fleet towards Cape Ortigal further east. There was a chapter of problems. His flagship, *The Repulse*, was leaking. The *San Mateo* and *San Andres* were again proving difficult to sail; the *San Andres*, was missing for three days, having lost its foremast in a storm, and the *San Mateo*, carrying their assault equipment and heavy guns, was disabled off Corunna. It took all George Carew's determination after rigging a jury mast to reach a French port for vital repairs before sailing home. After commandeering another vessel, he set out again but failed to catch the fleet.[16] The *Warspite* with Raleigh on board carried away her mainyard so that in an easterly she could only make south, but was followed by several vessels intended for use as fireships. Sir Christopher Blount and others believed (probably incorrectly) that Raleigh had purposely separated himself to act for his own account.

With Essex wanting any excuse to ignore the Spanish fleet at Ferrol, he received intelligence from captured fishermen that it was unlikely to sail that year. However unreliable this might be, it was enough for him to head straight for the Azores, and he was even able to claim that he had opposed his council's decision to ignore Corunna. While waiting with thirty ships off Lisbon, Raleigh heard that the fleet from Ferrol had already sailed for the Azores.[17] On hearing this, Essex sent him orders to rendezvous with the main fleet at Flores, despatching his uncle, Robert Knollys, to England to advise Elizabeth. After making a fast passage, Essex investigated Angra on Terceira, the harbour most likely to receive treasure ships, but found it empty. With forts on each side of its bay and a garrison of fourteen companies of Spanish troops, it seemed impregnable. His fleet then moved on 200 miles west to Flores to rendezvous with Raleigh, who arrived a few days later. To avoid a conflict on their meeting, Charles had persuaded Essex to tell Raleigh that he never doubted him. With no Spanish garrison at Flores, the mainly Portuguese locals greeted them with fruit and fresh provisions. It was not an ideal location from which to intercept a treasure fleet that could bypass the island out of view, so Essex decided to explore the whole Azores area, intent on arresting any ships that they found. He thus allocated ships to islands other than Terceira to source supplies. With Spanish troops having garrisoned Fayal and fortified a position on a hill above the main town of Horta, he reserved it for himself, proposing to make an attack with help from Raleigh.

Raleigh, who as usual on sea voyages was fatigued by lack of sleep, reached Fayal on 14 September with the *Warspite*, *Swiftsure* and *Dreadnought*. There was no sign of Essex, so he ordered his squadron to anchor away from Horta to take on water and transfer food from their store-ships. After three days, he held a council of war with his captains, who agreed to wait a further day before landing. With Essex still not in view, Raleigh's seamen disembarked at Horta under covering fire from his pinnaces. Although 600 Portuguese levies on shore offered little resistance, the Spanish caused considerable damage from their hillside position, until forced off it by gunfire. This allowed Raleigh to enter the town, which was now deserted.[18] When Essex at last appeared, Meyrick (his steward) on the Swiftsure filled him with embroidered tales of Raleigh's disobedience for having landed without orders and breaking an unwritten rule that the chief should not be deprived of the opportunity to take his prize. When an assembly of land and sea officers asked Raleigh for an explanation, he claimed that as rear admiral, he was not subject to any veto on his actions. Although Francis voted in Raleigh's favour, Howard had to step in to make peace so that Raleigh's apology was accepted. With the Spanish garrison still in the hills overlooking Horta, Francis was sent with 200 men to reconnoitre, but found their encampment recently abandoned with several English prisoners having had their throats cut. With pursuit being impracticable, they set fire to the town.

While Raleigh remained at Fayal to revictual, the main body of Essex's fleet patrolled between Terceira and Graciosa, about sixty miles to the north-east, which was the treasure fleet's likely route to Angra. Nevertheless, the master of Essex's ship, 'a dull, unlucky fellow, named Cover' (who seems to have been made the scapegoat) persuaded him to explore San Miguel, 100 miles further down wind to the south-east.[19] Four ships remained in the vicinity of Graciosa, probably being instructed to remain on station, with Sir William Monson in the *Rainbow* and Southampton in the *Garland* to the north, and Francis in the *Marie Rose* and Sir William Brooke in the *Dreadnought* further west towards San Jorge.

At this critical moment, the West Indies treasure fleet, the *flota*, consisting of twenty-five vessels, including eight galleons of the Indian guard, appeared from the north-west. Although Monson was near them, he was alone and would have been taken if the Spanish had attacked. The *flota* was aware of the English fleet's presence, but not how close it was. Although Monson fired flares and signal guns, which were heard by Southampton and Francis, the Spanish bunched their ships together and headed straight for Angra. When the fog rose next morning, Francis and Brooke could see Monson and Southampton chasing after the *flota*, and Southampton managed to capture a frigate carrying cochineal which was lagging behind, but the remainder arrived safely at Angra.

With the four English ships blockading Angra, a pinnace was sent to San Miguel to advise Essex. On his way back to Terceira, Essex sighted a big Spanish merchantman being escorted by two frigates and he captured all three. The value of this cargo alone covered the cost of the entire Azores expedition. On arrival, after struggling for two-and-a-half days into a north-west wind, he sent experienced captains to assess how they could reach the *flota's* anchorage, but they concluded that this would be impossible. It was anchored near the shore, dead into the wind, exposing attackers to close fire from the forts as they tacked into the bay. With the *flota's* vessels high in the water, they realised that their cargoes had been unloaded.

Essex now retired with his fleet to revictual at San Miguel. On reaching Ponta Delgada, its main town, the sea was rough, and his attempt at a landing met with fire from 400 entrenched musketeers. With Raleigh being left with the fleet off the town, Essex took Howard, Charles and Francis with 2,000 men in small crafts along the coast at night to find another place to revictual the fleet. Francis was sent ahead and found a suitable beach for disembarkation near Vila Franca do Campo, fifteen miles south-east. He then led 200 men to occupy the town and found a good supply of corn and fruit. Essex, Howard and Charles now returned to the fleet, leaving Francis to quarter the 2,000 men.

While Raleigh had waited, another opportunity was missed. A small Brazilian ship appeared followed by a large carrack. With the English ships at anchor having dropped their ensigns, both new arrivals assumed that they were the Spanish West Indies fleet. When Raleigh captured the smaller vessel with its cargo of sugar, the captain of the carrack realised the danger and ran it ashore to enable the townspeople to take off the crew and its cargo of untold wealth. It was then set alight in accordance with Spanish regulations to prevent it falling into English hands, and Raleigh's men in their remaining boats were unable to extinguish the flames.

Having returned to rejoin Raleigh off Ponta Delgada, Essex moved his vessels round the coast to Vila Franca to revictual and pick up water. Reloading the troops left with Francis and stocking with provisions took three or four days and everyone became drenched floating out barrels of water through the surf to one ship at a time. At 5.00 pm on 7 October, Francis's sentry at the church tower reported a large body of men approaching from Ponta Delgada. With only 500 men left on shore, he sent Sir William Constable to warn Essex and moved thirty shotmen forward to a wayside chapel with orders to give the enemy a volley as soon as they came within range. They were then to retire hurriedly to where the rest of Francis's men would be ready to repulse them. Essex seems to have doubted the story and reportedly lit a pipe, but there was a sudden volley of musketry and then another. The soldiers at the chapel did not retire as instructed, as the Spanish force halted and were kept at bay while Essex's remaining troops embarked. It took until midnight for this to be completed. With the outlying picket being withdrawn, Francis was the last man to leave the shore. (There is some doubt over the extent of the local opposition. The Spanish Governor claimed to have captured seven guns, seventy boats and water casks, and caused fifty English drownings in a rush for their boats, but the truth is difficult to establish.)

With the flota safely at Angra, and no other treasure ships likely to arrive before the spring, it was even more frustrating for Essex when he received a letter smuggled out of Terceira from Sir Richard Hawkins, who was being held as a prisoner on a treasure ship. He reported that the flota's heavily laden ships were small and the escort was 'altogether insufficient to withstand an English attack'.[20]

In the meantime, Essex had given no further thought to the Spanish fleet at Ferrol, which, unknown to him, was approaching the English Channel. A week after he left the Azores on 9 October, he received a message from Elizabeth, grumbling at him missing the flota and calling for his immediate return with enough ships to meet the Spanish threat. With discipline having been lost, his vessels took their own routes home out of contact with the flagship, just as on the return from Cádiz. Many ships were strained and had sick men on board. When a storm dispersed them even further, it was feared that any stragglers would be picked off.

Having moved from Ferrol to Corunna, the Spanish fleet was held up for three weeks by unfavourable winds, leaving it with insufficient time to avoid the threat of autumn storms. It consisted of 136 well-fitted ships carrying 9,000 troops (with further men in Brittany waiting to join them) under the command of Don Martin de Padilla. This made it larger than the Armada nine years earlier.[21] It included twenty warships belonging to the Spanish crown, of which eleven were of 400 tons or more. On 9 October, the day that Essex left San Miguel, Padilla set sail. His fleet was divided into four squadrons, one commanded by the best of the Spanish admirals, the Basque Pedro de Zubiaur, who would play a significant role in La Jornada de Irlanda three years later (see chapter 36). The Spanish plan was to garrison Pendennis Castle at Falmouth, taking control of its surrounding area. It was then to drop back to await Essex's return from the Azores. With Essex defeated, they next planned to tackle Plymouth.[22]

The English had no forewarning and would have had great difficulty raising even 500 military personnel to defend Falmouth. Essex's fleet was spread all over the North Atlantic with its crews exhausted and several vessels sailing under jury rig and in need of a refit. The *Warspite* was so badly strained that Raleigh was storing his bigger guns in the hold.[23] Even if they had been in seaworthy condition, the government recognised that the odds favoured the Spanish. It hastily recalled troops from France and commissioned its remaining 'great ships' lying at Chatham.

With the danger far greater than in 1588, it was again luck that saved the situation. The Spanish were forced to abort their mission when a massive gale dispersed its fleet and it crawled back to a disconsolate Philip II, who died the following year. It had failed to locate any of Essex's ships returning from the Azores. On 25 October, Charles reached Plymouth on the *Defiance* with four other ships, including the *Garland* under Southampton. They had seen nothing of the Spanish except for a pinnace that sailed into their midst before escaping, but this encounter warned them that an invasion was afoot. As Lieutenant General, Charles now showed his initiative. Having written to London, he assumed command of all shore-based forces, and developed a plan to combat a Spanish landing. Although Sir Fernando Gorges, the Governor of Plymouth, had put together 500 men to defend the harbour, he was short of artillery and ammunition. Charles stationed the five newly returned ships in the Hamoase (the estuary of the Tamar) so that in a wind allowing the Spanish into Plymouth Sound, he could still put to sea.[24]

When Essex arrived a day later, he rode off to Hampton Court expecting a chilly reception from Elizabeth, although she had already confirmed him as commander-in-chief of the English fleet to combat the new threat. Although he had prepared a long report on the Azores trip, setting out how unlucky they had been to miss the flota, he received a severe dressing-down for his shortcomings. After landing at St Ives, Raleigh rode overland to Plymouth and, in retaliation for the criticism of his failure to obey orders at Fayal, sent a report to Elizabeth on the expedition's failings. This arrived ahead of Essex, whose self-confidence had greatly outweighed his ability.[25] Not to have examined Ferrol had been imprudent. He should have left vessels to report any movement to him in the Azores, although news might not have reached him in time. In his defence, he had been unlucky, but the flota remained safely at Angra, reaching Lisbon in February 1598.

On 29 October, Howard, Raleigh and Charles wrote to Essex that nothing more had been heard of the Spanish, but Howard would put to sea with such ships as were serviceable. It was agreed that Raleigh should return to Cornwall, where he was Lord Lieutenant, and Francis's veteran troops went there with him. It did not take them long to realise that the immediate Spanish threat had evaporated. The troops were discharged, with the ships being laid up or returned to their owners.

Although Essex went to Wanstead 'in a dudgeon', he was soon restored to favour. Falls has argued: 'He was a man in whose spirit the spark of genius always burned but was only at intervals blown to a white flame. Of the men of action in a reign rich in them he was the greatest personality after Drake and Philip Sidney.'[26] It is hard to agree. With a calmer approach, he might have caught the flota and solved the Irish problem that was ahead of him. 'It is difficult to calculate how often [his] nervous collapses were real or imagined, and if imagined whether they were wholly exaggerated or the product of some underlying mental illness.'[27] He was undoubtedly unbalanced. He remained at Wanstead and did not return to court even to greet the French ambassador. Was he suffering from delusions of grandeur caused, like Darnley, by syphilis as suggested by Lopez? Steven Veerapen concludes that he wasn't, despite his indisputably licentious lifestyle and all Cecil's rumourmongering.[28]

Francis considered the criticism of Essex to be unjust, and he defended him to Elizabeth at court. It may have been this show of loyalty that resulted in Essex's appointment to command the English forces against Tyrone in Ireland. There can be no doubt that Charles would have been the better man to lead the Azores expedition (as he was to prove in Ireland) but he had not had the opportunity to show his worth. Elizabeth never doubted him. He was appointed a Knight of the Garter, and Cecil made overtures of friendship to him.

On Charles's return, his life was relatively uneventful, and he too avoided criticising Essex. The fortifications at Portsmouth had been completed in his absence under the supervision of Hampden Paulet, the Lieutenant-Governor. With no immediate overseas threat to keep him at his post Charles returned to London, where his standing at court continued to grow. He retained his roles as Governor and High Steward of Portsmouth, Warden of the New Forest and Lord Lieutenant of Hampshire (which he shared with the Marquess of Winchester, who died in November 1598). This more relaxed existence was brought to an abrupt end by the appearance of a Spanish fleet at Calais. With the need to mobilise soldiers along the south coast, he returned temporarily to Portsmouth, while Cobham, as Lord Warden of the Cinque Ports, went to Dover, and Raleigh conducted a tour of harbours to collect naval stores.

When the threat of invasion subsided, normality returned, although the Spanish arrival made Henry IV even more determined to restore peace.

It was Cumberland's capture of San Juan in Puerto Rico which did most to lift English spirits. With 1,700 men and a fleet of twenty ships, he succeeded where Drake had failed three years earlier. After grounding one of his ships to provide a stable platform, he bombarded the Boquerón Redoubt into submission and then landed artillery to bombard the El Morro Citadel, which capitulated twelve days later. Although he looted and sacked the town, nearly 700 of his men became incapacitated with dysentery, forcing him to leave. He returned to a hero's welcome, bringing seventy artillery pieces from the citadel, a Spanish ship and 2,000 slaves.

Chapter 30

Further action in the Low Countries, 1597–1602

Whilst Francis was in the Azores, Maurice had been actively employed against the Spanish. In the late autumn of 1597, Francis returned to find the Spanish, now under the command of the Archduke Albert, threatening Zeeland. As winter approached, Albert sent an army of 4,000 infantry and 600 cavalry, commanded by the inexperienced Count of Varras, to the village of Turnhout, twenty miles south of Breda, where its small castle was garrisoned by forty men. With Francis seeing this as an opportunity to challenge them, the States-General gave Maurice orders to gather troops at Gertruydenburg, twenty-seven miles further north. Francis joined him there with an English regiment, co-opting Sir Robert Sidney from Flushing with 300 of his garrison and a Scottish regiment under Sir Alexander Murray. All told, the allied force amounted to 5,000 foot and 800 horse with two demi-cannons and two fieldpieces.

On 23 January 1598, the allied expedition left Gertruydenburg in bitterly cold weather, reaching Ravels about three miles short of Turnhout two hours after dark. Varras only became aware of the approaching force at about midnight and, with his encampment not being entrenched, ordered a retreat to Heerenthals, twelve miles south. When Maurice, who had had little sleep, broke camp at dawn, he found the Spanish retreat well under way, and the allied force only reached Turnhout after the Spanish rearguard's departure. Francis advocated pursuit and found the rearguard defending a bridge they had broken down across the Aa. Having gone forward with 200 Dutch musketeers to dislodge them, his horse was killed under him as he crossed a brook. Nevertheless, he continued on foot until remounted. With some musketeers managing to cross the bridge, others forded the fast-flowing river with the cavalry.

With the enemy in full retreat, the issue was to prevent them from reaching thick woodland about three miles further on. Francis again went forward with a few officers to a point where he could see the enemy's route being impeded by wagons on a lane as it passed through trees and undergrowth. Beyond this was open heathland with a hedgerow to the left. He now moved his musketeers forward to the left of the trees with instructions to maintain a dropping fire to delay the enemy's movement. He then followed down the lane with sixteen horse in full view of the enemy after sending an urgent message for Maurice to advance with all his cavalry. With the enemy rearguard maintaining a skirmishing fire, Francis was slightly wounded in the leg, but his plan delayed the retreat for three hours.

After emerging onto the heathland, Varras formed his men into four squares of pikemen with shotmen on their flanks as they retired towards the protection of woods behind. Meanwhile, the Dutch musketeers moved forward behind the hedgerow on the left, from where they maintained their fire on the enemy. As soon as Maurice's cavalry appeared, it charged. The shotmen in the squares were able to fire only a single volley before fleeing, leaving the pikemen in their denuded squares easily broken. With the cavalry chasing after the fleeing enemy infantry, Francis knew that their well-ordered counterparts, who had not yet been in action, would appear from the woods to challenge them. Maurice's cavalry soon returned at the gallop, but Francis had positioned men to check the pursuers, who turned back on seeing fresh troops ready to challenge them. Out of the enemy's 4,000 foot, 300 were killed and 600 taken prisoner, with Varras among the dead. The allies lost ten men, and Maurice's infantry had not been brought into action. With the small enemy garrison capitulating, the Anglo-Dutch troops rested at Turnhout for the night.

After the battle, Francis returned to England. With Burgh, the governor of The Brill (and coincidently the Lord Deputy of Ireland) having died, Francis sought to take over his post there in addition to his own military appointments. He returned to take command of The Brill in September, after being fêted at court. He also received a letter from Elizabeth praising the Turnhout action. She did not make him a peer, as 'she held that the name of Francis Vere had become, through its owner's merits, more illustrious than any court title that she could bestow'.[1]

With Spain exhausted by war, Philip II was anxious to restore peace, even if it meant offering liberal terms to heretics. He had planned the marriage of his daughter, the Infanta Isabella, to the Archduke Albert, intending to grant Flanders to them as joint monarchs of an independent state, albeit owing suzerainty to Spain. Although Henry IV was already in peace negotiations with the Spanish, the States-General did not believe that a lasting settlement in the Low Countries would be achieved during Philip's lifetime. With England more sympathetic to calls for peace than the Dutch, Francis was appointed as a special envoy to negotiate a new agreement with them now that Spain had become less of a threat. (Dutch merchant shipping was already carrying produce from the Indies and Brazil to Spain and Portugal.)

When Francis met with the States-General, it was clear that they were not ready to come to terms with the Spanish but accepted the need to revise the Anglo-Dutch agreement. In a treaty signed on 13 September 1598, they acknowledged their debt of £800,000 to the English and agreed to contribute £30,000 annually towards the cost of maintaining garrisons at The Brill and Flushing, and to furnish aid in both ships and men if England should be invaded.[2] By December, Elizabeth was in desperate need of troops in Ireland and called on Francis to despatch 2,000 men, of whom 700 were drawn from the garrison towns. These set out from Flushing in January 1599.

On 18 May, with Philip II having died, the double marriages were celebrated in Valencia of his son Philip III to Anne of Austria, and of Archduke Albert to the Infanta Isabella, who became joint sovereigns of the Spanish Low Countries as planned. During the archduke's absence from Flanders, Don Francisco de Mendoza, Admiral of Aragon, was left in command and was determined to register a success by capturing the Bommel-waart, an island between the Maas and the Waal, which offered access into Holland. Francis was again called upon to join Maurice, who was assembling a force of 10,000 foot and 3,000 horse. On 4 May, Spanish troops under General Claude La Bourlotte [or Laberlot] had crossed the Maas, while Mendoza captured Crevecoeur and besieged Bommel. On 13 June, Mendoza was forced to raise the siege after Maurice's guns opened up 'a tremendous fire', but the Spanish general moved across the Bommel-waart to construct a fort, which he called San Andres, at the village of Hurwenen, while Maurice tried to hinder his progress by firing cannonades from across the Maas.

On 24 June, a force under William-Louis of Nassau-Dillenburg and Horace Vere, which had fortified Heerwaarden, was attacked by

3,000 Spanish and Italians under Jasper Zapena. Although the attackers forced the palisades, they were repulsed with heavy losses after hand-to-hand fighting. Maurice now built a bridge from Heerwaarden to the island of Voorn at the junction of the Maas and the Waal. Having crossed the river, Francis attacked the Spanish forts on the opposite bank and, on 22 July, forced the enemy to evacuate the Bommel-waart. Nevertheless, he was struck down by illness, and was confined to his tent at Voorn for several days, but wrote to Cecil to outline the success of the campaign. He also reported that the Spanish troops were close to mutiny for lack of pay, so that order was unlikely to be restored until the archduke's return.

At last, on 5 September, when the archduke reached Brussels with the Infanta, Mendoza redoubled his efforts, crossing the Maas and overrunning Cleves and Westphalia with shocking barbarity, despite this being in violation of the Holy Roman Empire's neutral rights. In November, he attacked Doesburg, but gained no permanent advantage. In the New Year, in order to resolve their troops' arrears of pay, the Spanish reached a deal to sell their forts of St Andres and Crevecoeur, including ordnance and munitions, to the Dutch for £22,500. At last the threat to Dutch independence was averted.

With the archduke embarrassed by both a lack of funds and mutinous troops, the States-General resolved to carry the war into enemy territory by attacking the walled town of Nieuport, set back about two miles from the sea and nine miles west of Ostend, which the Dutch were continuing to garrison. The ultimate objective was to renew the attack on Dunkirk to end the menace of 'Dunkirkers' marauding merchant shipping in the Channel. Both Maurice and Francis considered the objective extremely hazardous, as any failure would reopen Holland to the threat of invasion, but the States-General was determined to cast a blow for 'Christendom' and assembled a large fleet at Flushing. On 22 June 1600, the allied army, consisting of 12,000 infantry, 1,600 cavalry and ten pieces of artillery, disembarked at the fishing village of Philippine east of Ostend. It was led by Maurice as commander-in-chief, with Francis leading the van with 4,500 men. Meanwhile, the archduke concentrated a large army at Ghent ready to tackle them.

The allied army marched westward along the coast towards Nieuport, capturing the enemy forts and redoubts surrounding Ostend as it went. With these being on the archduke's route, Maurice left a garrison of 2,000 men at Ostend, while his main force built a road on which to move their guns forward to Nieuport, where the estuary of the Yser provided a haven for ships from the fleet to dry out at low water to unload provisions. On reaching the town early on 1 July, they left 3,000 troops on the east bank of the estuary, while their main force waded across the haven at low water.

The allies soon learned that the archduke's army had reached Bruges and was advancing with 10,000 infantry, 1,600 horse and six field guns under the command of Zapena and Mendoza. To protect their rear, Francis counselled Maurice to return to Ostend to defend the forts they had taken, but Maurice was slow to react and, with most of his force having crossed the Yser estuary, needed to await low water before he could return. By that evening, the forts at Ostend had surrendered, so Francis advocated moving the army back to await the enemy at Leffinghe, three miles east of Nieuport, where their right flank would be protected by a water-filled ditch. Although Maurice agreed to this, he sent forward only the 3,000 troops under Ernest of Nassau, who had remained on the east side of the haven, promising to provide his main force 'in due season'.[3] With the enemy reaching Leffinghe before him, Ernest's force fled when put under enemy fire. This caused the loss of 2,500 men without checking the Spanish advance. There was no further choice but to give battle in the strip of sand dunes between Nieuport and the sea.

At break of day on 2 July, Maurice ordered his troops to the west of the Yser to cross back over as soon as the tide had ebbed. It was still not fordable when Francis and Maurice received the news that the Spanish were marching towards them along the shore. They urgently needed to move their troops across. At 8.30 am, Louis-Günther of Nassau's cavalry, forming part of the van, swam the Yser with their horses, followed by Francis with the rest of his fully clothed vanguard of 4,350 men. Having arrived at the opposite bank, they could see the enemy in the distance marching towards them beside the sea. Francis handpicked 250 English foot and 250 of Maurice's guard, moving them forward to a narrower point in the dunes where two ridges which crossed them offered some protection. He placed the 250 English with fifty of Maurice's guard on the forward ridge, with the remainder on the one behind, where Maurice also positioned two culverins (long-barrelled cannons) at its seaward end. The two ridges were linked by a lower dune at their landward end, where he stationed 500 Frisian musketeers with orders to protect their right flank to the south. A further 700 English pike and shotmen were hidden in a ravine on the seaward side ready to support the men on the ridges as required. Meanwhile, Maurice lined up his remaining artillery on the shore with cavalry behind, and the remaining 650 English and 2,000 Frisians of Francis's vanguard waited behind Maurice's battery, ready to move forward as required. Although Maurice's remaining 3,150 infantry were stationed about a musket shot behind the vanguard's centre and right flank, they only latterly became involved.

Although Maurice contemplated moving forward to provoke the enemy into attack, Francis persuaded him to hold his position, as the archduke's hastily gathered troops, despite being tired after their night-time march, were short of provisions and would have to attack immediately. With the enemy's strength being in its infantry, it rested for a couple of hours, so that the rising tide would prevent Maurice from launching his cavalry along the beach. Soon after half-tide, the enemy's vanguard began to advance, shielded by light horse. When Francis ordered Louis-Günther of Nassau's cavalry forward to draw the enemy horse within range of Maurice's batteries on the shore, he misunderstood the order and failed to move. This ceased to matter when the enemy cavalry charged, only to be scattered by Maurice's artillery.

At 2.30 pm, with high tide approaching, the beach almost disappeared. This pushed the enemy foot back into the dunes, while its cavalry crossed over to the landward side. Francis took up a position with his 300 men at the top of the forward ridge. Very shortly, Spanish arquebusiers appeared over the opposite crest, and their vanguard of 500 infantry advanced down the slope towards Francis's handpicked line. His objective was to hold the forward ridge for as long as possible, hoping to wear out the Spanish attackers while he replenished his line from his 700 reserves as required. It proved an extremely hard-fought and bloody struggle at push of pike between crack troops on both sides, but the Spanish were eventually forced back. When their cavalry advanced along the landward side, they faced heavy flanking fire from the 500 Frisians and Maurice's culverins, so that, when challenged by Louis-Günther of Nassau's cavalry, they hurriedly retired back behind their infantry, closely followed for some distance by the young count. With the Spanish vanguard being reinforced, it rallied and took a round hill opposite Francis's vantage point. Francis brought up yet more men, who eventually dislodged it in hand-to-hand fighting 'with much slaughter on both sides'.[4]

With the archduke bringing up his centre, it was engaged in a long drawn-out battle for control of the forward ridge during which all the

English contingent became engaged. The archduke also moved men forward on the landward side fronting onto Maurice's reserve positioned further back. Although the Spanish were checked by the 500 Frisian musketeers, they sheltered in hollows, from where they sent out skirmishers. Francis sent repeated messages for 2,000 Frisian reserves waiting behind the seaward battery to be brought into the attack with further requests for part of Maurice's cavalry to be sent to prevent the enemy from rallying once driven back, but no one appeared. At last, Francis rode to join his men fighting below the forward ridge. They were still holding the enemy in check, but were in desperate need of the support he had requested. Although Francis was wounded in the thigh and in the leg, he concealed this from his men, but they were at last forced back by overwhelming numbers and retired in good order towards Maurice's battery. The Spanish followed 'at a respectful distance', although their skirmishing cavalry killed some of Maurice's men. Then Francis's horse fell dead, landing on him, and it took several of his officers to extricate him and he had to ride pillion behind one of them, staining his rescuer's uniform with his blood.[5]

On reaching the battery, Francis learned that his orders to advance, sent to the 1,000 Frisians and the 300 foot and horse under Horace, had never arrived. When the cavalry at last made their charge, they routed the Spaniards on the beach, forcing them back into the dunes. With Francis realising that he was gravely hurt, he was taken to the surgeon and played no further part in the battle.

With the Spanish infantry having gained control of the forward ridge, 2,000 of their men marched into the next valley to form tercios of shot and pike, which drove back the 500 Frisian musketeers (although they soon rallied). The archduke's arquebusiers now advanced on the landward flank, but his men were exhausted. With backing from the reserve and Horace's cavalry, the English force rallied. Maurice called up all his cavalry, some under Burghley's grandson, Sir Edward Cecil, with orders to charge as required, while he plied the enemy with shot from his demi-culverins. He also advanced his reserve divisions, which had yet to see action.

The renewed allied attack was decisive. 'The Spaniards broke and fled in all directions. The archduke never drew rein until he reached Bruges.'[6] Both Zapena and Mendoza were taken prisoner, with about one third of the Spanish army being killed or wounded, especially from among the elite units making up their van. In the allied army, 800 of the 1,600 English who had borne the brunt of the fighting were killed or wounded, but a complete victory had been achieved. The Dutch had lost 2,000 men, mainly at Leffinghe.

Elizabeth was ecstatic at the allied success and warmly congratulated Maurice, who attributed 'the victory to the good order and direction of Sir Francis Vere'.[7] She was 'often heard to say that she held Sir Francis to be the worthiest captain of her time'.[8] Nevertheless, his wounds proved serious, incapacitating him for several months. He was carried back to Ostend, where Northumberland (who may have escaped from England to avoid being closely implicated in Essex's rebellion) arrived at his bedside with a gracious letter from the queen. In August, Francis was conveyed to Ryswick, Maurice's home at The Hague, for convalescence. The bond between the English and the Dutch had never been stronger.

Despite the psychological impact of the victory at Nieuport, Maurice decided to withdraw without challenging Dunkirk. The Spanish were far from defeated and Ostend remained under siege. Although Francis recovered only slowly, he was inundated by 'fine gentlemen' wishing to claim that they had served under him. He was perfectly happy to employ career soldiers, but had no time for the likes of Northumberland, who swaggered about, happy to play their part as cavalry officers in a skirmish, but otherwise absenting themselves. If they did not measure up as soldiers, Francis felt obliged to dismiss them.

The most significant outcome of the Spanish siege of the little fishing town of Ostend was that they now recognised they could no longer hope to conquer the Dutch. The battle for this almost insignificant outpost occupied the efforts of most of their forces for three years. On 5 July 1601, when the archduke delivered 20,000 men and fifty siege guns to take it, its defence became a cause célèbre for the States-General. Having a garrison of only 2,600 Dutch troops under Governor Vandernood, Francis was detailed, once recuperated, to take control. He returned to England to gain Elizabeth's approval to recruit 3,000 men to supplement Maurice's main force. This allowed Horace to be detached with 800 English veterans to join his brother at the Ostend garrison. On their arrival on 9 July, they were obliged to land on the beach, as both the western and eastern harbours were within range of the archduke's guns, but their arrival strengthened the garrison to 3,500 men.

The town was strongly fortified, having a seawater moat, the Geule, surrounding its walls. There was a network of marshy ditches to the south with fortified outworks, the most significant of which were 'the Polder' to the south-west, and 'the Spanish Half-moon' to the south-east. The Geule held deep water on the town's east side but was fordable at low water to the north-west, where the town's defences were correspondingly stronger. An area of sand dunes on the seaward side left it vulnerable to attack by troops fording the Geule from the west, but it was also strongly defended by walls linked to three forts. The siege was thus a struggle to gain control of the sand dune area, from where the walls and palisades could be approached on dry land.

Francis's objective was to keep the besiegers fully occupied. His first task was to entrench and improve the ramparts of the Polder, manning it with 200 men. He realised that if it were accessed by the enemy, water could be drained out of the surrounding ditches protecting the walls. He also improved access for shipping by cutting a passage from the Geule, at the point where it joined the sea to the north-east, into the town's harbour, which could safely unload 100 vessels at the same time, once they had run the gauntlet of the Spanish batteries on their approach.

With the Spanish maintaining a continuous bombardment, few buildings were left standing, but the garrison dug underground quarters in the marketplace for protection. On 4 August, Francis was severely wounded in the head and was forced to leave six days later after developing a fever. Having convalesced at Middelburg, he was sufficiently recovered on 19 September to return. Meanwhile, on 1 August, Elizabeth had sent a further 1,200 properly provisioned troops from England with contingents of French, Scots and Frisians. These landed a week later, increasing the garrison's complement to 4,480 men. Unfortunately, an English traitor called Conisby, employed by the archduke, accessed the garrison with these latest recruits. He now conveyed intelligence to the besiegers in messages left in a boat stuck in the mud beyond the Polder, from where a Spanish soldier recovered them at night. After trying to persuade a sergeant to blow up the powder magazine, Conisby was reported and whipped out of town.

With the besiegers concentrating their efforts on the north-west corner of the town, its walls were so peppered with shot that they became coated with iron. This shattered any new missiles fired at it. On 4 December, the archduke was ready to launch a night attack after building foundations for gun batteries out into the Geule. After a fierce struggle, the besiegers were pushed back leaving 500 dead. From 12 December until Christmas, there was a south-east gale preventing the delivery of provisions and reinforcements. This left the garrison, which was wasting daily, short of ammunition. Although another assault was imminent, they could muster only 2,100 able-bodied men, although they needed a minimum of 4,000 to man the walls. Francis had to buy time in the hope of receiving reinforcements. With the archduke awaiting a spring tide to launch a major attack after fording the Geule, Francis called a parley. He sent two English officers to act as hostages for the safe return of the two Spanish negotiators, who arrived with every expectation that Francis was about to capitulate. When they arrived, Francis avoided meeting them and, on the following day, they were landed on the east side so that they had to walk outside the town's perimeter to report back to the archduke. They returned the following evening and Francis feasted them on their arrival, calling many toasts. He then stunned them by proposing that the archduke should raise the siege, before leaving them to sleep it off in his chamber. At the break of day, as if by a miracle, men-of-war carrying 400 men with provisions anchored off the town. Although they faced heavy fire on their approach, only three sailors were hurt. The Spanish negotiators were now exchanged for the two English hostages. It was not what the Spanish had expected. 'The Infanta Isabella, gorgeously attired with twenty ladies and gentlemen in her train, had walked before the walls of the town' to await a victorious entry.[9]

The Archduke was furious. On 7 January 1602, two of the Spanish batteries began a massive bombardment. By now, 163,200 cannon balls of 40–46lb had been fired at the walls.[10] In the evening, the Spanish waded across the Geule with scaling ladders, hand-grenades and ammunition to challenge the north-western defences and seaward facing walls.[11] At the same time, attacks were launched on the Polder and on the east side. Francis had demolished ruined houses for beams and spars to shore up the palisades and, at high water, closed the west sluice next to the north-west defences to keep the Geule as full as possible. He then positioned most of his garrison to cover the seaward side, where the curtain wall had been much damaged by waves during a recent gale, placing two demi-culverins loaded with musket shot on the north-west battlements to sweep the Geule as it was forded. At the seaward side breach, he collected an arsenal of missiles to hurl at the attackers.

These included firkins of ashes to blind the assailants, barrels full of tenter-nails, stones and bricks from the ruined church, hoops bound with squibs and fireworks, hand-grenades and clubs.[12]

During a lull, while the besiegers cooled their guns after firing all day, he called in fifty sappers to throw up a small breastwork and drive in palisades across the breach.[13] A soldier, who had crept forward to watch for the enemy's arrival, reported back that Italian troops were wading across the Geule. With Francis standing at the top of the north-western battlements, he gave orders for his troops to delay firing until he gave the signal. As soon as the besiegers rushed into the assault, he caused carnage by opening a hot raking fusillade. Although the advancing assailants released one great volley, the garrison lay flat to let it pass harmlessly over them. Those reaching the breach were met by Francis's cocktail of weapons and ordnance hurled from the bulwarks. Despite this, the assailants bravely rallied three times only to be beaten back. Meanwhile, similar assaults were launched elsewhere, with an attack on the eastern side challenging the Spanish half-moon, which Francis used as a decoy to keep the besiegers on the eastern side from coming to the assistance of those on the west.

With the Spanish on the sand dunes at last being driven back, they waded across the Geule on a rising tide. Francis opened the sluices sending a torrent of water down on them, washing many out to sea. The enemy lost 2,000 men, but the garrison suffered thirty dead and 100 wounded with Horace having been shot in the leg. Francis's troops now crossed the walls to plunder the dead.

Francis and Horace left Ostend two months later, but a succession of Dutch governors continued to hold the town until, on 20 September 1604, it at last fell to the enemy. By then, it was 'a confused heap of smouldering ruins'.[14] When Francis returned to The Hague, he found the Dutch offensive stalled for want of men and resources. With the States-General seeking to raise 20,000 foot and 5,000 horse, he returned to England to ask Elizabeth, yet again, to provide more recruits. He then returned with them to reassume command. While in England, the tiresome Northumberland challenged him to a duel. When this was brought to Elizabeth's attention, she instructed Northumberland to forebear, but he still issued a letter describing Francis as 'a knave, a coward, and a buffoon'.[15] Although they agreed to meet on Francis's return from Holland, Northumberland was by then safely ensconced in the Tower.

By May 1602, Francis had 8,000 English troops under his command in the Low Countries. This formed nearly half the complement of the allied army, in which Burghley's grandson, Sir Edward Cecil, was now in command of the English horse. Francis's force immediately joined Maurice to advance into Brabant, but on finding Mendoza strongly entrenched they retraced their steps to besiege Grave. It was to be Francis's last military operation. While working in the trenches he was shot in the face, with the bullet passing below his right eye and lodging near his ear. He was invalided back to Ryswick in a critical condition.

In August, with Ireland facing the threat of La Jornada de Irlanda (see chapter 36), Elizabeth called for more troops to be made available from the Low Countries. Initially, the States-General refused her request, claiming that 'the sword was now over their heads', but they offered ships. Despite his wounds, on 10 August Francis found himself having to attend a full assembly at the Hague to persuade them to send 2,000 of his men. Nevertheless, he was not able to return to his military duties until October, by when Maurice had taken Grave.

PART VI

CAMPAIGNS IN IRELAND

Chapter 31

Background to efforts to pacify Ireland, 1588–97

For many generations, Ireland's disgruntled and belligerent population of warring Celtic clans had threatened English security by challenging their self-appointed overlords, Plantagenet and Tudor kings. After the Reformation in England, Henry VIII needed to establish Protestant authority and, for the first time, he attempted to unify Ireland into a single kingdom. With the cost of military intervention being prohibitive and the Irish Catholic Church proving a bastion against reform, he adopted a more persuasive approach. He restored English rule over much of the country by offering support to Gaelic chieftains against rival clans and granting peerages to those who would accept his paramount authority. His objective was to achieve their subservience not expropriation.[1] By 1543, nearly all Irish chieftains had visited England to receive grants of titles. This did not prevent local warlords from maintaining armies of clan members to settle neighbouring conflicts and to impose law in their own fiefdoms.

To settle Ulster, Henry granted the Earldom of Tyrone to Conn Bacach O'Neill out of what had previously been the kingdom of Tír Eóghain, even though Conn Bacach's belligerent eldest son, Shane, was in league with the Spanish. With encouragement from the Dublin authorities, Tyrone drew up a will to bypass Shane as his successor, nominating his illegitimate (or more likely adopted) son, Matthew, Lord of Dungannon, in his place. Shane armed his followers and in the ensuing conflict killed Matthew and his eldest son, Brian, leaving the 12-year-old younger son, Hugh, as the heir. To protect Hugh, the English whisked him off to the Pale, the area around Dublin, from where he was sent for his education to England under the protection of the Sidneys at Penshurst. On Conn Bacach's death, Hugh duly became Earl of Tyrone and was later restored to the substantial O'Neill estates. Even then the English never wholly trusted him, and built a network of forts across his lands to monitor his movements. They also incited conflict with rival groupings to keep his power in check.

Although Edward VI's accession heralded an aggressive campaign to implement an Irish Reformation, his Lord Protectors' policies were motivated by a need to establish English authority rather than religious observance. Nevertheless, they formed an Anglican Church of Ireland with its own panoply of bishops and imported Protestant settlers to occupy lands expropriated from any chieftain daring to challenge English supremacy. By these means, they hoped to dilute opposition by weight of numbers.

Tyrone began to fear that the English were bent on seizing back the lands already restored to him. It seemed a more fruitful course for him to build his authority among the Gaelic clans, particularly the O'Donnells, who occupied most of present-day Donegal, and to maintain a dialogue with the Spanish. In 1588, he made a point of offering food and shelter to the crew of an Armada vessel wrecked at Inishowen. His action resulted in arms and provisions being delivered from Spain, enabling the Ulstermen to become better organised. In 1592, he helped the 15-year-old Hugh Roe O'Donnell to escape from Dublin Castle. On returning to Ulster, O'Donnell's father abdicated, and Hugh Roe became The O'Donnell and Lord of Tyrconnell. Catholic bishops in Tyrconnell called on Irish chieftains to seek Spanish aid for a rebellion to install Philip II as their rightful monarch. Tyrconnell recognised that to achieve this he would need the support of the powerful O'Neills. Despite Tyrone's Protestant English upbringing, he realised that his authority with hitherto rival Gaelic chieftains depended on him launching a Counter-Reformation as champion of the Roman Catholic Church. After receiving support from Spain and from Catholics in northern Scotland, he galvanised the other Gaelic lords as never before. In February 1595, his half-brother Art O'Neill had captured the Blackwater Fort after receiving gunpowder and updated military equipment from Scotland. Although Tyrone received Spanish support, Philip II turned down his proposal that the Spanish should appoint an Irish governor. In 1596, with the Spanish needing to divert English troops from the Low Countries, they landed good quality armaments in Donegal with the promise of a Spanish expeditionary force to follow.[2] With assistance from Spanish drill sergeants, 6,000 of Tyrone's clansmen were trained to use pikes in the European style, with a further 4,000 becoming musketeers and 1,000 being mounted as cavalry. In May, the O'Donnells, Maguires and O'Neills were on the move, recapturing Enniskillen, which had been taken by the English, ravaging Louth as far as Drogheda and defeating a small English army under Bagenal at Clontibret.

In March 1596, Cumberland was sent to prevent the Spanish from providing Tyrone with further support by giving instructions for him to bring Tyrone as a prisoner to London. Elizabeth had greatly underestimated the difficulty, and Cumberland returned empty-handed, but she now recognised the threat posed by Spanish involvement. Realising that her military policy in Ireland had been overly cautious, she tried to pre-empt the Spanish threat by sending troops under Sir John Norreys, but these were mainly raw recruits, who arrived later and in smaller numbers than needed, so that Norreys 'obtained no appreciable success'.[3] Furthermore, Tyrone had been able to end rivalries between Irish tribes. He was now viewed as 'the last and greatest of Gaelic Kings', the king of Ulster.

Without having Spanish troops at his side, Tyrone adopted guerrilla tactics to enable him to remain 'elusive' and 'strike without warning'.[4] Despite combining with Tyrconnell and Hugh Maguire of Fermanagh, he dared not risk open warfare, attacking only if the enemy was weakened and worn out. He continued to disrupt English supply lines to their forward garrisons, while, at the same time, temporising with them to defer their incursion onto his estates. In 1598, having negotiated a cessation of hostilities, he was formally pardoned but used the lull to build up his forces.

When Burgh, the English Lord Deputy, died in the autumn of 1597, possibly as a result of poison, there was no great clamour of candidates to replace him, and his role was left unfilled. Then Cecil heard that Tyrconnell and Maguire had linked up with Tyrone to attack Portmore fort in Armagh. Although Sir Henry Bagenal brought a large English army to relieve its garrison, including hardened troops from the Low Countries and the Azores expedition, on 14 August he was ambushed at the Yellow Ford on the Blackwater River. His force suffered the heaviest defeat ever inflicted by the Irish on English troops, with 800 killed and a further 400 wounded. Despite this Irish success, Tyrone 'was curiously hesitant at moments of crisis'.[5] He missed his opportunity to march on Dublin and allowed the English survivors to retire to Newry, giving them 'more respite than they deserved'.[6] His limited objective was to become 'the unchallenged ruler of Ulster, not of Ireland as a whole'.[7] It was still a serious English setback. More troops were needed, and Tyrone's success led to renewed outbreaks of unrest elsewhere. The English abandoned Armagh, so that Tyrone and Tyrconnell were able to send forces south into Munster to assist in the destruction of English settlements.

Cecil sent Raleigh to Ireland to report on the worsening situation. Raleigh arrived to find his estates in Munster under threat, with many English settlers fleeing. Spenser returned to London in October after his castle at Kilcolman was destroyed by Tyrone's forces. Raleigh's report to Cecil shows that the English were even contemplating Tyrone's assassination, although Raleigh was told to avoid Cecil being implicated, 'presumably in the hope that [Raleigh's] loyalty would pay back dividends'.[8] He was 'well aware that things were done in war time from which leaders wished to distance themselves', and Cecil was 'not to be touched in the matter'.[9] Even now, Raleigh was doubtful of Cecil's friendship, despite having warned him that Essex was a 'tyrant', whose 'malice is fixed'.[10]

Chapter 32

Re-establishing Devereux influence, 1597–1600

Essex and Charles were now firm friends through their mutual affection for Penelope, and she was overjoyed at their safe return from the Azores. With the older generation having died, it was Penelope who exerted political influence on their behalf. To assuage former rivalries, she was at pains to develop a warmer relationship with Cecil, who had been appointed Chancellor of the Duchy of Lancaster. Despite the Azores expedition's failure to intercept the flota, reports of Essex's bravery made him more popular than ever. This did not please Elizabeth, and his enemies saw him as a 'warmonger and a powerseeker'.[1]

A peace party was forming around Cecil, who saw Essex's anti-Spanish policy as dangerous and unaffordable. Cecil deflected suggestions of his personal antipathy for Essex by persuading Elizabeth to help restore his rival's ailing finances by allowing him to purchase some of the booty accumulated in the Azores on favourable terms. In his efforts to regain Elizabeth's affection it was Raleigh who saw Essex, with his insufferable arrogance, as his foremost enemy. This resulted in Bess's close friendship with Penelope coming to an end.

In late November 1597, Lettice, now aged 54, took a coach to London to attend the birth of Penelope's fourth child by Charles. On 8 December, the boy was baptised Scipio Rich at St Clement Danes. Choosing the name of a Roman general may have reflected Charles's growing reputation as an army commander.[2] Nevertheless, the child seems to have become known as St John. (There is no further mention of 'Scipio', who may have died in infancy, but no baptismal record has been found for the child named St John mentioned in Charles's will, so it is assumed that they were one and the same.)

With Essex as 'the warlike voice of aggression', he would always oppose accord being reached with Spain.[3] His *Apologie*, written as an open letter to Anthony Bacon, was designed to demonstrate his continued concern for England's security. However, with Henry IV having recovered Amiens, and Philip II bankrupt and close to death, the superpowers had a strong incentive to come to terms, and a peace process was begun, to which the English were invited. Nevertheless, Elizabeth did not want to desert the Dutch, who were on the front foot after their successes in the Low Countries, and she asked Essex to act as a peace commissioner. When he wriggled out of such an unpalatable role, Cecil was tasked with joining the negotiations in France, leaving his position of Secretary temporarily in Essex's hands.

Fortuitously for Essex's hawkish stance, the Spanish delivered a fleet up the Channel with 4,000 troops to support their garrison at Calais. This greatly diminished the risk of a peace accord being reached. In December Elizabeth recalled him to court, offering him the post of Earl Marshal, the highest chivalric role under the sovereign.

With Essex back in favour, Lettice, who had remained in London, hoped that Elizabeth might at last be prepared to receive her with Sir Christopher Blount. In December she asked Essex to make overtures on her behalf, but he suggested that she should consult with Elizabeth's ladies, Anne Russell (Warwick's widow) and Elizabeth Leighton (her younger sister). By mid-February, she still had heard nothing from the queen, so, with Cecil in France, Essex took the opportunity to lobby on his mother's behalf, but Elizabeth remained full of malice over her marriage to Leicester. Although she agreed to a meeting, whenever Lettice was escorted to the privy galleries, Elizabeth found an excuse not to appear. On 27 February 1598, Lettice was left waiting with her gift of a 'fair jewel of £300'.[4] This public slight was repeated on several occasions, until Essex went to the queen's rooms to persuade her to relent. On the following day, Lettice 'kissed the queen's hand and her breast, and embraced her, and the queen kissed her ladyship'.[5] There was no warmth in it, and Elizabeth refused a second meeting.

While Lettice was waiting for an opportunity to see the queen, Essex arranged entertainments. On Valentine's Day, 'a very great supper at Essex House' involved music and dancing.[6] This was attended by family and friends including Charles, Penelope and Dorothy, but not Rich. With two plays being performed, it did not end until 1.00 am. With Southampton being another close ally of both Essex and Charles, and a promising soldier, he would have expected to attend this event. Unfortunately, he too had fallen foul of the queen.

Southampton had suffered a dysfunctional upbringing. His father had lived openly with his manservant, while his mother took her pleasures elsewhere. On his father's death in 1581, the 8-year-old became Burghley's ward. After attending St John's College, Cambridge, his marriage was arranged to Burghley's eldest grand-daughter, Elizabeth Vere, the daughter of the 17th Earl of Oxford. With Southampton being openly homosexual, he had to pay £5,000 to extricate himself. Being fascinated by theatre, he became a patron of Shakespeare, who admitted to their relationship and seems to have written: *'Shall I compare thee to a summers day?'* in Southampton's honour. In 1593, he dedicated *Venus and Adonis* to him. His 1594 dedication of the *Rape of Lucrece* states: 'The love I dedicate to your lordship is without end ... What I have done is yours; what I have to do is yours; being part in all I have, devoted yours.'

It can be no surprise that Elizabeth intuitively mistrusted Southampton, who spent much time at court. Probably to his own complete surprise, he fell passionately in love with Penelope's cousin, Elizabeth Vernon, another lady-in-waiting. During their 'stormy erotic courtship', she became pregnant, although this remained secret. When Southampton sought the queen's consent to marry her, Elizabeth strongly disapproved and, in February 1598, sent him abroad for two years to join the peace negotiations between Spain and France.

In August, with Elizabeth Vernon having moved into Essex House, Essex and Penelope sneaked Southampton temporarily back so that they could be secretly married. They were taking a great risk in defying the queen but hoped to preserve what remained of Vernon's honour. When the queen discovered the deception, Vernon was committed to one of the 'better apartments' at the Fleet Prison with instructions for Southampton to join her there on his return from France.[7] There can be no doubt of the intensity of their relationship. She wrote to him: 'My dear Lord and only joy of my life ... I am severed from you whom I do, and ever will, most infinitely and truly love. I beseech you, love forever most faithfully me, that everlastingly will remain your faithful and obedient wife.'[8]

The 'Vernon affair' did not improve Essex's relationship with the queen. She was also furious to find him back to his lascivious ways, bedding her ladies. It was reported: 'He is again fallen in love with his fairest B (Elizabeth Brydges, daughter of the 3rd Lord Chandos).' Having boxed the fairest B's ears, she told Essex that he could only remain at court if he desisted, and she would not overlook any future philandering. This did not end his belief that he could do no wrong.

Unfortunately for Essex, the negotiations in France came to a premature end and Cecil sought consent in mid-April to return to England. He had been given the run-around by Henry IV, who reached a secret agreement with the Spanish and, on 2 May, signed the Treaty of Vervins, under which, to everyone's relief, the Spanish were required to abandon both Calais and Blavet in Brittany, but it did not end their continuing support for the Irish rebels. Cecil secretly warned Essex of his imminent return, which would enable him to spend time with his elderly father before his death on 4 August. Elizabeth was distraught at losing Burghley, the man who had been the architect of her reign. The last remnant of the greatness of the Elizabethan age seemed to be over.[9]

With the Dublin government remaining disorganised, and Cecil absent in France, Francis Bacon alerted Essex to his opportunity to improve his standing by involving himself in what had always been England's Achilles' heel. A new Lord Deputy was urgently needed. Both camps in the privy council nominated opponents for the role. Essex suggested Raleigh, while Cecil proposed Sir William Knollys. When Knollys was vetoed by Essex, he proposed Cecil's and Raleigh's ally, Sir George Carew, but Elizabeth turned him down. When Essex advised Elizabeth to send a well-equipped army, there was strong disagreement over what was required and, as he considered her an ignoramus on military matters, he lost his temper. After turning his back on her, she 'boxed his ears'. This caused him to put his hand to his sword, and swear 'a great oath that he neither could nor would swallow so great an indignity'. Although he was restrained by Nottingham, he was still throwing insults as he left for Wanstead.[10]

With Burghley's death making government roles available, this was not the time for Essex to absent himself from court, and Cecil's policy to restore peace started to gain the upper hand. Raleigh was reappointed captain of the queen's guard and retained all his West Country posts, including that of Lord Lieutenant of Cornwall, but a coveted position on the privy council still eluded him. Essex had had great respect for Burghley as his guardian and attended his funeral on 29 August, but after joining the 500 mourners who walked solemnly beside his coffin from the Strand to Westminster Abbey, he immediately returned to Wanstead, 'tired of the shallowness and deceit' of the elderly queen.[11]

With the queen believing that Essex had the arrogance to make a challenge for the crown, William Knollys was one of many of his allies who warned him to be reconciled to her.[12] It was only at about this time that she discovered that Elizabeth Southwell's son, Walter, born at the end of 1591, was Essex's child and not that of Thomas Vavasour, whom she had jailed. She insisted on Essex making provision for Walter in his will and was furious, as an omnipotent queen, at having been kept in the dark. To Frances's great disappointment, with her own younger children not surviving infancy, she now learned that the young Walter, who was abundantly healthy, was living with Lettice in Staffordshire.

It was Cecil's allies who benefited from Burghley's death. Although Elizabeth arranged the Garter ceremony at Windsor as a low-key affair, Cobham was installed as one of the new knights and, in May, Cecil replaced his father as Master of the Court of Wards. With Elizabeth having dangled this lucrative role before Essex for months, knowing that it would solve his financial difficulties at a stroke, Cecil's appointment was a disaster for him. With him still remaining at loggerheads with the queen, Penelope turned to Cecil when in need of favours but this was to little avail. When she tried to arrange Sir William Knollys's appointment as Treasurer of the Household, it was offered to Roger, Lord North of Kirtling. Knollys had to make do with the lesser role of Comptroller, but became a privy councillor and, a few years later, did gain the coveted post of Treasurer.[13]

Meanwhile, Penelope took Rich and three of her children to visit her mother, who was with Sir Christopher at Drayton Bassett. On an impulse she decided to invite everyone to Chartley, sending her cook ahead to warn the steward, William Trew, that they would arrive on the following day. On the cook's arrival, Chartley's staff spent the night preparing beds and rooms, while Trew sent to York for food and extra horses. By four o'clock that afternoon everything was ready. Then a second message was received that they would not arrive until the following day.

There was consternation when news reached Chartley of Essex's row with the queen. Lettice wrote to him: 'I cannot be quiet until I know the true cause of your absence [from court] and discontent.'[14] She was confident that if the problem were Ireland, he would deal with it wisely, and if it were 'men's matters', he had the courage to cope with them. If it were 'women's matters', he 'should be skilful' enough in those sorts of problems by now! She wanted him to maintain his honour, but it was his honour that made it difficult for him to offer Elizabeth the abject apology she was demanding.[15]

Back at Wanstead, Essex had collapsed with a fever, stewing 'in his own neuroses, worrying over enemies at court, both real and imagined'.[16] As Steven Veerapen has explained:

> Essex truly thought that he had done no wrong. As such he could barely understand his situation and he never understood his feelings for the queen, so warped were they by the division between hatred of her politics, chaste attraction to her mind and image, and the required, mawkish expostulation of physical attraction to her person. At any rate it did nothing to warm Elizabeth to him. 'He hath played long enough upon me. I mean to play upon him.'[17]

Appointing a new Irish Lord Deputy was now urgent. With Burghley dead, and with the need to balance Cecil's growing authority, Elizabeth continued to believe that Essex had a role to play. He still held offices, and the government's smooth running required his presence.[18] The family closed ranks behind him, and Lettice sent Sir Christopher to establish how he was, while Sir William Knollys assured Elizabeth that his illness was genuine. At last, in mid-September, Essex swallowed his overbearing pride and apologised, admitting his fault – albeit through gritted teeth. He was now restored to court. Dorothy wrote to him: 'Dear Brother, I cannot but desire to know how the court air and humours agree with you. If both sort with your health and contentment, none shall be more glad [than] your most affectionate sister.'[19]

Earlier in the year, Dorothy's son, the heir to the Northumberland Earldom and a 'goodly boy', had died at just a year old, but another son, Henry, was born at Syon House a few days later. On 24 June 1598, Northumberland reported to Essex that the birth 'recompensed his last loss'.[20] Essex became a godfather, but sadly this child also died at under 6 months. By the autumn, despite having to endure a difficult relationship with her husband, Dorothy was again pregnant.

During this period, it was Penelope who Essex credited with being his strongest influence and support. It was her charm and diplomacy which maintained his vital channel of communication with Elizabeth. When he needed to see his sister at short notice, despite her being unwell and without her finery, she arrived at court early in the morning to avoid being seen. She also helped Elizabeth Vernon when freed from the Fleet, taking her to Leighs for her baby's arrival. When a daughter was born on 8 November, Penelope became a godmother and the child took her name.

In October, Charles came from Nonsuch Palace to spend a month with Elizabeth at Richmond. Although it was rumoured that he would be made a privy councillor, Elizabeth and most of the council wanted him as Ireland's Lord Deputy. Nevertheless, Essex vetoed his ally's appointment, arguing that Charles's experience in 'martial affairs' was limited, being a scholar not a soldier.[21] This may have been for Penelope's sake, as Ireland was considered unhealthy, and Charles was probably not disappointed. By now, Essex realised that although it was unwise for him to be absent from court, he would need to go himself. As he warmed to the idea, he wrote to Elizabeth: 'Duty was strong enough to rouse me out of my deadliest melancholy.'[22]

Essex was unquestionably regarded as England's most able general, beloved of his soldiers. Furthermore, the role called for a person of prestige.[23] To encourage him to agree, Elizabeth and Cecil offered him the lord lieutenancy rather than the lesser title of Lord Deputy. He was also appointed Lieutenant General and Governor General of Ireland with a promise of 16,000 foot and 1,500 horse, by far the largest English army ever sent there. Raleigh saw his appointment as a personal slight, but Elizabeth 'valued [Raleigh's] perspective on Ireland, appointing him to a commission to advise on the conduct of the war'.[24] He soon came to realise, as Essex did, that the role was a poisoned chalice, and Essex had been given 'inadequate resources to fight an impossible war against a relentless enemy'.[25]

The lord lieutenancy of Ireland was Essex's last opportunity – a time to do or die.[26] There can be little doubt that Cecil expected him to fail and, like Raleigh, probably hoped that he would, although both realised 'that English control of Ireland was essential to the nation's security'.[27] This was not simply a military expedition. Essex was given instructions to assess the state of the country, to assemble a council, to monitor religion and justice and to reform corruption.[28] He was also discharged of £10,000 of his debt by the crown. Penelope realised it was a chance he could not refuse and would be an opportunity to redeem his father's reputation. He announced: 'I have beaten Knollys and Mountjoy in the Council, and by God I will beat Tyrone in the field.'[29] Nevertheless, in his absence, Cecil and his cronies were left to monopolise the queen's ear.

Essex made preparations enthusiastically, but his finances were so parlous that he was forced to sell Wanstead. With Penelope distraught at the thought of losing the place she had treated as home since her mother's marriage to Leicester, Charles scraped together £4,300 to acquire it as a home for them within reach of her children at Leighs. By Christmas 1598, the deal was done, and Rich remained unfailingly obliging. The only shadow was Essex's departure to Ireland which he viewed with gloom. He prepared a new will, which only highlights his recognition of the risks involved.

On Twelfth Night 1599, Essex attended the festivities in honour of the Danish Ambassador, and Elizabeth chose him to dance a galliard with her. Perhaps she recognised that she was sending him to his fate. On 13 January, Edmund Spenser died suddenly in London, and Essex paid the costs for his burial at Westminster Abbey. Spencer had been a staunch Devereux ally, writing poetry to commemorate Essex's successes. On 5 March, Essex's 13-year-old stepdaughter Elizabeth, the daughter of Philip Sidney, married his ally, the 22-year-old Roger Manners, 5th Earl of Rutland. This proved to be an unhappy relationship. With Rutland being homosexual and suffering from syphilis they had no children, and it has been assumed that the marriage remained unconsummated. All these events caused a 'dangerous delay' to Essex's departure, but, on 27 March, he at last left London. Soon afterwards, Shakespeare's *Henry V*, modelled on the new Lord Lieutenant, opened at Shoreditch.

Essex's entourage included Thomas, 15th Lord Grey de Wilton, an experienced soldier but Cecil's watchdog, who soon quarrelled with the Lord Lieutenant. Other 'diverse noblemen' included Southampton, Rutland, Sir Christopher Blount and Essex's steward, Sir Gelli Meyrick, not a group that Elizabeth would have picked. Appointing Sir Christopher and Southampton, even in an unofficial capacity, expressly contravened her orders.[30] Being married to Lettice, Sir Christopher was refused a seat on the Irish council. With Southampton having returned from the Continent for the birth of his son, he was yet again in disgrace after brawling at court, and Elizabeth refused to appoint him as Master of the Horse in Ireland. There may have been more to his appointment than met the eye. Notwithstanding Essex's promiscuity with ladies at court, like so many of the attractive men in his entourage, he was not averse to male relationships on campaign. Despite their undoubted bravery, young men like Rutland, Southampton and the Danvers brothers carried little military weight, but provided other services. On 13 February 1601, William Reynolds (probably a brother of Essex's secretary):

> marvelled what had become of Piers Edmonds, the Earl of Essex's man, born in the Strand near me, who had many preferments by the Earl. His villainy I have often complained of. He was Corporal General of the Horse in Ireland under the Earl of Southampton. He ate and drank at his table and lay in his tent. The Earl of Southampton gave him a horse which Edmunds refused a hundred marks for him, the Earl of Southampton would [embrace and hug] him in his arms and play wantonly with him.

Edmonds was 'so favoured as he often rode in a coach with [Essex] and was wholly of his charges maintained, being a man of base birth in St Clement's Parish'. (For a man to ride in a coach was effeminate of itself. To ride with another man was practically a proclamation of homosexuality.)[31] What their wives thought remains unknown.

To avoid the tensions of court life, Penelope took some of her children and again retired to Chartley with Elizabeth Vernon, who brought her baby, Penelope, and was again pregnant. Neither Charles nor Rich went with them. Although Elizabeth Vernon suffered a miscarriage, this did not disturb their enjoyment, and Penelope reported to Essex that Cobham, still nicknamed 'Sir John Falstaff', had fathered a son by his mistress. They remained at Chartley for two months, but, in June,

Essex's infant daughter died at Walsingham House and was buried at All Hallows by the Tower, so Penelope returned to comfort her sister-in-law. It was some compensation for Frances that she was again pregnant, but she lived in fear of losing another child. On 8 July, Elizabeth Vernon wrote to Southampton that Rich had 'importuned' Penelope to return to Leighs by 24 August to assist him in dealing with a serious land dispute. Penelope did not want to upset him any further, so she invited Elizabeth Vernon to come there with her daughter, but it would require Southampton's influence to persuade Rich to agree.

Essex set off for Ireland through crowds, who lined the old post road to Holyhead two deep for four miles, shouting: 'God bless your lordship. God preserve your honour.'[32] On 3 April, he detoured to Drayton Bassett with Sir Christopher for a brief farewell to Lettice. Despite contrary winds, they reached Dublin on 15 April. Charles had warned him that Cecil 'possesses the mind of her that rules' and promises of support from London might not be honoured.[33] Essex knew that many of his enemies at court would be happy to see him fail but relied on Sir Christopher and Sir Charles Blount of Mapledurham to report on any hostility among his troops.

London was full of rumours of a Spanish invasion, but stories that James VI in Scotland was backing a Catholic uprising to revenge his mother's execution could not have been further from the truth. The night watch was doubled, and Nottingham was appointed general (presumably because he was considered too old to take command at sea) with Charles as his deputy. All available naval and military forces were mobilised after an unfounded story of a Spanish landing on the Isle of Wight. Nevertheless, there were concerning reports of a build-up of Spanish warships at Corunna, and Charles remained at Somerset House assessing the threat of an invasion of London.

Although the so-called 'Invisible Armada' never approached English shores, Spanish warships were undoubtedly being readied at Corunna. On 1 June, news arrived that a powerful Dutch fleet had approached Corunna but, finding its batteries well-fortified, had moved on down the coast after a brief exchange of fire. When it was later learned that the Dutch had taken Grand Canary, it was feared that the Spanish fleet would be able to leave Corunna unchallenged. However, when it at last ventured out, it followed the Dutch fleet as it moved on to the Azores. This had been Holland's first great expedition independent of the English. Despite it being undone by disease, it kept the Spanish away from England. By September, with rumours of a Spanish invasion of England subsiding, Nottingham's defensive force was stood down.

The Spanish were not daunted. In early 1600, Frederico Spinola spirited six Spanish galleys from Santander to Sluis to challenge English and Dutch shipping. In June, a 'Dunkirker' took nine coasters off Flamborough Head in a single day. In October, Dunkirkers captured three ships out of Falmouth bound for Ireland, driving ashore a warship trying to intercept them and threatening Plymouth Sound.[34] Elizabeth called for a public subscription to fit out a protective squadron of ten or twelve ships but her plan gained little support.

Chapter 33

Essex's campaign in Ireland and its aftermath, 1599–1601

Elizabeth had become exasperated by Ireland. She reluctantly invested huge sums in military operations there, rising to a staggering £2 million by the end of her reign, about a half of her total wartime expenditure between 1585 and 1603.[1] Having lost 40,000 men, she was in no mood to take prisoners.

Tyrone knew that he needed foreign support to drive out the English. He was not an experienced field commander and his army was unpopular after feeding on plunder as it moved. To gain Spanish support, he promoted his rebellion as a Counter-Reformation. With Philip II having died in September 1597, his son Philip III promised Spanish troops, notwithstanding the reluctance of his father's more experienced advisers.[2] He knew that Ireland remained England's weak spot, and eventually agreed to launch an expedition, despite his pressing need for reinforcements in the Low Countries.[3] He argued, correctly, that it would deflect English troops to Ireland, reducing their support for the Dutch. With the Spanish having made peace with the French, they had 6,000 experienced troops available to make Ireland their base for a renewed attempt to place the Infanta Isabella on the English throne. This would become known as La Jornada de Irlanda and Tyrone and Tyrconnell agreed that a force of this magnitude should land at Cork or Waterford, but, if in lesser numbers, should disembark at Limerick or Donegal.

When Essex reached Ireland in April 1599, he found that most of his promised troops were inexperienced levies and in lesser numbers than agreed, and 2,000 veterans being sent by Francis from the Low Countries were still awaited. He recognised the need to deal with Ulster before the Spanish arrival, but, with the rebels already having 20,000 well-trained and properly armed men, he was outnumbered by two to one. Although there were reports that he rushed blindly into action, it was the Irish council who advised him to clean up unrest in Leinster before marching north. They argued that, by waiting until June, there would be ample grazing for his horses. He should have followed his instinct.

When the seasoned troops arrived, Essex deployed men to strengthen the Pale and regarrisoned castles in Meath and Louth, before setting out on 10 May for Leinster. His plan was to drive a wedge between Tyrone in the north and the Leinster and Munster lords in the south, but the Anglo-Normans, being Catholic, proved unreliable as allies. He faced several sharp skirmishes before reaching Athy, forty-five miles south-west from Dublin, to meet Elizabeth's former favourite, Thomas Butler, 10th Earl of Ormonde, the Irish Treasurer who retained responsibility for Munster. Ormonde endorsed the Irish council's advice to resolve rebellion in the south before tackling Tyrone.

Although Essex was warmly welcomed by English settlers and gained their military support, Elizabeth was extremely critical of his failure to accost the Munster rebels and considered his detour into Leinster to have had little military value. Furthermore, a detachment left to subdue the O'Byrnes was routed in Wicklow, and a larger force was annihilated by Tyrconnell in the Curlew Hills in County Roscommon with its commander, Sir Conyers Clifford, the governor of Connaught, being killed. With Tyrconnell having now gained control of Connaught, Tyrone marched south to destroy the fragile English plantation in Munster. With support from the Fitzgeralds, their combined force reached the Dublin suburbs before withdrawing.

After meeting up at Limerick with Carew, who was acting as his treasurer-at-war, Essex brought his men back to Dublin, harassed by the Irish at every opportunity. Nevertheless, he showed great energy, marching his men off their feet as he fought his way along the Wicklow coast, despite many of them suffering from disease. He was determined to appease the queen, despite her complaining, unhelpfully, that 'much time and excessive charges have been spent to little purpose'.[4] He was undoubtedly surprised by the level of Irish resistance; reinforced, as he realised, by the Spanish. He was beginning to share the view of the Irish council that taking Ulster might be insuperable, but Elizabeth had no time for excuses. She wrote:

> We have perceived … that you have arrived in Dublin after
> your journey into Munster, where though it seemeth, by the

words of your letter, that you have spent diverse days in taking an account of all things that have passed since you left that place, yet have you in this despatch given us small light either when, or in what order, you intend particularly to proceed to the northern action.[5]

Her anger had been brewing up for some time, and she now considered him disgraced. He was not the man, if he had ever been the man, to deal with Tyrone, who was far more powerful and well-organised than she had realised. Even the privy council considered her unfair, sending their own more sympathetic response.[6]

On 25 July, Essex provided Elizabeth with a detailed and rational assessment of the challenge ahead. He had found the Irish troops, with their Spanish training and arms, to be hardy and mobile with a self-confidence born out of military success. With Tyrone having every expectation of Spanish military support on the ground, the war would be long and costly.[7] The raw recruits at his disposal were unnerved by guerrilla tactics. He needed officers, whose 'example and bravery in the field would be 'of more use than all the rest of [his] troops'.[8] He also needed superior English cavalry. With the rebels lacking the means to storm walled towns, he wanted them kept well-garrisoned as bases for operation, where merchants could source provisions otherwise available to the enemy. To cut off rebel food supplies he destroyed local produce, but this required him to supply his own forces from west and north-west England with everything being shipped in when needed. He also wanted a cordon of ships blockading ports to prevent the rebels from receiving deliveries from either Scotland or Spain.

Before heading north, Essex drew up a resolution signed and approved by all the members of the Irish council at Dublin. It laid out their opposition to an invasion of Ulster. 'Then, surprisingly, he changed his mind and, at the end of August, sent his secretary, Henry Cuffe, to England with both the resolution and a note indicating that he was making the attempt despite it.'[9] This may have been intended as an insurance policy against failure to demonstrate the difficulty of the task being forced upon him. It was late in the season for him to be setting out. He was left with only 4,000 combatants, was exhausted and Elizabeth was refusing his request for more troops and money. Despite involvement in a few inconclusive skirmishes, he was losing the 'spell which is so great a gift of leadership', and his troops began to desert.[10]

Having returned to Donegal, Tyrone received a message of papal encouragement. More tangibly, Don Martin de la Cerdá resupplied him with 2,000 Spanish arquebuses, powder and 20,000 ducats. Although there was news of a further delay in La Jornada de Irlanda, Tyrone was in a sufficiently commanding position to march on Dublin but chose to await the Spanish arrival, although this was hardly needed. On 28 August, he appeared in superior strength on the opposite bank of the Lagan at Ardee in Louth and called for Essex to parley with him.[11] The two commanders met across a ford on the River Glyde, with Tyrone's horse standing in water up to its belly as a gesture of humility.[12] Inexplicably, they talked out of earshot, without witnesses and with nothing written down. They agreed a renewable six-week truce, which was probably the most Essex could hope for. According to Tyrone (who Elizabeth considered a traitor and an arch dissembler), the terms agreed were completely one-sided. He claimed that he was authorised to retain control of all the lands he had acquired without fighting a battle; no further English garrisons were to be established; English and Irish 'zones of influence' were agreed; the Roman-Catholic faith was to be restored and the English clergy were to leave Ireland; a Roman-Catholic university was to be established; all great offices of state were to be held by Irishmen, who would be free to travel to the Continent at will; and all their forfeited lands were to be restored.

It is hard to imagine that Essex would genuinely have approved such terms. He did not believe that he had agreed anything unreasonable. Although expressly forbidden from doing it, he provided knighthoods to his senior officers in recognition of their efforts against unassailable odds.[13] Like his father before him, Ireland had got the better of him and he was completely deflated, demoralised and unwell from dysentery. Back in Dublin, he received another vitriolic letter from Elizabeth, highly critical both of him and those, like Southampton, who had arrived in Ireland against her wishes. He was convinced that she had not grasped the realities. It was only now, encouraged by Southampton, that he contemplated rebelling against Cecil's government. At his later trial, Sir Christopher Blount claimed to have dissuaded him from taking a nucleus of 2,000 men back to England hoping to gather further support as he travelled south. Instead, he was persuaded to return to discuss his predicament with Elizabeth personally to reassert his standing, despite being expressly forbidden to leave his post without authority.[14]

Communicating by letter would take at least a fortnight. He had little choice, despite her instruction not to return before 'the northern action had been tried'.

On 24 September 1599, Essex handed responsibility for Ireland's government to the two Lord Justices: Adam Loftus, who was both Archbishop of Dublin and Lord Chancellor, and Carew, before setting out for London with a handful of men to protect him from arrest on landing. At the same time, Southampton left for the Low Countries hoping to raise support among English troops stationed there. Essex reached the court at Nonsuch in a little more than three days. He went straight to the queen's bedchamber, spattered with mud, only to find her 'newly up with her hair about her face'.[15] Although she welcomed him, she was deeply shocked by his arrival. After dinner, she became more critical, and by nightfall he was ordered to his chamber. She did not know his intentions but was furious at him deserting his Irish post. He was visited by Francis Bacon, who warned him of the build-up of opposition to him, advising that he should behave modestly, demand nothing and seek more personal interviews with Elizabeth. 'Only she ... could shield him', but he needed to secure her favour.[16]

Essex believed he should try to establish control over the council. He was paranoid that Cecil, surrounded by his cautious peace party, was 'encouraging Elizabeth to refuse his requests for more money, men and horse'.[17] He believed that they were 'grouped comfortably round the Council table keeping the home fires of criticism burning'.[18] The rival factions were now clearly drawn. On 29 September, Cecil dined with Shrewsbury, Nottingham, Cobham, Grey de Wilton, and Raleigh, all of whom were hostile to Essex. As captain of the guard, Raleigh had Essex in his sights, but his own star failed to rise. He was 'acutely disappointed' not to be appointed vice chamberlain and was still not a privy councillor. When the queen made him governor of Jersey, he left court in disappointment. Meanwhile, Essex met separately with Rich, Charles, Edward Somerset, 4th Earl of Worcester (Huntingdon's brother-in-law), Rutland (Essex's stepson-in-law), Lord Henry Howard (later Earl of Northampton, who was probably neutral), Sir William Knollys, Sir Edward Dyer (Chancellor of the Order of the Garter) and John, Lord Lumley (Keeper of Nonsuch Palace).

Penelope was at Walsingham House, awaiting the arrival of Frances's baby. At least she could be relieved that Charles had not been in

Ireland with her brother. Frances's daughter (named Frances) was born on 30 September and was baptised with little ceremony. On the day following the birth, Essex was placed in the charge of the Lord Keeper, Sir Thomas Egerton, at York House in the Strand. Penelope immediately moved with Elizabeth Vernon to Essex House to be nearby. Dorothy, who had had a row with the tiresome Northumberland, also arrived. Essex House now became the rallying point for Essex's supporters, but when Elizabeth became offended at this 'open-door' policy for government opponents, Penelope realised that it was unhelpful. On 11 October, she and Elizabeth Vernon left for the country, although Penelope seems to have appeared regularly at court to keep abreast of developments.

With Essex under arrest, his supporters rallied round, concerned that he was 'distracted in mind' by his confinement. His doctors considered him gravely ill and feared for his life. Despite his philandering, and the recent birth of her daughter, Frances asked to see him and offered to move into York House to be with him, but he 'coldly refused to see her' or anyone else unless sent by the queen.[19] When she asked the queen's permission to join him, she was rebuffed. At the beginning of November, Penelope and Dorothy, dressed 'aggressively all in black', went to court to plead 'as humble suitors' to move him to 'more airy quarters', but Elizabeth refused.[20] Elizabeth was undoubtedly distressed at his sickness and recognised that his continued detention would only increase his popularity, but this did not prevent her retaining the jewels sent by Penelope and Dorothy to support their plea. Their black garb gave rise to rumours of his death, and a bell was tolled at St Clement Danes.

Penelope now turned to Cecil for help to gain better accommodation for her brother, but to no avail. Essex had a swelling on his legs and received communion in the belief that he was dying. Despite suggestions that he might not survive the month, others said that his illness was feigned. While Elizabeth and her Council deliberated, the Accession Day tilt took place without the man who had been its star turn for the previous decade.[21] The crowds were hugely sympathetic at his predicament. This was not what Cecil needed. At the end of November, the privy council, through the Court of Star Chamber, issued a public declaration of his misdeeds and his failure to resolve the sorry state of Ireland.

With Penelope back at Essex House, her brother's continued detention increased her concerns for his well-being, and she pressurised Elizabeth to release him, but rumours persisted that he would be sent to the Tower. Southampton and Sir Christopher Blount met with Charles hoping to develop a plan to spring him from York House and to smuggle him to France or Wales. Charles was involved in another plan to bring him to court and to confront Elizabeth with demands for his reinstatement. Essex refused all such offers of help, believing he could answer all the charges made against him. When Elizabeth permitted him to receive daytime visits from his uncle, Sir William Knollys, and from Frances, broad daylight and the company of others did not prevent her from becoming pregnant![22] To make it more difficult to bring him to trial, he commissioned an engraving depicting him as a war hero in full armour.[23] On 29 November, William Trew, who had arrived at Essex House from Chartley, became hopeful of his release after hearing that Elizabeth had gone to York House with Worcester and the Countess of Warwick, but this was to censure him for claiming to be too unwell to attend the Star Chamber.

'Elizabeth celebrated Christmas with bravado, filling Richmond Palace with lords and ladies to show that she could enjoy herself without Essex', and she even played cards with Cecil.[24] A German visitor described the 65-year-old queen as:

> Oblong, fair, but wrinkled, her eyes small, yet black and pleasant; her nose a little hooked, her lips narrow and her teeth black; her hair was of an auburn colour, but false; upon her head she had a small crown. He bosom was uncovered, as all the English ladies have it till they marry. Her hands were slender, her fingers rather long, and her stature neither tall nor low; her air was stately, and her manner of speaking mild and obliging.[25]

Commentators needed great tact. The scholar and humanist, Thomas Platter, wrote: '[Elizabeth is] very youthful still in appearance, seeming no more than twenty years of age.'[26] It was claimed 'that her sexual intactness had brought with it resistance to bodily decay'. For others 'the mask of youth' was a 'grotesque falsity', but it was wise not to suggest it.[27] Her age was a taboo subject, but the principal concern was her failure to name a successor.

Penelope again appeared at court in an attempt to gain Essex's release, using the excuse of his need to resolve money matters, but to no avail, although the queen 'spoke with her and used her very graciously'.[28]

She now solicited Cecil's help to gain access to York House to see her 'unfortunate sick brother', but once more without success.[29] At New Year, she attended the traditional present giving with Rich and Charles, but Elizabeth rejected Essex's gift and he received nothing in return.

By this time, Essex had been at York House for three months. With his life seemingly in jeopardy, Penelope wrote to the queen in a florid style imploring sympathy for him. She unwisely suggested that, 'if the Queen's "fair hands do not check the course of their unbridled hate", his enemies will pursue him to "his last breath". And having removed him they would make "preparation of greater mischiefs", and then "make war against heaven" – Elizabeth herself'.[30] This was a hint at the queen's failure to curb Cecil's vindictiveness. On 2 February 1600, Cecil's ally Thomas Sackville, Lord Buckhurst, the Lord Treasurer, took Penelope to task. Although she managed to convince him of her loyalty to the queen, she was obliged to send a conciliatory apology.

Meanwhile, Essex was feeling better and agreed to attend a public hearing in the Star Chamber. Although this was set for 7 February, it was postponed when, at Cecil's instigation, he wrote a submissive letter to Elizabeth. It appears that Cecil was nervous of having to shoulder the blame for bringing down a popular man. Messages were scrawled on his front door saying: 'Here lieth the toad.'[31] With Essex's blessing, Charles, Southampton and Charles Danvers all wrote secretly to James VI to imply that Cecil opposed his succession. They proposed that he should ready an army on the Scottish border, and they would raise an English force to pressurise the government in London into confirming his claim. Although they sent Sir Henry Lee to Scotland, James remained cautious but was still considering their plan when Charles was appointed Lord Deputy of Ireland, even though Cecil clearly knew what was going on.

In early March, Penelope became convinced that the queen would allow her brother to return to Essex House, but Elizabeth took 'umbrage' when Penelope assembled there with Dorothy, Southampton and Elizabeth Vernon, so that he remained where he was.[32] It was not until 20 March that he was, at last, released to Essex House under guard to await his hearing, but he was still under house arrest. He was undoubtedly severely depressed, fearing that there were spies in his household and his handwriting had been forged.[33]

There was further trouble when copies of Penelope's letter to the queen were published abroad. She hotly denied responsibility but, on

29 March, was called before the council to explain how it could have happened (although it may well have been arranged by Cecil). When she claimed illness and failed to attend, rumours were spread that she had something to hide and had fled the country, but she had gone to Leighs with Elizabeth Vernon. On 26 May, Danvers, who was acting as her go-between with Essex, Southampton and Charles, warned her to return to London.

It was Essex who faced trial first. In May his *Apologie,* which had irritated Elizabeth in the previous year, reappeared in print without his authorisation. Yet again, Cecil may have been responsible. There was a further problem when a young lawyer, John Hayward, published *The First Part of the Life and Raine of King Henry IV,* dedicated to Essex. This likened Elizabeth to the deposed Richard II, and implied that Essex was behind this criticism of the queen.

On 5 June, Essex was brought before a special commission at York House. Although he was spared the ignominy of a public trial in the Star Chamber, he faced savage interrogation from Coke, who set out a litany of his faults while in Ireland. These included his appointment of Southampton as Master of the Horse against Elizabeth's express orders, touring Leinster and Munster instead of going straight to Ulster, conferring knighthoods without good cause, agreeing a truce with Tyrone rather than fighting and arresting him, and his return without authority. Coke described him as 'proud and ambitious ... disobedient and contemptuous ... notorious and dangerous'.[34] Nevertherless, there was sympathy for him being required to spend two hours kneeling on a cushion during a twelve-hour hearing.

Despite accepting some failures, Essex refused to admit insubordination or having any connection with Hayward's book. Even Francis Bacon was called to provide evidence of his criticisms of the queen. In the final outcome, Essex was censured and stripped of his offices including membership of the privy council and his role as earl marshal, but he had avoided a treason trial and was permitted to return under house arrest to Essex House. '[He] was no longer a prisoner ... [and] the attitude of the Queen held out the promise of complete freedom, which indeed soon followed.'[35] Bacon apologised for being forced to give evidence against him and suggested that he should concoct a correspondence full of contrition with Anthony Bacon, which could later be brought to Elizabeth's attention.

Cecil soon realised that there was no evidence linking Essex to Hayward's book. In early July, the guard was removed and, in August, he had little alternative but to allow him to go where he chose, although he was banned from court. Essex left London to stay with Sir William Knollys, at Caversham, hoping to restore his health. From here he returned to Essex House where, for the time being, he lived quietly, but in a fragile mental state. His finances depended on him being able to retain the monopoly of the farm of sweet wines, which would soon be up for renewal. He wrote abject letters of contrition to Elizabeth hoping to retain them. In October, she let it be known that she would keep them for her own benefit.[36] At a stroke his finances, which had always been parlous, were in ruin.[37] 'Stripped of offices, titles, income and his good name, Essex had no option but to bid for power.'[38]

It was those who depended on Essex for preferment, like Meyrick and Cuffe, who wanted to avoid him disappearing into obscurity. They encouraged him to believe that his popularity would attract support. Francis Bacon was conspicuously absent from the coterie of malcontents who now surrounded him, implying that his more balanced advice was no longer sought. Penelope was encouraging him to challenge the circle of ministers surrounding Cecil. As his most stalwart ally and a more able politician, she undoubtedly egged him on, while managing to remain continuously in Elizabeth's favour.

When Penelope faced trial, Charles had already replaced Essex in Ireland (see chapter 35). The publication of her letter was described as 'an insolent, saucy, malapert action'. Although she was retained under house arrest during July, she defied her detention order. It took Buckhurst some time to find her and she did not reappear until 13 August.[39] Cecil was furious, not only at Penelope's delaying tactic, but at Buckhurst being too easily won over by her answers on the letter's content. She had run rings round him, and he was warned not to fall for her charms a second time. He told Cecil:

> [She] prayed me give her majesty most humble thanks for her favour, which she acknowledged with her follies and faults committed and assured that this should be a warning to her for ever not to commit the like; concluding still with her most humble desire to have the happiness to see her majesty, until which she should never enjoy a day of comfort to her heart.[40]

She also gave Buckhurst a letter for the queen's eyes only, to prevent Cecil from magically 'losing' it. Cecil was thoroughly unsettled but reported back to Buckhurst that the queen had read her letter 'and then caused it to be burned'.[41] As he realised, Penelope had undoubtedly complained at being maliciously handled. Elizabeth responded that Penelope had shown 'stomach and presumption' in writing, but 'magnanimously' accepted that she was not responsible for the letter's publication, despite being 'so negligent that others might come by it'.[42]

Although Penelope was banned from court, she was permitted to travel where she chose. With Rich being apparently gravely ill, she took Elizabeth Vernon to nurse him at Leighs, using this as an excuse to defer returning to London. She remained in the thick of the plotting and if she needed to, could easily escape from a nearby port to the Continent. On her final evening in London, she dined with Essex, Frances, Southampton, Sir Christopher Blount, Sir Charles Danvers, and Sir Robert Vernon (Elizabeth Vernon's brother) at Essex House, following a scuffle between Southampton and Grey de Wilton, in which Grey drew his sword.

At New Year 1601 Penelope visited Barn Elms, the Walsingham's Surrey home, to visit Frances with her new daughter, Dorothy, born a few days before Christmas. Frances's elder daughter Elizabeth, now Countess of Rutland, also joined them with her husband. When Penelope returned to London, she threw 'herself with gusto into the plotting', recruiting support for a coup.[43] Cecil did his best to blacken her name. Although Elizabeth had never mentioned her infidelity to Rich, the official history of the reign, which Cecil commissioned from William Camden, records: 'The Lady Rich the Earl's sister (who having violated her husband's bed, was in the Queen's heavy displeasure) visiteth [Essex] daily.'[44] This has provided history with the spin that Cecil wanted.

Chapter 34

Essex's rebellion, 1600–02

The targets of Essex's rebellion were Cecil and his fellow 'parasites', including Cobham, Raleigh, Nottingham, Grey de Wilton and Buckhurst. With Essex having established links with James VI, Raleigh cultivated Cecil, worrying what would happen when the queen died. He also became friendly with Cobham, who had entertained the queen at his house at Blackfriars and remained Lord Warden of the Cinque Ports. Raleigh stayed away from London until the autumn of 1600. Although he was governor of Jersey, he believed that Cornwall was the principal target for Spanish invasion and, as Lord Lieutenant, considered that he could best serve Elizabeth by being there. Nevertheless, with Essex out of favour, Raleigh returned to London reassuming his post as captain of the guard with 'double the usual number of men'.[1] He also fulfilled ambassadorial duties, taking Virginio Orsini, Duke of Bracciano, a nephew of the Grand Duke of Tuscany, to court for the first night of Shakespeare's *Twelfth Night*.

It had never been Essex's objective to usurp the throne, as Cecil tried to imply, but he relied on his popular support to assist him in removing Elizabeth 'from infamy in as smooth and orderly a fashion as possible'.[2] The English succession had still not been resolved and was likely to provoke bloodshed. Although James VI was the obvious claimant, the descendants of Queen Margaret of Scotland were ignored under Henry VIII's will. Although Arbella Stuart was the next dynastic heir, common sense pointed to James. With Cecil immersed in the peace negotiations with Spain, which began in May 1600, Essex implied that his rival preferred the Infanta Isabella, but this was scaremongering. He argued that if Cecil was left in control of English government, 'the queen might have to be ignominiously deposed'.[3] In retaliation, Cecil let it be known that Essex, with all his Plantagenet, even if not Tudor, blood was tilting at the Crown. There is no evidence for this, and it does not fit with his support for James's accession.

Essex and Cecil had known each other since childhood, and Essex could not believe that this little hunchback was now in charge and, as he saw it, thwarting his every move. He blamed Cecil for keeping the English army in Ireland starved of resources and of blackening his name with the queen. He believed obsessively in his own popularity and thought that everyone would recognise that Cecil was dishonest and grasping. His government was detested. 'The poor were worse off than at any time for two centuries, food prices were rising, plague and apprentice riots were endemic.'[4]

Although Essex had been released, there was no thought of returning him to Ireland. It was Charles who was to replace him, even though 'he laboureth the contrary'.[5] The Irish posting would take a long time (and eventually lasted three-and-a-half years). Initially, Charles had every expectation of Essex being reinstated. Essex remained on cordial terms with Tyrone, who might break the truce if he were withdrawn. This was unrealistic. Both Elizabeth and her ministers considered the terms he had negotiated with Tyrone to be ignominious. By mid-October, she had decided that Charles, her protégé, now aged 36, should become Ireland's Lord Deputy. At the end of October, he was told to prepare himself, but Cecil informed him privately that there was no urgency. He had undoubtedly been at the heart of the plotting to bring down Cecil, who may still have been hoping to persuade Elizabeth to appoint Francis Vere, now conveniently in England. On arrival from the Low Countries, Francis had been warmly greeted by Cecil and the queen and was appointed Lord Marshal of the army in England. It was certainly recognised that if Charles did not go, Francis would be appointed Ireland's Lord Deputy.

Choosing Charles was controversial. When Sir Charles Danvers was interrogated in February 1601, he confirmed that Charles had written to James VI, prior to Essex's return, seeking his support against Cecil. He had probably been pushed into this by Penelope, whose 'love and zeal for her brother was rashly expressed'.[6] With the prospect of having an army in Ireland under his control, he undoubtedly contemplated repatriating 4,000–5,000 troops, and again sought James's support, believing that, together with men raised by Essex in England, they could overthrow the government.

Even after Charles's arrival in Ireland, he was still contemplating a plot in support of Essex. According to Southampton's confession made in February 1601, Charles remained fearful that Cecil preferred a Spanish succession. He admitted to having approached James 'to take some action to prevent England from being wholly given over to his enemies'.[7] With Charles's undoubted loyalty to Elizabeth, he must have been seeking James's assistance against a Spanish invasion. He apparently told Essex: 'I pray God the Queen may with all prosperity outlive [the government's] negligence.'[8] When Charles arrived in Ireland, Essex sent first Southampton and then Sir Charles Danvers to seek his backing, but his attitude had begun to change. With Penelope no longer whispering in his ear, Charles wanted to assess the extent of support for Essex in London. He became less wedded to the Devereux cause and had no intention of marching into folly. He was, by then, corresponding with Cecil over the conduct of the war, and they had developed a degree of mutual respect. By now Cecil had a full appreciation of the magnitude of the Irish task.

By this time, Essex's allies were trying to save him from himself, but Southampton and Danvers were too bound up in conspiracy to desert him. Already nervous of the outcome, Danvers claimed that he had begged Essex not to request troops from Charles, convinced he would not agree to send them. Although Cuffe asked Danvers to persuade Charles to write a letter summoning Essex to redress England's misgovernment, Charles refused, advising him to be patient and recover the queen's favour by 'ordinary' measures.[9] For Charles 'to commit treason – and wreck his own career in the process – would be mad as well as wicked.'[10] By holding back, he avoided censure.

From the distance of Scotland, James probably overestimated the strength of Essex's support and became convinced that an uprising was imminent. That he did not become involved was a matter of luck. He sent his cousin, Ludovick Stuart, 2nd Duke of Lennox, to tell Essex that he would back him, and John Erskine, 2nd Earl of Mar, came with the diplomat Edward Bruce of Kinloss to report that he had his army assembled north of the border, but by the time of their arrival in London, Essex had been executed and James could confirm that he had not been involved. With Mar in London, Cecil asked his ally Lord Henry Howard to approach him. Howard, who was Norfolk's brother and had long been a political outcast, warned Mar that Cecil knew exactly what the Scottish king had been up to. Mar was told that James was Elizabeth's 'common sense' heir and should not jeopardise his succession hopes with a scatter-brained invasion plan. She had for years maintained a maternal and tutorial correspondence with her godson, but would never recognise his claim, seeing any heir as a catalyst for rebellion against her rule. Howard warned Mar to discourage him from pressing his suit or becoming involved in further interference until his succession was generally accepted. There was no English candidate to compete with the modest military presence he could command in Scotland, and he could be installed as king in London well before the arrival of any competing Continental claimant. Most Englishmen saw him as the obvious and desired successor and wanted to avoid another female ruler. James was very rapidly reinvented as a model monarch and supporter of Cecil's government.

Prior to Essex's attempted coup, 'friends in the City' warned that Raleigh, as captain of the guard, 'had a band of men ready to murder him and that an ambush had been prepared if he went to the Privy Council'.[11] Essex formed his own council with Southampton, Sir Charles Danvers and Penelope as its principal members. They generally met at Southampton's lodgings at Drury House, but sometimes at Charles's London home in Holborn, where Penelope was living. They made a plan to seize Whitehall Palace to force the queen to dismiss Cecil, Raleigh and Cobham.[12] After returning to Essex House, its doors were opened to anyone who would join them.[13] With unpaid soldiers from Ireland milling around London, Essex continued to spread rumours that Cecil favoured the Infanta Isabella and brought in radical preachers to attract support with Puritan sermons. This gained him a following from those traditionally loyal to his stepfather, Leicester. He also tried to attract Roman Catholic support with 'half-promises' of toleration. At Christmas, he again turned to James in Scotland and Charles in Ireland but was forced into precipitate action. He had the backing of a nucleus of only 300 'gentlemen', but hoped to 'move the city' by encouraging the 'citizens to take arms on his behalf' and bring out the trained bands.[14]

On 4 February 1601, Essex's allies at Drury House failed to agree a coherent plan. His supporters, including Southampton, Sir Christopher Blount, Sir Charles Danvers, Sir Robert Vernon and Penelope, continued to advocate securing Whitehall Palace after arresting Raleigh. Essex would then throw himself at Elizabeth's feet to demand the removal of Cecil and his allies to allow him to take control. On 7 February, they paid Shakespeare's company forty shillings to perform *Richard II* at the Globe as an allusion to the monarchy's weakness. This was not lost on Elizabeth. When Essex was summoned to the privy council, he again pleaded sickness, but some of his allies suggested that he should flee abroad or to Wales.[15] Although he remained, he had become dangerously unbalanced. On the evening of the play he entertained the ringleaders and was still being encouraged, particularly by Cuffe and Meyrick, that his muster of the City on the following day would be strongly supported. Being well aware of his plans, the privy council allowed the plot to develop.

On the morning of 8 February, the rebels assembled at Essex House, but 'little of what was happening went unreported to the council'. Cecil had left Essex with just enough rope to hang himself, and seems to have fomented unrest in Essex's name, perhaps trying to escalate it into a full-scale rebellion.[16] When the march began, the conspirators were full of confidence. Gorges intercepted Raleigh on the Thames and told him to return to court as 'he would have a bloody day of it'.[17] With Essex's movements being watched, Elizabeth sent instructions with Egerton, Worcester, Chief Justice John Popham, and Sir William Knollys (now firmly sided against his nephew) to dissolve their gathering and come to court, 'where his griefs would be graciously heard'.[18] Essex shouted out that his life was in danger and he needed the assemblage as a bodyguard.[19] He took Elizabeth's messengers hostage 'in honourable confinement' at Essex House and, sometime after 10.00 am, set off down Fleet Street with his followers brandishing rapiers to confer with the Lord Mayor in the City. They shouted: 'For the queen, for the queen my masters,' claiming to have foiled a plan led by Raleigh, Cobham and others for Essex's murder.[20] He gathered no more than 300 additional supporters. Although Penelope persuaded Edward Russell, 3rd Earl of Bedford, to join them, and he admitted setting out for the City, when he reached a cross street, he left and went home.

On reaching Ludgate Hill, the rebels passed St Paul's Cathedral and marched down Cheapside to the home of the sheriff, Thomas Smythe, but gained no appreciable increase in supporters. Although Smythe promised to call the Lord Mayor, Essex knew that backing for him was faltering and the game was up. He mounted a horse to return to Essex House but, on reaching Ludgate, found the gates locked. He was now trapped with the City under martial law. Cecil had sent Cumberland from court with pikemen, who re-established control with help from the Bishop of London. When a shot carried off Essex's hat, he instructed

Sir Christopher Blount to make a stand. This resulted in Sir Christopher, who was 'sore hurt in the head', being left behind, but it gave Essex and his allies time to escape. With the revolt doomed, Gorges went on to Essex House intent on releasing the hostages. Meanwhile, Essex commandeered a boat on the river at Queenhithe which rowed him to Essex House stairs.[21] With his supporters having melted away, Essex House was surrounded by forces commanded by the 64-year-old Nottingham.

With the hostages at Essex House having become restless, they asked to join Penelope and Frances 'the better to pass the time'.[22] Unfortunately, Penelope taunted Popham, who was to become a judge at her trial. On his arrival, Gorges faked a message from Essex authorising the hostages' release and he escorted them back to court. Penelope, Frances and their gentlewomen now barricaded the entrances with furniture and the windows with books. When soldiers entered the courtyard after breaking down the gates, they were put off from sniping through the windows by the servants' screams. With the ladies staying put, Essex and Penelope had time to burn his papers, including his correspondence with James.[23] Its content never came to light, even though one of Penelope's messengers was picked up and held in the Tower. Their action to protect James was to reap great rewards when he became king.

When Southampton tried to seek terms by shouting from the roof of the great hall, it was to no avail. Nottingham would accept no conditions and trained two cannons on the building, which had been brought from the Tower. Sir Robert Sidney went into the garden to call on the rebels to surrender before the house was blown up. Although Southampton negotiated a temporary ceasefire to enable the doors to be unblocked to let out the ladies, Essex admitted defeat. At 9.00 pm he opened the doors and, with his remaining supporters, surrendered with their swords on their knees.[24] He was rowed across the river to spend the night at Lambeth Palace before being moved to the Tower (to what is still known as the Devereux Tower), while his followers filled various of the London prisons. Although Thomas Lee, one of Essex's captains, broke into Elizabeth's presence chamber to demand a warrant for Essex's release, he was arrested and executed.

Essex and Southampton, as the declared ringleaders, were charged with high treason having sought to 'deprive and depose' Elizabeth and 'procure her death and destruction'. This infuriated Essex, whose only objective had been to depose the leading members of the council.[25] He had wanted to become the council's preeminent member to smooth the way for James VI's accession.[26] Cecil expected them to lose their heads as an example to the troops still mooching around London. When the trial opened at Westminster Hall on 19 February, the two prisoners were dressed in black. Rich was among the twenty-five peers summoned to hear the case but remained silent. With the prisoners pleading not guilty, Coke again led the prosecution with help from Cecil. Raleigh, as a key witness, confirmed his conversation with Gorges that 'he would have a bloody day of it'.[27] Although Gorges confirmed this, he was terrified of being branded a turncoat, but Raleigh was now seen as Essex's 'number-one enemy'.[28]

Cecil, who was full of 'pent-up resentment', sneered at Essex's displays of contrition.[29] He also pointed to the strongly Catholic bias among his allies, saying: 'I stand for loyalty, you stand for treachery. You would depose the queen; you would be king of England.'[30] Rumours being circulated by Cecil of Essex's ambitions for the crown were now so strong that even Northumberland believed them. Nevertheless, these were hotly denied by Essex, and Charles later assured James that there was no truth in them. Despite being Essex's close associate, Francis Bacon was forced to interrogate witnesses and to provide damning evidence against his friend. This confirmed that the rebellion had been planned for several months. Although Francis averred that it had James VI's support, this was not mentioned in court, and he later enjoyed a successful legal and scientific career when James came to the English throne. When he ultimately became Lord Chancellor he was accused of corruption, and in 1621 his old enemy Coke oversaw his downfall.[31]

Although a unanimous guilty verdict was a foregone conclusion, Essex heard it with great dignity and professed to welcome death. On returning to the Tower, he asked for a preacher to give him comfort, and 'humbly desired her majesty would send some of the council to him' to hear his side of the story. When Cecil and Nottingham visited him, Essex failed to adopt the expected chivalrous persona by which he wanted to be known. He broke into 'a passion of penitence', and failed to shoulder responsibility, implicating all his co-conspirators including Penelope.[32] According to a letter from Nottingham to Charles in Ireland, Essex claimed that Penelope, 'did continually urge me on with telling me how all my friends and followers thought me a coward, and that I had lost all my valour'.[33] Essex had also divulged her 'affection' for Charles, hinting that, if pressed, she could reveal more [presumably of Charles's involvement], but would not be easily broken.[34] He confirmed Charles's original offer to send a force from Ireland to support him, although evidence from other conspirators confirmed that, when Essex was released from York House, Charles had refused his help. Penelope was distraught that her much loved brother would 'throw her to the wolves', writing: 'Yet so strangely have I been wronged, finding the smoke of envy where affection should be clearest.'[35] Lettice, who had remained at Drayton Bassett was appalled at her beloved son implicating his sister. Penelope shared none of the 'self-doubt and depression that dogged him, the self-pity and paranoia that ruined his political judgement'.[36] Essex never criticised the loyal Frances, who gave some of his more incriminating letters to a servant for safekeeping. When Elizabeth heard that the servant's husband was trying to blackmail her, she fined him and gave Frances the money. She wanted the matter dropped.

Elizabeth revoked her first warrant for Essex's execution but, to Frances's consternation, another was soon prepared. Frances wrote to implore Cecil to dissuade Elizabeth from signing it. When she did, Essex refused to crawl for forgiveness, but a 5,000-strong mob of London apprentices was rumoured to be planning to storm the Tower to free him. Cecil needed to act quickly. Five days after the trial, on Ash Wednesday, 25 February 1601, Essex was beheaded at Tower Hill, while Raleigh, in his capacity as captain of the guard, watched from a window in the Tower armoury. Although it took three swings of the axe to sever his head, he died calmly and bravely. He probably knew nothing after the first blow, but the mob attacked the executioner as he left the scaffold.[37] Although Southampton was 'up to the neck' in it, Cecil arranged his reprieve on the grounds of his penitence and youth, but he remained in the Tower. Others were less lucky. Sir Christopher Blount and Sir Charles Danvers were beheaded at Tower Hill, while Meyrick and Cuffe were disembowelled at Tyburn. These were the only rebels to face death, but Bedford, Rutland and most of the remainder faced heavy fines, which were generally left unpaid.

Elizabeth was distraught at having to approve Essex's execution, but Penelope believed that she could have pardoned him had she wanted to. 'The prevailing mood at Court and in the capital was one of gloom and melancholy.'[38] Many linked Shakespeare's moody Hamlet, first performed at the end of 1601, to Essex, 'a man of whom great things were expected, but whose indecision destroyed him'.[39] Christmas without Essex at court was altogether a sad little affair.

Rumours that Raleigh smirked and smoked during Essex's execution are unfounded, but it was he who faced the people's venom for engineering his death.[40] With his continued occupation of the Sherborne estate, he took over many of the ambassadorial duties previously handled by his rival. In September 1601, he entertained Charles de Gontaut, Duke of Biron, who arrived with a large retinue as an emissary for Henry IV. When he felt that the duke was being neglected, he took him to Westminster to see the monuments and later to the bear garden, but eventually escorted him to be entertained by the queen at the Vyne in Hampshire.

Essex House was now placed under Nottingham's control, but before the end of the year, Frances had moved there with her mother, after appealing for the water supply to be restored. To help to resolve Essex's debts, she sold Walsingham House and leased Essex House to Northumberland. On 29 September 1602, Dorothy at last gave birth to a surviving son, Algernon, and Elizabeth became a godmother. The Northumberlands' show of marital harmony was short-lived and by November, Dorothy was living alone at Syon House. In the spring of 1603, Frances married Richard Burke, Earl of Clanricarde, eventually providing him with three children. He was a staunch anglophile, having grown up in the Devereux household and fought beside Essex in Ireland. Charles later knighted him after his valiant role at the battle of Kinsale.

Penelope had undoubtedly been one of the ringleaders and was the only lady to be detained, as Cecil wanted to avoid her helping her brother or disappearing off to cause further mischief. She was separated from her servants and confined under the control of Henry Seckford, Keeper of the Privy Purse. She was soon appealing for 'a cook to dress her meat', and Rich was later directed to send bedding to her.[41] Although there is no evidence that Rich was at Essex House, he was temporarily committed to the Tower but had been freed by the time Penelope's bedding was being requested. She had probably been the rebellion's dominant force, but her gender saved her from imprisonment and a treason trial. Cecil knew that she was aware he had profiteered from provisioning contracts in Ireland. When she was interviewed, Nottingham and Cecil reported that she 'used herself with that modesty and wisdom' for which she was known. Nottingham fell under her spell. He delivered a letter from her to the queen, in which she claimed to have been treated by Essex 'more like a slave than a sister, which proceeded out of my exceeding love rather than his authority'.[42]

Despite Elizabeth having Penelope interrogated, she was released without trial.[43] To Cecil's frustration, she was returned to Rich's care. She believed that Nottingham had been responsible for her lenient treatment and wrote him a most courteous letter. It was probably Nottingham who shielded Charles from further criticism.[44] When asked to provide a list of those involved in the plot, he named only those who had been executed and Southampton, who was likely to remain in the Tower indefinitely. He did not name Penelope or Charles, and an unspoken pact was formed to protect them.

Penelope never again visited Elizabeth's court. With Essex dead, Rich disowned her, but paid her an allowance out of her dowry. She probably retired to Drayton to join the grieving Lettice, who had lost both a husband and a son, but made occasional visits to Wanstead to be closer to her children. Her trump cards were that James was now an unfailing ally, and her lover in Ireland was delivering undreamt-of military successes.

Chapter 35

Charles's arrival in Ireland, 1600–01

Charles's period in Ireland singles him out as one of the great military commanders of his day with a strategic flair that even Francis Vere was never called upon to provide. Ireland had been a graveyard for its administrators, and only Sir Henry Sidney had managed to enhance his reputation there.[1] Charles may have fought shy of the appointment, but his 'unquenched ambition' pushed him into achieving a success where Essex had failed.[2]

With terms for his appointment as Lord Deputy agreed, Charles left London on 7 February 1600, almost exactly a year before Essex's rebellion. His departure was much lower key than that of Essex, but he was reportedly 'very gracious'.[3] It must have been a poignant parting with Penelope, as he was likely to be away for a long period and she was expecting his fifth child. On her boy's arrival, he was named Charles after his father, but his future prosperity depended on his father's safe return. Carew, who was, in effect, Charles's second-in-command, travelled with him. He was an ideal colleague, despite being Raleigh's friend and Cecil's protégé. He had been appointed Lord President of Munster with instructions from Elizabeth to carry 'her gracious pleasure' into effect and 'to put suspected Irish to the rack when they should find it convenient'.[4] On reaching Chester on 14 February, Charles and Carew spent five days inspecting troops and dined with the mayor before embarking at Holyhead on 26 February for the Head of Howth outside Dublin.

On arrival two days later, Charles was sworn in as Lord Deputy. He was a born leader, who knew how to restore discipline and get the best from his men. He was good tempered, sharing jokes with them, but could reprove with a look and spoke 'straight and to the point when annoyed'.[5] He found English authority to be in great jeopardy, with the troops under his command suffering from disease and an acute shortage of provisions. He very quickly gained their confidence, punishing non-attendance at sermons or morning and evening prayers as he believed his men's poor morale reflected a disregard for religion.[6] His intense interest in theology and growing Roman Catholic sympathies had made him deeply religious. He criticised blasphemy and adultery, oblivious of his own situation as he was unable to accept the validity of Penelope's arranged marriage to Rich. He managed the resources available to him with great care and his secretary, Fynes Moryson, branded him 'parsimonious'. Although he accumulated money while in command, the careful auditing of his accounts made no 'accusations affecting his handling of funds'.[7]

Charles did not enjoy a strong constitution. He smoked the finest tobacco, convinced that it protected him from the 'Irish ague' and eased occasional bouts of migraine.[8] His regime worked, and, despite pushing himself to the limits, he was never seriously ill in Ireland until struck down with influenza aggravated by fatigue after the battle of Kinsale. Nevertheless, his addiction to nicotine would have ominous forebodings for his future.

On his arrival, the weather was unseasonably cold, and frost during April and May threatened the harvest. His remedy was to stay warm and eat well. He was always splendidly attired and 'caught the eye' in Dublin, wearing ruffs, black beaver hats, bright waistcoats and his garter ribbon over his silk stockings. In the field, he would wrap up in as many as three waistcoats, jerkins, cloth cloaks lined with velvet and a russet scarf.[9] Over the 'ordinary stockings of silk, he wore, under [his] boots, another pair of woollen or worsted, with a pair of high linen boot-hose'.[10] Moryson commented: 'I never observed any of his age and strength to keep his body so warm.'[11] Tyrone scoffed at his dress – but not for long. He soon recognised Charles as an inspired and fearless commander.

Seeing Ireland as England's Achilles heel, the Spanish were determined to make amends for the failures of their earlier invasion attempts. With most Irish staunchly Catholic, they knew that their invasion force would gain strong local support to evict the English. With Ireland becoming a Spanish suzerainty, it would provide a base from which to invade Britain. That they failed was down to a combination of incompetence, bad luck and Charles's astute leadership.

At first, Charles was wary of over-challenging his men, but later 'demanded heavy sacrifices and incredible exertions'.[12] His approach inspired them to achieve hitherto unseen feats of arms. He wrote to Cecil: 'And now that being a nurse to the army as well as a general, I have given it more health and strength, you must hereafter look to hear of deeper blows that we shall either give or receive.'[13]

Charles was required to consult with the Irish council and was careful to seek their advice, taking half of them with him on major expeditions. Nevertheless, military decisions were his own and he kept discussion to a minimum and his plans to himself. He was surrounded by able subordinates. In addition to Carew as President of Munster, he was lucky to have Sir Arthur Chichester, Governor of Carrickfergus, and Sir Henry Docwra, who had served under Essex at Cádiz and at Rouen, and under Francis Vere in the Low Countries. He expected his officers to show absolute discretion, realising that careless talk would be reported to Tyrone, but was not averse to chatting up ladies about his earlier exploits. Once he had made a decision, he implemented it with dispatch. He confided in only three colleagues, Sir William Godolphin, a long-time friend from Cornwall; Sir Richard Moryson, brother of his secretary; and Sir Henry Danvers, Sir Charles's younger brother, despite the queen being nervous of the Danvers' association with Essex. Although Carew, Docwra and Chichester acted independently out of necessity, he otherwise delegated little. He would listen to his officers but was critical of experienced men who lacked originality. He personally reconnoitred the ground he was to fight over 'often to within musket shot of the enemy', and was exposed to even greater danger from Irish guerrilla tactics.[14] Miraculously he remained unscathed, although many of those beside him were wounded, and a horse was killed from under him.

The main issue on Irish campaigns was to contain rebel groupings within their own lands. In the previous month, Tyrone had denounced the truce he had agreed with Essex and marched south to Munster, where most local chieftains swore allegiance to him. Although Charles intended to delegate Munster's military supervision to Carew and his commissioners at Cork to act on his general instructions, there was difficulty in installing Carew to undertake the role. With his predecessor, Sir Thomas Norreys, having died, English troops in the south were commanded by the elderly but loyal Ormonde, based at Kilkenny in Leinster, who left the Munster commissioners holed up by Tyrone at Cork. With Carew unable to reach Cork overland, Charles retained him at his side, grateful for the advice of a trusted colleague with good experience of Ireland.

Tyrone's campaign in Munster faced a setback in March when Hugh Maguire was killed, but in April Mateo de Oviedo, who had been appointed by the Spanish as titular Archbishop of Dublin, landed in Donegal with arms, money and ammunition. He also brought news that the long awaited Jornada de Irlanda was being readied. His arrival in Donegal required Tyrone to travel north. Despite Ormonde receiving 5,000 men for the purpose of intercepting him, Tyrone gave him the slip by marching twenty-seven miles per day through the Tipperary hills. Even though Charles had troops at Trim, north-west of Dublin, Ormonde failed to send him warning in time, resulting in Tyrone being missed. Although bitter, Charles treated Ormonde, the revered elder statesman, with his usual courtesy. At least he was able to restore the troops supplied to Ormonde to protect the Pale, and Carew set out for Cork, escorted by the English ally Donogh O'Brien, 4th Earl of Thomond. On arrival at Kilkenny, Ormonde asked Carew and Thomond to attend a parley with the rebel Owen MacRory O'Moore, during which Ormonde was treacherously seized. Carew and Thomond escaped, but Thomond was stabbed by a pike in the back. When at last Carew reached Cork, Charles set up garrisons in Munster and Connaught, and stationed Sir Arthur Chichester at Carrickfergus while retaining 400 horse and 4,600 foot in the Pale.

The strategic plan, agreed before Charles's arrival in Ireland, was to establish a powerful force at Lough Foyle in northern Ulster, with the objective of creating a line of forts to segregate the O'Neills from the O'Donnells. There was a similar plan to garrison 4,000 men at Ballyshannon at the mouth of the River Erne to the south of O'Donnell territory and to station gun boats at Belleek on Lough Erne to prevent Tyrconnell from making incursions into Connaught. Charles moved quickly. On 7 May, Sir Henry Docwra sailed from Carrickfergus to land in the Foyle at Culmore north of Derry with 4,000 men and 200 cavalry, which could be provisioned by sea. Having murdered the Roman-Catholic Bishop of Derry, Docwra fortified his old ecclesiastical settlement to become his headquarters. Although Tyrconnell harassed Docwra's men if they ventured out, stealing 200 of their horses, Docwra brokered an alliance with Niall Garbh O'Donnell, Tyrconnell's brother-in-law, who wanted to claim the O'Donnell chieftaincy and had a great reputation as a warrior. Docwra also formed alliances with the O'Cahans in Coleraine and O'Dohertys in Inishowen, who were seeking freedom from their O'Neill and O'Donnell overlords. With their help, he overran Inishowen, fighting on towards Strabane.

Meanwhile, Sir Oliver Lambart, who had served under Charles at Portsmouth, defeated rebels in Offaly (after which his bravery was mentioned in Charles's despatches). This enabled Charles to concentrate against Tyrone when he duly reappeared from Ulster with 2,300 horse and 18,000 well-armed foot. Although Chichester attacked from Carrickfergus, and Charles, with the signal support of Southampton leading the English cavalry, intercepted him at the Moyry Pass between Dundalk and Newry, they failed to break the O'Neill defences despite weeks of intense fighting. Charles now realised that 'the rebels were more numerous, superior in physique, and better versed in the use of arms than the raw recruits sent over from England'.[15] Luckily not all the Irish were trained to the same level, and Charles believed that if tackled in open country, he would eventually be able to regain control.

Charles received plenty of advice from England. Buckhurst sent an instruction to require officers to maintain diaries with a copy for the Lord Deputy. He also received Elizabeth's instruction to prevent absence without leave (which had been a problem during Essex's command), to require troops to attend church services as soon as clergy were reassembled and, as might be expected, to retain proper records of victual consumption to prevent the defrauding of the Exchequer.

Although Charles had 1,200 horse and 14,440 foot, his army was suffering continued wastage from disease and desertion. With sanitation being inadequate, 'night soil' piled up outside cabin entrances harboured infestation. Friend and foe became a prey to cholera, dysentery and even plague. With his men often out of contact in different locations, Charles found it difficult to assess their fitness. The impact of disease on his troops was not understood in England, and when the queen threatened to cut his infantry complement to 12,000 men, he protested that he needed reinforcements.

Charles adopted Essex's earlier policy of keeping the rebels short of provisions by:

> laying waste the countryside and starving the people. He preferred to fight in winter, when it was more difficult

for the Irish to hide in the leafless woods, when their stores of corn and butter could be burned and when their cattle down from their summer pastures could more easily be slaughtered.[16]

With his foodstuffs being delivered from England, he believed that his men could withstand the winter conditions better than the Irish.

With Tyrone dominating Ulster, Charles realised that he needed better seasoned troops to enable him to launch a challenge. He wanted more men and needed to buy time for Docwra's Lough Foyle force to prepare the way. On 28 May, he returned to Dublin, only to find trouble on his arrival. Bands of rebels were carrying off cattle and burning villages in Meath and Westmeath. The Anglo-Irish lords and gentry condoned these attacks and bypassed Charles by sending a deputation to Cecil to complain at having his forces in the Pale billeted on them. Although Elizabeth told them to raise their complaint with Charles, she also told him to redress it.[17]

Docwra faced other difficulties. Although he had established useful alliances with rival branches of the O'Neill clan, Niall Garbh O'Donnell proved a difficult and truculent ally and did not appear until the following summer. This slowed Docwra's progress against ever more committed rebels. Furthermore, his men were dying 'in scores', probably after drinking contaminated water. This resulted in his failure to pin down Tyrconnell, who raided Connaught in June and reached the Shannon almost unopposed.[18] Charles had no troops there, other than the garrison at Athlone, although Galway was held for the Crown by its own levy.

Charles now received instructions from London to appoint Thomond and Richard Burke, Viscount Dunkellin, as joint governors of Connaught, but this would never be an ideal arrangement. Although Thomond had recovered from the wound he received at Kilkenny, he preferred campaigning with Carew or living on his lands (later named County Clare). As the son of the 3rd Earl of Clanricarde, Dunkellin, who had been brought up in the Sidney household at Penshurst (and later married Frances), was an enthusiastic anglophile. Nevertheless, he complained, quite reasonably, that he had been promised command in Connaught but was now told that this did not include Athlone or Galway, without which he could not maintain effective control. He made no attempt to oppose Tyrconnell's raid and probably lacked the means to do so. When he offered his resignation, Charles was told to accept it, but did it so graciously that the young man was invited to serve directly under him. (On 20 May 1601, Dunkellin succeeded his father as the 4th Earl of Clanricarde and was to prove an invaluable ally for Charles at Kinsale.)

When Elizabeth at last increased Charles's English complement from 14,000 to 16,000 men, he began to make better progress. He offered a large reward for Tyrone's capture and renewed bribes to gain alliances with rival Irish clans. He also built a network of forts behind enemy lines to impede Tyrone's hit and run tactics. With his support falling away Tyrone retired into Armagh, enabling Charles to sever his links with the Munster insurgents, who were dependent on bonaghts (mercenaries) from Ulster and Connaught, led by Dermot O'Connor, to stiffen their resistance. Furthermore, the Munster gentry began to stand aloof from what they saw as Tyrone's personal quarrel with the English. Carew now played on clan rivalries to gain submission and even service from most of them, forcing O'Connor's bonaghts back into hiding in Connaught. As an artillery expert, Carew systematically captured castles in rebel hands and moved on to campaign in Limerick. During August 1600, Charles joined him to campaign in Offaly, Kerry, and Leinster, before returning in the autumn to the offensive in Ulster, where he managed to break through Tyrone's lines between Dundalk and Newry.

Although Charles was instructed to appoint Sir Arthur Savage, the commander at Athlone, as provisional governor of Connaught, he became irritated by criticism of his campaign emanating from England. He believed that some of this came from Essex's supporters. Although Charles had refused Southampton's request for him to bring a force to England to support Essex, he respected Southampton as an outstanding soldier and trusted friend. Although Southampton was not officially a part of the English military presence, he had fought with distinction. Believing that it would be preferable to appoint a peer of 'greatness and reputation' as Connaught's governor, Charles proposed him, telling Elizabeth that he had 'saved her honour' at the Moyry Pass. He knew that Southampton was not in her good books after his marriage to Elizabeth Vernon and was no friend of Cecil. Furthermore, Elizabeth had previously vetoed his appointment as Essex's master of horse, but Charles claimed that 'he would take great joy in the assistance and company of so dear a friend and so noble a gentleman'.[19] Cyril Falls has suggested that he may have been trying to prevent Southampton from becoming involved in Essex's rebellion, but Elizabeth refused his appointment. This resulted in Savage being confirmed as Connaught's provisional governor. Southampton claimed that he was not offended, but as a volunteer he could not afford to remain in Ireland unpaid. He left for the Low Countries, perhaps trying to drum up support for Essex among the English forces there, but soon returned to London with the inevitable consequences for his future.

In mid-June, Ormonde managed to negotiate his own release from the O'Moores in exchange for hostages to deter him from proceeding against them. He had been severely shaken but immediately paid a ransom to enable some of the hostages to be released, and others were later rescued by Charles. Although Charles visited him 'reverentially' at Kilkenny, he was suspicious of his kidnap and wanted reassurance of his loyalty. In mid-July, Charles marched through Meath almost into Cavan, where he forced Connor Roe Maguire, one of the rival chiefs of Fermanagh, to submit, although his lands remained under rebel control.

Charles now focused his full force against Tyrone and, by marching into Armagh, pinned him back into Ulster, while Chichester caused much slaughter in Coleraine in reprisal for attacks on English settlers. In December, Tyrone was reinforced with more Spanish gold and arms arriving in Donegal. Although Charles offered £2,000 for his capture (and £1,000 for his head), winter was approaching, and his cavalry was forced back to Carlingford to obtain fodder.

In the spring, Charles kept Tyrone hemmed in by pressing forward to Benburb, while Niall Garbh captured Donegal Abbey. This enabled him to deal with continuing resistance in Leinster led by the O'Moores and Kavanaghs, who remained strong and defiant. He delivered troops from four directions with Lambart arriving from Kildare, Savage from Athlone and Ormonde from the south to join him at Cullanagh. He was determined to end the burnings in the Pale and wanted them hit hard. After destroying their standing corn and livestock, and capturing 700–800 horses, he forced them into the open. In a heavy engagement, his horse was shot from under him, but when Owen MacRory O'Moore was killed, his followers 'disperse[d] in all directions'.[20] With Carew driving the remaining Ulstermen out of Munster, English supremacy there was gradually restored until there was no castle left in rebel hands. A regiment surplus to his needs could now be provided to fight in Leinster.

With southern Ireland relatively settled, Charles again focused against Tyrone after receiving a further 2,000 men from England. He set out north with 375 horse and 3,500 foot, leaving 157 horse and 2,700 foot with Ormonde in the Pale. He had to pledge his own money to revictual his men while awaiting provisions from England to garrison Armagh. Furthermore, wet autumn weather had made streams impassable.[21] With Charles's departure having been delayed, Tyrone was able to establish three lines of trenches 'covered by great ramparts of earth and stone, barbed with thorn bushes' at the Moyry Pass. These were protected by crossfire from the steep hills on each side.[22] Charles realised that this was a trial of strength. Thanks to the bravery of Dunkellin's brother, Sir Thomas Burke, they cleared the first line after he sprang forward with the regimental colours when his men faltered. Despite suffering 152 casualties, they failed to clear the two remaining trenches, but Tyrone had had enough and withdrew to Armagh.

It was now too late in the season to tackle Ulster. Charles remained short of victuals, and Docwra's force was still incapacitated by sickness. Despite this, Niall Garbh seized the O'Donnell castle at Lifford south of Derry and retained control even when Tyrconnell returned from the south. In November, Charles established a garrison of 400 men in an earthen fort eight miles north of Newry, from where it could easily be supplied. He named it Mountnorris, after his old mentor, Sir John Norreys [or Norris]. He then returned to the Pale via Carlingford.

Charles complained bitterly to London at their failure to provide him with supplies on time. He also objected to being 'scolded like a scullion' by Elizabeth. On 3 December, she replied:

> Mistress Kitchenmaid – Comfort yourself therefore in this, that neither your careful endeavour, nor dangerous travels, nor heedful regard to our service, could ever have been disposed upon a prince that more esteems them, considers, and regards them, than she for whom chiefly, I know, all this hath been done, and who keeps this verdict ever in store for you: that no vainglory nor popular fawning can ever advance you forward, but true vow of duty and reverence of prince, which, too, after your life, I see you do prefer ... There is no man can rule so great a charge without some errors, yet you may

assure yourself I have never heard of any that had fewer. Your Sovereign that dearly regards you.[23]

'No vainglory nor popular fawning' was a veiled hint that he should avoid supporting Essex, but the letter greatly boosted his self-confidence.[24]

Charles continued to show tireless energy while keeping his plans to himself. He did not stay long in Dublin but pronounced publicly that he would spend Christmas at Monasterevin Abbey in Kildare, previously used by Essex. This implied that he was proposing further action against the O'Moores and O'Connors, although they had already become submissive. Before reaching Monasterevin, he suddenly turned east into Wicklow to challenge the O'Byrnes, who had regularly raided the Pale and had ignominiously defeated an English force during Essex's time.[25] By arriving at nightfall on 24 December after a twenty-nine-hour march, he caught their chieftain, Phelim McFeagh O'Byrne, by surprise at his fortress at Ballincor. Although Phelim McFeagh escaped by jumping naked from a window into the winter snow, his son was arrested, and Charles's men enjoyed their Christmas sustenance. In March, with his lands despoiled and many of his cattle taken, Phelim McFeagh was forced to submit. Although some of the O'Byrnes offered to join Charles, they were required 'to perform some useful service against their former allies before being received into submission. This served as an insurance against their subsequent relapse, though not a complete one.'[26] Having installed garrisons at Wicklow and Tullagh to maintain control, Charles moved back to Monasterevin. Despite all his exertions, he did not stay long, moving on to Maynooth in Kildare and then to Trim in Meath to rest his men.[27]

During his four-month absence from Dublin, Charles had maintained contact with the council by messenger, but had to handle a stream of complaints and job recommendations. On learning that Tyrone was sending reinforcements into Munster, he moved quickly to cut him off, and although Tyrone reached Cavan in force, he retired on learning that his route was blocked. Charles now moved on to Athlone. With Savage being on leave in England, Charles was seeking a briefing from his deputy, Sir John Berkeley, before returning to Dublin.

On 4 February 1601, Charles asked for leave to visit England to report personally on his progress, as was the custom. With Essex about to launch his rebellion, Charles's timing was unfortunate, but he knew

Penelope was up to her neck in conspiracy and he offered not to see her. Unsurprisingly, his request was turned down.[28] Elizabeth called on him to remain to consolidate his victories, but confirmed that a visit would be reconsidered when the Spanish threat was resolved.[29]

Charles learned of Essex's rebellion while at Donore in County Meath. According to Fynes Moryson, it 'wrought strange alteration' in him, causing him to eat in silence and become uncommunicative. Although he had refused to support Essex, his earlier involvement would probably come to light. His first step was to destroy any incriminating papers, greatly upsetting Moryson at the loss of such important historic material.[30] He spent time contemplating what to do but, on 24 February, wrote a carefully worded personal letter to Cecil to confirm his 'love and duty' towards Elizabeth and his steadfast allegiance to her. While admitting his 'long and inward familiarity' with the rebellion's participants, he assured him that his proceedings while in Ireland had stemmed from 'a root without corruption'.[31] 'Nothing on earth, neither an angel from Heaven [Penelope], shall make me deceive the trust she [Elizabeth] hath reposed in me.' He also confirmed his army's loyalty to the crown and commended Cecil as the queen's most 'watchful and worthy servant'.[32]

Charles was right to be nervous of the confessions of Essex allies, and he readied a ship to take him to France if he should be recalled. When interrogated they revealed his involvement, including the missions of both Southampton and Danvers to Ireland.[33] It was also known that he had changed his mind and had refused to support them. Furthermore, his role in Ireland was of too much strategic importance to recall him for questioning. Elizabeth was determined to pardon anyone who had been 'seduced and blindly led' by Essex.[34] When he eventually returned, Elizabeth was dead, and James was on the English throne.

Charles received a friendly letter from Nottingham admitting the privy council's embarrassment at Essex's revelation of Penelope's part in the rebellion. Charles must have known that this was true, but Nottingham confirmed his admiration for her. His tone implied that although the government knew of his involvement, they did not intend to proceed against him.[35] It may have taken him time to become assured of this, but Southampton was instructed not to discuss Charles's involvement again and was only liberated from the Tower after James became king. With every scrap of evidence being suppressed, Charles's anxiety subsided.

Elizabeth considered Charles to be both irreplaceable in Ireland and personally devoted to her. Charles made it a matter of policy to remain on good terms with Cecil, forging a link with him through Carew, which gives the appearance of them becoming genuine friends and colleagues, but he never liked Raleigh. On James's accession to the English throne, it became clear that Cecil was likely to become his chief minister and Charles needed to remain his ally.[36] 'He was succeeding where others had failed, but the final test would probably come in the shape of a Spanish expeditionary force.'[37]

Chapter 36

La Jornada de Irlanda, 1601–02

Neither Charles (in the south) nor Docwra (in the north) 'relaxed their campaigns of attrition during the winter of 1600/01'.[1] Charles mopped up pockets of resistance in Offaly, Meath and Monaghan, forcing Tyrone's ally, Ever MacCooley, into submission when 3,000 of his cattle with horses, sheep and pigs were captured. By taking the crannog (timber-structured) fortress of Lough Lurgan, holding much of the enemy's foodstores and gunpowder, Charles caused a local famine. He also ravished Clandeboye, where the powerful Turlagh MacHenry O'Neill agreed to join him. At Lough Foyle, Docwra received crucial help from Niall Garbh, who was now well-established to the west of the Swilly, and from Cahir O'Doherty in Inishowen. At Lough Neagh, Chichester kept up the pressure by crossing in boats to ravage its western shore, while a naval blockade of the north coast cut off the rebels from powder being delivered from Scotland. Although Ulster was not subdued, Tyrone's power was severely diminished, even though Docwra's men continued to suffer intermittent sickness and his musketeers were short of match.

During the summer of 1600, there had been persistent rumours of the arrival of a Spanish invasion fleet, although it was not certain whether its destination was Ireland or the Low Countries. At last, news arrived that La Jornada de Irlanda had set sail. With Cerdá having contracted malaria, Don Diego de Brochero y Añaya had become the Spanish naval commander, while the experienced Àguila took control of their land forces. Despite Àguila's distinguished military record, he had been 'convicted of ill-treating his men and dipping his hands into government funds', and had to be released from gaol to take up his appointment.[2] Splitting the Spanish command caused disagreement over where to land. With the Spanish being short of available ships, Brochero wanted to disembark in the south to enable him to return home more quickly. Àguila would have preferred to join Tyrone and Tyrconnell in Donegal in the best defended part of Ireland, but this involved sailing 250 miles further north.[3]

The Spanish fleet of thirty-three ships set out from Lisbon on about 1 September 1601 with 4,464 combatants, six pieces of artillery and large quantities of provisions and arms for the Irish. A further eleven ships under Zubiaur joined them from Andalusia. These included the *San Felipe* of 960 tons, carrying 650 troops and a considerable part of the provisions, including most of the powder and match for the arquebuses. After a month at sea, during which atrocious weather pushed them well off course, they were still 300 leagues from Ireland when Brochero called a conference on his flagship. Archbishop Oviedo, who was with them, was suffering from seasickness and wanted to make landfall at the first opportunity. With their objective being a Counter-Reformation, he believed that they were arriving in sufficient strength to land in the south and to march in triumph straight to Dublin.[4] With Àguila being outvoted, they agreed to disembark at Kinsale, south of Cork. Carew was expecting this and reckoned that if they landed in Munster, he could hold Cork and Limerick until English reinforcements arrived.

Although Cecil in London received word that the invasion fleet had been seen by English pinnaces in the western approaches, it took three weeks for the news to reach Carew in Cork. Soon afterwards, it was scattered by a violent storm off Ireland's west coast. Zubiaur on the *San Felipe* with six accompanying vessels made an abortive attempt to sail north to Donegal, before returning with nine ships and all their provisions to Spain. Àguila, with 3,814 troops, many of whom were suffering from seasickness, eventually reached Kinsale. Not realising the lack of Irish support for them in Munster, Àguila issued a proclamation to every Irishman that, with Elizabeth excommunicated, they should join the Spanish in attacking heresy.[5]

On learning of the Spaniards' imminent arrival, Charles rode quickly south with a small escort to meet Carew. They moved on to Kilkenny, where Ormonde was joined by Sir Richard Wingfield, the Marshal of the Army, and Sir Robert Gardiner, the Chief Justice. On 22 September, they learned that the Spanish fleet had been seen off the Old Head of Kinsale. On the following day, it disembarked its troops and left immediately. Carew advised Charles to show his intent to the Irish by challenging the Spanish immediately and by cutting them off from access to Irish reinforcements. When Charles worried that he was short of provisions, Carew confirmed that he had stockpiled food in Munster after granting his men a cash allowance to purchase their immediate needs. This enabled Charles to march his army south. After seizing two of Tyrone's more powerful Munster allies, James Fitzthomas and Florence MacCarthy, intent on reinforcing the Spanish, he shipped them off to the Tower of London. He was still awaiting delivery of transport animals and provisions from England, but his main problem was the late arrival of English troops. To overcome this shortfall and to consolidate a force at Cork, he withdrew every man he could spare from garrisons around the Pale.

By mid-October, regiments from England had at last been delivered, but Charles reported that the men 'were wholly wasted, either by death, sickness or running away'.[6] By 25 October, illness in his camp left him with only 7,000 foot and 600 horse out of a theoretical complement of 12,000 men, and his defences at the Pale remained undermanned. The weather was 'dark, wild and thunderous', with 'intolerable cold, dreadful labour and want of almost everything'.[7] Being unable to surround Kinsale, he subjected the Spanish to constant artillery fire from higher ground above the town and used his cavalry to destroy nearby crops and livestock. Although he exuded confidence, he warned Cecil that, from his experience in Brittany, Àguila was 'one of the best generals in the service with veteran captains and good, well-armed troops'.

With Cecil recognising the vital need for a supreme effort, he hastened to deliver the reinforcements which Charles had requested five months earlier. Despite his promise of 4,000 men with munitions, victuals and money, only a half of these had been landed. To meet the huge outlay required, Elizabeth had been forced to sell former monastery lands and jewels. At last, Admiral Sir Richard Leveson with a fleet of ten warships delivered the remainder to Cork and, on arrival on 12 November, visited Charles outside Kinsale. In late November, Thomond brought a further 1,100 men from England, but they landed at Castlehaven, thirty miles west of Kinsale, after being blown off course. Another contingent of 2,000 men and 200 horse arrived at Waterford, but the new arrivals 'were so raw and sickly from the bad weather' that they needed time at 'Cork for rest and training before they joined in the siege'. Importantly, two culverins were also delivered.[8]

With the Munster Irish failing to support them, the Spanish in Kinsale found themselves isolated. With Tyrone and Tyrconnell and their disorganised band of Gaelic chieftains facing continued hostility in the north, they were reluctant to risk the long march south in the depths of winter. They were unsure how they would be received as they came and wanted to avoid open battle. Although the Spanish had arrived with saddles, they had hoped to source horses locally. Without cavalry, Àguila realised that he could do little more than shore up the town's inadequate defences. Charles could see them hard at work strengthening the walls for a siege. He thus prepared the ground by digging parallels (trenches parallel to the walls).

On their arrival, the Spanish had occupied two forts outside Kinsale, Rincurren and Castle Ny Park in the Bandon estuary. When Carew was sent to batter Rincurren, he met stiff Spanish resistance from the fort and a bombardment from Kinsale. At last, on 1 November, the Spanish garrison at Rincurren called a parley. Their offer to lay down their arms if permitted to return to Spain was accepted. On 17 November (auspiciously Elizabeth's birthday), Castle Ny Park was bombarded by the English fleet under Leveson. Although the attack was initially repulsed, it was renewed three days later, and the seventeen Spaniards remaining surrendered after a gallant defence.

By 23 November, Charles was pounding the walls of Kinsale with nine guns, and on 30 November, a length of the walls near the east gate collapsed. Nevertheless, the cellars in the town offered the Spanish ample protection from the English bombardment, and when 2,000 English troops launched an attack on the breach, they were met with stalwart resistance. This ended further attempts to storm the town. The Spanish sallied out the following night, knocking out the English battery, which fled after at least one of its guns was spiked. Although Charles brought up reinforcements, which pushed the Spanish back into the town with considerable loss, the artillery was withdrawn to the main camp for protection.

After three months at Kinsale, Àguila was becoming depleted of provisions and was frustrated by the Irish failure to provide assistance. He wrote reproachfully to Tyrone and Tyrconnell pointing out that the English were undermanned.[9] Charles was now reduced to 6,595 combatants and was desperate for fodder for his horses. By now, the Ulstermen with their 6,500 troops, if added to the Spanish in Kinsale, significantly outnumbered Charles's dwindling force. The Ulstermen were only too aware that if defeated, the Spanish were unlikely to attempt another expedition but always hoped that by delaying their arrival, a shortage of provisions would force the English to raise the siege. After further weeks of hesitation, they realised that they had to take their chance, even if it involved fighting in the open. To ease the problem of provisioning their 5,000 infantry and 700 cavalry on their 300 mile trek south, they marched in two groups. When Tyrconnell set out on 23 October, Charles sent Carew to intercept him. Even Carew was given the slip when Tyrconnell made a forced march of forty miles in icy conditions through the seemingly impassable Slievephelim Mountains.

Meanwhile, Zubiaur had set out again from Spain and, on 1 December, landed a further 621 men, five guns and stores at Castlehaven. Although Leveson sank one of Zubiaur's merchantmen and drove another ashore, his own ships became bottled in by a contrary wind and were severely damaged. Zubiaur's force was not large, but it acted as a catalyst to gain support from Munster chieftains, resulting in several Gaelic strongholds being handed over to him. This opened up the south-west for the delivery of Spanish provisions.

After joining up with Gaelic contingents in the south, Tyrconnell reached Bandon with 3,000 men to be joined by Zubiaur's Spaniards. Tyrone, who left seven days later, ravaged Leinster as he travelled south, hoping to cut Charles's supply lines from the Pale, before he too joined the encampment at Bandon. By 5 December, the combined army was camped a few miles north of Kinsale in good spirits and confident of victory.

During Carew's absence from Kinsale, the Spanish had sortied out from the walls to attack the English trenches, hoping to provoke Charles into a frontal attack, but instead he outflanked them, forcing them back with enfilade fire along their line. On Carew's return on 25 November, he found that Thomond had arrived with enough troops to set up a second camp to the west of Kinsale, thereby severing Àguila's communication with the Irish. Charles linked the two camps with trenches and was now receiving supplies delivered to Oyster Haven further east. Even now, his call for the Spanish to surrender was treated with disdain.

To maintain the blockade along the whole coastline, Charles called urgently for Leveson's fleet to be strengthened. He also reported that he had provisions only until 20 January. With his men housed in improvised shelters, 6,000 died from the winter cold and dysentery, and many of the newly arrived raw recruits deserted. Although desertion was punishable by death, he advocated compassion, given the horrendous conditions under which they were having to serve. He set up a rest house at Cork, where Gardiner, the Chief Justice, acted as welfare officer. Even the officers contributed £50 per week to provide food for the sick and wounded.

Leveson's blockade left Àguila desperate for provisions and reinforcements. With time being critical, he called on Tyrone and Tyrconnell to make their advance at night, hoping that with the English turning to face them he could sally out to attack from the rear. The Ulstermen remained nervous of open conflict, particularly as Zubiaur had retained most of his men at forts protecting his supply lines and sent only eighty men from Castlehaven. Although Tyrone and Tyrconnell agreed Àguila's concept, no detailed plan of action was developed. On 21 December, the Ulstermen appeared in force on the road from Cork but their hope of making a surprise attack was doomed when they were confronted by two regiments of Charles's foot and most of his cavalry which forced them back into woodland.

The next day, Christmas eve, Carew received an obscure message from Tyrone's son-in-law, Brian MacHugh Oge MacMahon, requesting a bottle of whiskey. With his son having been one of Carew's pages, it was duly provided. On the following night, a message of thanks arrived with information that the Irish assault would be launched on the next day, with the Spanish sallying out from Kinsale in support. This was invaluable information. Charles strengthened his guard and held his troops in readiness. He set up a 'flying regiment' of 449 men under Sir Henry Power, and when the moon went down, Power's force was moved to the west of the main camp. Charles's main concern was that his half-starved war-horses might be too weak for effective action.

The Irish planned their attack in three columns. Richard Tyrrell, an English mercenary (who had served Elizabeth and greatly respected Charles) led the Irish left, with Tyrone in the centre and Tyrconnell on the right. With Charles having learned their detailed plan from captured dispatches and prisoners, he waited in a 'hut' on a ridge north-west of Kinsale, from where he sent out scouts to monitor the enemy's movement. Before dawn, Power with his advanced force could see the Irish lighting slow matches and reported their likely route to Charles, who was with Carew and Wingfield. When Tyrone moved forward at daybreak, Charles called his men to arms but retained his main force to guard his camp and to cover Kinsale. A little later, Graeme's cavalry reported Irish musketeers lighting matches while advancing from the west. Charles sent Wingfield forward to the line of English outposts, from where he reported back that the Irish had halted.

Charles's initial intention had been to reinforce Power's flying regiment to fight a defensive battle at Thomond's fortified camp, which was linked by a trench to an outpost further south. Although he brought up two troops of foot to support Power, the Irish did not attack. Tyrone's problem was that Tyrconnell's men failed to reach their rendezvous by dawn, and he was nervous of facing the English, who were clearly well prepared, in open warfare on his own. Without Tyrconnell, he aborted a plan to move Tyrrell and 800 of his best troops (including 200 Spanish from Castlehaven) into Kinsale to reinforce the garrison. Àguila, who had also seen the Ulstermen halting, was now left waiting in vain for Tyrrell to arrive. Although he watched Charles lining out his infantry, he did not expect him to challenge Tyrone with so few men.

Under cover of a violent squall, Tyrone pulled his 6,000 infantry and 600 horse back over a 'ford' or causeway behind boggy ground, which he hoped would mire an English cavalry charge, but Wingfield reported that they seemed 'somewhat disordered'.[10] Charles then took the bold decision to 'follow up the enemy' with only 1,500 men, despite them being outnumbered by more than four to one.[11] This left three-quarters of his infantry under Carew to counter any Spanish sally out from Kinsale.

When English cavalry under Sir Henry Danvers were sent forward, Wingfield went with them, followed by Power's flying regiment. Almost immediately the three great bodies of Irish foot retired, under cover from their horse.[12] After advancing for about a mile, Danvers' horse reached the ford across the boggy stream. Although Wingfield could see Spanish officers marshalling their Irish troops beyond it, they still seemed 'confused'.[13] He immediately sent Clanricarde with a message to Charles seeking his agreement to attack. Charles did not hesitate, ordering the advance and leading his remaining infantry forward 'as fast as they could march'.[14]

Having reached the ford, Wingfield gave orders for Power's flying regiment to use 100 of its musketeers to drive back the Irish rearguard. After a sharp exchange Power's men were forced back, but as soon as reinforcements arrived the Irish rearguard broke, leaving the way open.[15] With Wingfield bringing Graeme's horse across, the cavalry charged Tyrone's pikemen, but they stood firm, forcing the English cavalry to wheel back. By this time, Power's men, with two infantry regiments in support, had also crossed the ford, and more cavalry arrived to increase Graeme's strength to 500 men. Wingfield now ordered a second charge headed by Danvers, Clanricarde and himself. Although the Irish cavalry on their lightweight horses attempted to challenge them, they broke as soon as the English cavalry rode into their midst, and were followed by the Irish pike. Although Tyrrell sent men to Tyrone's assistance, a flanking attack by Charles's infantry forced them back to a hilltop. This left Tyrone's Ulstermen in full flight, and with Tyrrell's force being 'discouraged', it followed suit. Although Tyrconnell's men at last arrived, they were too late to offer assistance and '[threw] away their arms to run the lighter'.[16] One small Spanish contingent was left to make a stand but was hacked down until their commander and forty-seven survivors surrendered, but other Spanish reappeared later at Castlehaven.

Tyrone had an estimated 1,200 casualties with many more dying from wounds and exposure in the ensuing days. Although these numbers may be exaggerated, they could have been greater as the English were forced to pull back from the chase after 1½ miles on their half-starved horses. Tyrone's survivors headed for Ulster at top speed, leaving their route strewn with dead men and horses. Some of those who had had their houses burned as the Ulstermen came south 'took their revenge by throwing stragglers into bogholes and treading them down'.[17] Tyrconnell joined Zubiaur at Castlehaven from where, on 27 December, he sailed to Spain to seek further assistance; he died soon after arrival, possibly from poison. His men remained largely unscathed apart from their loss of 2,000 weapons with powder drums and nine regimental colours, which were recovered by the English. The English hanged their Irish prisoners but spared the well-respected Spanish. Although they claimed to have lost only three men, Danvers and a few others were slightly wounded, and there was a heavier loss of horses. Having knighted Clanricarde on the field, Charles returned to his camp, calling on his men to give thanks to God that his calculated risk had paid off. Carew recorded: 'Never any general in this Kingdom had a more fortunate day, or in his own person and direction has better deserved; for the dice was cast, the kingdom being ready to sway on that side that proved victorious.'[18]

The English now fired a volley to celebrate their victory. After hearing this, and confident of an Irish victory, Àguila sallied out from the walls, but on seeing the English with Irish and even Spanish colours, he retired back into the town. The siege was not over, and the Spanish still had plenty of fight in them and were expecting reinforcements to arrive at Munster ports, where Zubiaur retained 400 men supported by Munster rebels. On 25 and 26 December, Àguila made two further sallies from Kinsale. Although these were repulsed, Charles did not relish having to storm the walls. His position was far from secure. The fleet blockading Kinsale needed provisions, and the countryside was eaten bare of fodder for their horses. His problems were outlined in his despatches of 27 December, which reported the victory. He asked Danvers to carry them in the hope that as the bearer of good news, it would mitigate his brother Sir Charles's leading part in Essex's rebellion. Charles wrote privately to Cecil, excusing the despatches' brevity, as he was exhausted from a cold and severe migraine.

On 31 December, Àguila called a parley in which he complained that he considered the Irish 'barbarous, untrustworthy and weak', and felt no further obligation to support them.[19] He offered to surrender Kinsale and other forts in Spanish occupation on honourable terms. This suited Charles, but Àguila refused to hand over those Irish who had bravely helped him to defend Kinsale to face certain execution. Charles did not persist. He treated the Spanish with great civility after their stalwart defence. On 2 January 1602, terms were agreed for Àguila's 3,200 survivors from an original force of 4,464 men to be shipped to Spain on English transports. He was unaware that reinforcements being sent to his assistance only turned back on learning of his surrender. Nor did he know that the English were reduced to six days' provisions with a desperate shortage of powder.

The Spanish departure from Ireland ended any future intervention and would prove as crucial as the victory against the Armada in 1588. Nevertheless, Cecil considered Charles's terms overly generous, but on 8 March their remaining forces embarked unmolested, despite having to wait eight days for a favourable wind before leaving harbour. Charles left for Dublin on 9 March after re-establishing control at Castlehaven and dispersing his troops into garrison towns. He felt no elation and worried about the consequences of the war. His leadership had won the day, but he had received invaluable help from 'Carew in the siege and Wingfield in the battle, and the men of his old companies had fought magnificently'.[20]

On reaching Waterford, Charles met 2,000 reinforcements who had arrived too late to assist him. He was accompanied to Kilkenny by Carew, but the strain had taken its toll. He was laid low by the influenza afflicting many of his troops and had to be 'carried on a horse-litter, and so all the journey until he came to Dublin'. On arrival, he was warmly greeted but, after taking to his bed, there were fears for his life. Carew, who was also struck down, reached Cork by easy stages on 28 March.[21]

Chapter 37

Settling Ireland, 1603

The departure of the Spanish did nothing to resolve underlying pockets of rebellion all over Ireland, and Carew's efforts to impose Protestantism in Munster met strong resistance. After leaving Kinsale, Tyrone had escaped north with sixty men. Although he sought a pardon, he was determined to fight on, but many of his former allies, enraged at his failure, melted into the forests of Glenconkeyne when the English destroyed their cattle and crops, only to die of starvation. This left him fatally weakened. Charles needed to bring him to heel but saw him as the means of establishing control of Ulster's belligerent Gaelic chieftains as a poacher turned gamekeeper. Although rival clans had seen his downfall as their opportunity, they offered no better prospect for settling the country, and his removal only heralded continuing discord between them. Unfortunately, neither Elizabeth (initially at least) nor his senior officers agreed with him.

Elizabeth's principal concern was to end the crippling cost of the Irish campaign. Large parts of England had been denuded of men of fighting age to join Charles's army. Cecil's government had been forced to devalue the Irish currency by one quarter to pay its army. Elizabeth wanted Tyrone forced into submission and his earldom removed, but perhaps leaving him as Lord of Dungannon. Cecil advised Charles that if Tyrone made an abject apology, he could promise him his life, but no more. Neither Charles nor Cecil saw any purpose in keeping him alive if he were to remain incarcerated, but wanted him demoted from his paramount role among the Gaelic chieftains. They feared that calls for his unconditional surrender would push him into escaping to Spain at a time when Cecil was trying to negotiate a Spanish peace. With Elizabeth having little time to live, her likely successor, James VI, was expected to advocate mercy in line with his policy for dealing with rebels opposing his rule in Scotland.

Being too unwell to take to the field, Charles, who was continuing to suffer from migraines, wrote a detailed report to Cecil to outline why his campaign had taken so long. He explained that the Irish had received better arms and training from the Spanish than that obtained by the raw recruits arriving from England. Although his policy of destroying Irish crops and cattle had forced the enemy into submission, it had entailed the provisioning of his troops by sea, causing the English government additional cost. To protect against a further Spanish invasion, the Dublin Council had, on 28 April, advocated building a new fort and magazine at Cork, with the forts at Waterford and Limerick being strengthened and additional ones being constructed at Kinsale, Galway and Carlingford.

Without the Spanish presence, Irish unrest became more muted with the Pale and Leinster reasonably quiet. Nevertheless, Munster was still causing Carew anxiety, and Connaught remained unsettled. In Ulster, Docwra had made good progress in Tyrone's and Tyrconnell's absence by occupying the lower Erne as a barrier between Ulster and Connaught. On 25 March 1602, he had taken Ballyshannon Castle, after shipping cannon by sea from Lough Foyle. Although he and Chichester still faced unrest, the Ulster clans, particularly the O'Neills, were now greatly weakened. Although the O'Donnells had returned to Donegal relatively unscathed, Tyrconnell's death in Spain left his more amenable brother Rory as chieftain, and they were without most of their arms.

The queen continued to seek Tyrone's unconditional surrender. In early June, Charles was at last well enough to come north. On reaching the River Blackwater, the Ulstermen retreated into the woods and he established a crossing at a bridge protected with a fort, which he named Charlemount (now Charlemont). He then met up with Docwra and Chichester at Omagh, which Docwra had garrisoned. With Danvers having returned from England after being rehabilitated by the queen, Charles appointed him Sergeant-Major of the army to replace Sir John Berkeley, who had been killed by a stray shot during a skirmish with the MacMahons in Monaghan. Charles promptly wasted their lands in retaliation before moving forward in earnest against Tyrone. At the end of July, with many of Tyrone's former allies having submitted, Charles retired to Newry to rest his men.

In the south, Carew took Dunboy Castle after bombarding it with artillery, and by winter, 'the last flicker of revolt' in Munster had been stamped out.[1] In Connaught, the new governor, Sir Oliver Lambart, secured Sligo and sent a galley to deal with piracy along the coast, but when he threatened to expropriate rebel lands, Charles objected, believing that it would only force them to fight to the death. In the final English setback of the war, Clanricarde and Sir Arthur Savage were ambushed while marching through the Curlew Hills, but by then the rebel cause was as good as lost.

When Carew heard rumours that troops were being readied in Spain for another expedition, Charles left 1,500 men in Munster, despite needing every man he could spare against Tyrone. Eventually, Cecil confirmed that his agents could find no evidence to suggest that an invasion fleet was being prepared and this was confirmed by an English squadron which was patrolling the Spanish coastline as a deterrent.

On 20 August, Charles headed after Tyrone, realising that he had to be arrested if peace were to be restored. When he fled into Fermanagh, Charles did not follow him but again destroyed his harvest. He directed those who had submitted to move their cattle south of the Blackwater where there was fodder, and seed could be sown. With Tyrone's lands being deserted, Charles destroyed the stone chair at Tullahogue where the O'Neills' paramount chief was proclaimed.

Charles now extended his more lenient policy and, on 18 November, visited Athlone to reinforce it on Lambart. On 14 December, Rory O'Donnell submitted to him, and Charles gained the backing of the Dublin government to take a conciliatory line, even though the O'Donnells had not suffered at Kinsale and still retained their cattle. To the horror of Charles's senior English officers, the Dublin government considered Rory to be manageable and confirmed him as Lord of Tyrconnell, with most of the barony's estates being restored to him. This incensed Docwra, who, with Charles's blessing, had previously offered the lordship to Niall Garbh, but Charles concluded that his 'ambition, insolence, covetousness, ill temper, and generally bad promise made him unsuitable as a paramount chief'.[2] In April 1603, Docwra took Niall Garbh to Dublin to establish Charles's intentions, but Charles ignored his former undertakings. Niall Garbh now had himself named to the forbidden Gaelic title of 'The O'Donnell', and, although Docwra imprisoned him, he may have connived in his escape.

O'Doherty at Inishowen, Donal Ballach O'Cahan at Coleraine and MacMahon at Monaghan had also been offered lands by Docwra in return for support against Tyrone, but Charles thought it better to free them from Tyrone's overlordship. Together with smaller O'Neill clan chieftains, they were permitted to negotiate formal tenancies to avoid future disagreement. O'Doherty was knighted and restored to the Inishowen Peninsula, including the island of Inch. O'Cahan was told to ignore rental undertakings previously due to Tyrone. When he set aside his marriage to Tyrone's daughter, Tyrone threatened court action, but the new Irish Solicitor General, Sir John Davies, appointed by Charles, handled O'Cahan's defence.

Charles spent Christmas at Galway, Ireland's most remote fortified port, where he persuaded Connaught's principal rebels to submit to him and to sign a document swearing allegiance to Elizabeth. He was now able to reduce the army's strength to 12,000 foot and 1,000 horse. On 20 January 1603, he wrote to Cecil to object that the Irish Lord Chancellor, Archbishop Adam Loftus, had imprisoned several Dubliners, including six aldermen, for failing to attend Protestant services. Charles believed that being confrontational would 'breed a new war', arguing that persecution only strengthened religions.[3] His approach was in advance of its time by a good hundred years, but Cecil agreed and the privy council in London authorised him to tell Loftus to desist and to discourage the adoption of similar policies elsewhere.[4]

Cecil eventually brought Elizabeth round to Charles's more lenient approach for dealing with Tyrone. On 17 February, she authorised him 'to offer life, liberty and pardon', but Cecil warned that she would have much preferred him to submit with his earldom being forfeited.[5] Charles concurred with her call for the lands being restored to him to be reduced, and he maintained all forts under English control.

At last, Tyrone wrote a grovelling letter asking for a meeting with Charles. He received a safe-conduct on 25 March and arrived at Mellifont Abbey near Drogheda five days later. While Charles waited, he heard unofficially through Fynes Moryson that Elizabeth had died, but told his secretary to keep the news secret. He knew that if true, his commission for dealing with Tyrone was invalid. If Tyrone were told, he would try to delay having to submit, hoping for more lenient treatment from King James. (Elizabeth had, in fact, died on 24 March.)

On 30 March, Tyrone knelt at the threshold of the hall at Mellifont with Charles sitting in state as the representative of royal power. Having been bidden to approach, he lay at Charles's feet in humble and penitent submission, making protestations of repentance and loyalty.

He undertook to be governed by the advice of the crown's magistrates and to aid them in its service. He also forewent his titles. Charles insisted on this being put in writing. On the following day, Tyrone provided a lengthy submission, renouncing any further dependency on Spain or any other foreign power. He wrote to Philip III to confirm this, asking for his son, who was now in Spain, to be returned to Ireland. Charles at last pardoned him, agreeing to restore his English earldom with new letters patent. The death-knell of Gaelic Ireland had been sounded.[6]

On 3 April, Charles escorted Tyrone to Dublin, and two days later Danvers arrived, carrying the official report of Elizabeth's death. He also brought a 'gracious' letter to Charles from James in Scotland. With his appointment as Lord Deputy expiring on the queen's death, Charles was appointed as a Lord Justice until 17 April, when his reinstatement was confirmed by the new king. Tyrone burst into tears of frustration on hearing the news, believing that James might have been more sympathetic, but made a submission to the new king and signed the proclamation of his accession. Those Gaelic chieftains who had assisted the English were infuriated at Tyrone recovering so much of his former property, but both Cecil and Charles knew that James preferred to work through magnates to maintain peace, so it was in keeping with his policy to seek to win Tyrone over.

Charles now believed he had a breathing place to return home to the 'land of good meat and clean linen' for a reunion with Penelope and his family.[7] He proposed to James that he should become Lord Lieutenant with two-thirds of his vice-regal stipend while supervising Ireland from England. He also suggested that Sir George Carey of Cockington (a half second-cousin of William Carey, who married Mary Boleyn), the treasurer-at-war, should become his Lord Deputy based in Ireland and receive the remainder of the stipend, together with his existing salary as treasurer. James agreed to this except that, in May 1603, Carey was appointed the king's, not Charles's, deputy. (In February 1605, Carey was replaced by Chichester and returned to England, where, at the age of 66, he married Penelope's daughter, Lettice Rich, who was 22.)

Unfortunately, Charles was held up in Ireland until June. Unrest had broken out in the southern towns, caused in part by the unsettling effect of Elizabeth's death, in part by the debasement of the Irish currency (out of which Carey was rumoured to have benefited), but mainly because of Roman Catholic concerns that James would be intolerant of their faith.

The unrest only became serious in Munster and southern Leinster, where Carew had attempted to enforce Protestantism, but Mass was regularly celebrated in small chapels. Although Carew had been withdrawn from Ireland in March at Cecil's 'earnest request', unrest continued. While Cecil remained his close friend, Carew's confrontational religious approach was proving unhelpful to Charles's more tolerant policy. With most of the difficulty arising in Cork, Waterford and Kilkenny, on 27 April Charles arrived with a strong force. This was enough to overawe most areas, but when Waterford remained insolent, he arrested those who opposed James on the grounds of his perceived intolerance and enforced the oath of allegiance on the principal citizens. After leaving a garrison under Sir Richard Moryson to provide security, he moved on to Cork, where its citizens had seized the munitions and bombarded Shandon Castle where Lady Carew was continuing to live apparently undismayed. Although Sir Charles Wilmot drove the citizens back into the town and established a truce, he was short of munitions. Having hanged three of the ringleaders and imprisoned the Recorder, William Meade (who ended his life living on a pension in Spain), Charles permitted the citizens to practice their religion privately if they swore allegiance to James. He then installed a garrison of 1,000 men, before moving on to Limerick. This area proved less contentious, as the locality willingly took the oath of allegiance, despite taking Mass. Before returning to Dublin, Charles gave orders for its castle's fortifications to be strengthened. 'He did not believe in extremes or in pushing men too hard', and this approach settled southern Ireland.[8]

While Charles was on his way to Limerick, he received advice from Tyrone that he was invited to meet the privy council in London. Charles decided that he would also take Niall Garbh O'Donnell. On 29 May, they left Dublin for Beaumaris, Anglesey, on the *Tramontana,* a ship with a long history of action against the Spanish. Having narrowly missed the Skerries in a fog off the Anglesey coast, it arrived unscathed apart from damage to the boat on its stern davits.

PART VII

WITH JAMES I AS KING

Chapter 38

The end of the Elizabethan era, 1601–03

In early 1601, when Cecil's peace negotiations with Spain came to nothing, Henry Wotton came to Scotland to assess James's suitability to become the English king. Wotton was impressed, describing him as a man of charm and intelligence at the heart of a court of loyal subjects. James had asked Mar and Bruce, who were still in London, to contact Cobham, Raleigh and Northumberland, who had secretly approached him through Lennox. As always, Cecil was aware of what was going on. With his alliance with Raleigh being paper-thin, he was determined to prevent them interfering. He again turned to Howard to warn Mar and Bruce that they could not keep their mouths shut, and continued contact with them was counterproductive. This did not prevent him from covering himself by investing £2,000 in one of Raleigh's shipping ventures.

Howard now became Cecil's conduit for building bridges with James. This involved a secret correspondence with coded messages to advise the Scottish king how to protect his claim to the English throne. This was kept from Elizabeth, whose 'age and orbity joined to the jealousy of her sex, might have moved her to think ill of that which helped to preserve her'. Names were given as numbers, with Elizabeth being 24, James 30, Cecil 10, Mar 20 and Northumberland 0. Cecil eventually signed himself as James's 'dearest and most truest 10', and arranged for his English pension to be increased to £5,000 per annum. James accepted Cecil's advice, writing that 'good government at home, firm amity with the Queen, and a loving care of all things that may concern the weal of the State [England] are the only three steps whereby I think to mount upon the hearts of the people'.

Elizabeth remained oblivious of the negotiations taking place behind her back but saw Mar as a 'courtly and well-advised gentleman'. She appointed him to her council of war against the Irish rebels and made James a Knight of the Garter. Although Howard's voluble writing style brought wry complaints from James, he was created Earl of Northampton after James's accession. Raleigh now saw James, with his close affiliation to the Essex faction, as a threat and, with Spanish money to grease his palms, he tried to promote the rival claim of Arbella Stuart, despite Elizabeth keeping her out of the limelight.[1] It has been suggested that Bess Throckmorton, as a close friend of Arbella's grandmother, Bess of Hardwick, also helped to promote Arbella.[2] Certainly Howard viewed Bess and Raleigh with equal suspicion. This did not bode well for them if James should become king. In the spring of 1602, Raleigh went to Jersey, where he remained governor, politically impotent and despondent at finding himself in the 'wilderness' and cut off from court.[3] Despite being Cecil's brother-in-law, Cobham's position was no better.

Raleigh was pleading poverty, although the extent of his financial difficulties is hard to gauge. On 7 December 1602, he sold his Irish estates to Sir Richard Boyle. He also placed his Sherborne property in trust. If he should face trial for treason, any lands in his ownership would 'lapse' to the crown, and he wanted Sherborne protected for his 10-year-old son, Wat. Was he, even then, contemplating a treasonable plot? We do not know, but James was later to accuse him of it, a charge which he hotly denied.

Elizabeth was feeling older and, in late 1601, hinted in parliament that she was finding her role stressful, and would be 'glad to be freed of the glory with the labours, for it is not my desire to live nor to reign longer than my life and reign shall be for your good'.[4] At an audience with Sir Robert Carey on 19 March 1603, she admitted: '"Robin, I am not well!" On the following day, she heard Sunday service propped on cushions on the floor at the door of her chapel.'[5] She became speechless, but, according to Cecil, made signs to indicate that James should succeed her. After prayers led by John Whitgift, the Archbishop of Canterbury, she expired 'easily like a ripe apple from a tree', at Richmond Palace at 2.30 am on 24 March, 'as the most resplendent sun setteth at last in a western cloud'. She was in her seventieth year, the first English monarch to reach such an age. It may not have been a 'golden' period, but chroniclers tried to guide her successors to emulate her brand of monarchy.

Carey's sister, Philadelphia, Lady Scope, one of Elizabeth's ladies, held a sapphire ring which James had sent south with orders for it to be returned as soon as Elizabeth died. She passed it to Carey, who had posted horses along the North Road to outpace the official messenger and be the first to bring James the news. On arrival in Edinburgh, he was appointed a Gentleman of the Bedchamber, only to have it countermanded later when the English privy council objected. In what was a personal triumph for Cecil, James was proclaimed king immediately, without any commotion, being 'lineally and lawfully descended' from Margaret Tudor, daughter of Henry VII.

On 5 April, within a fortnight of Elizabeth's death, James left Edinburgh after borrowing an additional £6,660 Scots from his long-suffering bankers. As he travelled south, his new subjects flocked to see him, showing 'sparkles of affection'. Although Raleigh headed north, hoping, optimistically, to be recognised by the new king, both he and Cobham were stopped on Cecil's instructions and forced to return to London. Although Raleigh wrote to James with *A Discourse touching a war with Spain,* which advocated continued support for the Dutch, it was reported that his 'opinions' 'hath taken no great root here'.[6] So long as James had vied with the Infanta Isabella to be recognised as Elizabeth's heir, he had had no interest in peace with the Spanish, but once king, he became much more conciliatory.[7] Raleigh's future looked bleak. Much later, the diarist John Aubrey reported that James met him at Burghley House at Stamford, but Howard and Cecil had already poisoned James's mind against him.[8]

James timed his arrival in London for 29 April, the day following Elizabeth's state funeral. This was perhaps the biggest ceremonial event ever staged in England, although her body, which had been poorly embalmed, was decomposing. Rich was one of twelve barons who walked beside her coffin, 'carrying tall lances with flags fluttering at the tip'.[9] In a final demonstration of his ostensible standing, Raleigh led his 150 men as captain of the guard.

James's arrival with his motley entourage of Scots was, by comparison, lacklustre. According to Horace Walpole, it initiated the nursery rhyme:

> Hark, hark, the dogs do bark,
> The beggars are coming to town,
> Some in rags, and some in tags,
> And some in velvet gowns …

Queen Anne did not travel with the new king, partly because the English ladies-in-waiting were unable to attend her until after Elizabeth's funeral, and partly because she was again pregnant, although she later suffered a miscarriage. Early in May Penelope, who did not know when Charles might return from Ireland, left London to greet Anne as she travelled south. She was one of six ladies-in-waiting chosen by Cecil for this purpose. This may seem surprising given her involvement in her brother's rebellion and her separation from her husband, but James ignored these concerns. Cecil had already sent some of Elizabeth's jewels and gowns to Edinburgh, so that Anne would look the part on her arrival. Further jewellery was sent with the ladies-in-waiting, but to prevent its disappearance on arrival in Scotland, they were instructed to await Anne at Berwick.[10] Meanwhile, other ladies went straight to Edinburgh, hoping to ingratiate themselves with the new queen before the official party could do so. One of these was Lucy, Countess of Bedford, the attractive young daughter of Elizabeth's godson, Sir John Harington. With her husband having been an Essex ally, she was soon enjoying a close familiarity with the new queen. Bess Throckmorton arrived, but was not so welcome. Cecil sent a spy to watch her every move, and she received no more than 'idle graces' from the queen.[11]

Anne left Edinburgh on 1 June, bringing her own first lady, the Catholic Jean, daughter of Patrick 3rd Lord Drummond. Although Anne had been brought up as a Lutheran, she was already flirting with the Catholic faith. Despite retaining official Protestant chaplains, she surrounded herself with Catholic attendants and clandestinely celebrated Mass with Jean.[12] On reaching Berwick, it was soon recognised that she was more impressed with Lucy and Penelope than the dowdier ladies with whom she had been saddled. As they travelled south, Anne and Penelope developed a close rapport. Despite being ten years older, Penelope was still glamorous with gleaming dark eyes. Like Penelope, Anne spoke fluent French and some Italian. She played the lute, virginals and several other instruments. She loved partying and dancing, and ran up huge debts on plays, masques, extravagant clothing and jewellery. They also shared an interest in politics and foreign affairs.[13] Travelling north proved to be 'an excellent investment of Penelope's time', beginning 'a royal friendship that brought her to the peak of her influence' as one of the court's most celebrated figures.[14] It was 'the ladies of Bedford, Rich and Essex [Frances] [who were] especially in favour'.

Jean Drummond and Lucy were appointed as Anne's ladies of the bedchamber. Although Penelope was one of six ladies of the drawing chamber, her greater rapport with Anne caused jealousy when Lucy found herself being treated 'indifferently'. 'Competition was intense. "The plotting and malice" among the ladies was so bad that it was feared they would "sting one another to death".'[15]

The queen travelled south by easy stages, visiting Cecil's elder brother Thomas, now Lord Burghley, who, as President of the Council of the North, occupied King's Manor at York, where Penelope had been schooled by the Huntingdons. Wherever the royal party stopped, it was greeted by local gentry, often petitioning for more Catholic toleration.[16] Anne's entourage grew so large that many had to be billeted around the community. On reaching Althorp in Northamptonshire, she was greeted to a 'magical two days', with Ben Jonson's 'Masque of the Fairies' depicting her as Oriana.[17] On reaching Easton Neston in Northamptonshire, she was met by James, who took her to Windsor, where Penelope and Charles were at last reunited. Being Charles's mistress was no bar to her status at court but they were left with no time to escape to Wanstead.

Raleigh's former standing quickly unravelled. He was stripped of his captaincy of the guard and lost his former monopolies. On 31 May, he received notice to vacate Durham Place by 24 June, and it was returned to the Bishop of Durham, but the stables and gardens were granted to Cecil to make place for his 'New Exchange'. Raleigh found it 'very strange' not to receive more notice to leave a property he had occupied for twenty years and on which he had lavished £2,000.

Chapter 39

Life under James I and Queen Anne, 1603–05

'As [Charles and Tyrone] rode to London the widows and orphans of soldiers who had died unpaid in Ireland lined the roads pelting the "arch-traitor" Tyrone.'[1] On reaching Dunstable, Charles sent a message to Cecil that he was taking Tyrone to Wanstead, but 'protested that nothing, save the honour of serving King James, afforded him greater pride than the love of his correspondent [Cecil], which he would try to deserve'.[2] This may have seemed genuine, but in the light of Charles's previous support for Essex's rebellion, Sally Varlow does not accept that Cecil reciprocated Charles's overtures of friendship. It is difficult to disagree with her view that he was determined on revenge on all those who had been Essex's supporters. She argues that he methodically developed his rapport with James so that, one by one, he could engineer the downfall of his enemies.

As soon as he was proclaimed king, James recognised his debt to Essex's allies and arranged their rehabilitation. Although Southampton was still in the Tower, James sent instructions from Edinburgh for his immediate release. On James's arrival in London, Southampton joined his coterie of mignons and, to Cecil's frustration, was made a Knight of the Garter. Sir William Knollys and Sir Robert Sidney became barons, as did Essex's secretary, Henry Wotton, and Danvers became Lord Danvers of Dauntsey. Even Frances, who was about to marry Clanricarde, was warmly received, and Essex's three children were reinstated 'in noble blood ... as though the earl had never been attainted'.[3]

Cecil would need to wait for his moment to pounce on his rivals, particularly Penelope. His apparent rapport with Charles in Ireland would not prevent him, when the moment was right, from using his misalliance with her to blacken her name with James. She knew that she needed to be careful and before Charles's arrival had written, 'thanking [Cecil] for his noble favours to "his absent friend [Charles]" and to herself'.[4] On reaching London on 6 June, Charles was exhausted, but was warmly greeted by the king and became the principal beneficiary of his munificence. James spent much time with him, admiring his erudition and holding his views on divinity in 'high esteem'.[5] On 7 June, Charles was appointed a privy councillor. Tyrone was also well received, and James reconfirmed the promises that Charles had made to him. Rory O'Donnell was made Earl of Tyrconnell, although Niall Garbh retained his original possessions, enhanced with the Finn Valley.[6] Tyrone never proved a reliable ally. While staying at Kingston, he was reported to have taken Mass, which cannot have pleased Charles. Niall Garbh also proved treacherous, spending his later years in the Tower.

After meeting Charles, James visited Syon House. With Dorothy having temporarily patched up her differences with Northumberland (and in 1604 she produced a second son, Henry), James was 'entertained with great ceremony'.[7] Northumberland became a privy councillor and was appointed Commander of the Gentlemen Pensioners, the sovereign's bodyguard. He had little respect for James, who was easily bored by administrative chores, but indulged in hunting and was often to be found overly sentimental and drunk with mignons, who satisfied his bisexual pleasures. Northumberland also considered his forthright views on Anglican dogma to be lacking in tact.

On 2 July, Charles attended the Garter ceremony at Windsor, and on 21 July, 'resplendent in crimson velvet robes', was created Earl of Devonshire in the great hall at Hampton Court, receiving lands forfeited from the previous titleholders, his distant kinsmen, the Courtenays. He was rewarded with a rent of assize from the Exchequer of £200 per annum together with Duchy of Lancaster lands of a similar value, and further lands in Ireland.[8] To these were added lucrative customs duties on French and Rhenish wines. Particularly appreciated was his recent success in gaining acceptance for James's accession in Munster. His retention of two-thirds of the stipend as Lord Lieutenant of Ireland was also confirmed, but this was no sinecure, and, until his death, 'all Irish affairs passed through his hands' with very little interference from James.[9] He was responsible for 'general policy, defence, appointments [and] finance'.[10] All correspondence for Carey and Chichester, as Lords Deputy, was addressed in the first instance to him. One of his shrewdest actions was to employ Sir John Davies as Solicitor General. Despite being an able poet, Davies had had a chequered career at the Inns of Court in London after striking a fellow member with a cudgel, but his abilities shone through in Ireland. Charles was also able to cut the military establishment there to 234 horse and 880 foot. 'His policy was to make the Irish realise that the reduction in the army was due to the king's confidence in their loyalty, which allowed him to ease the people of their burdens.'[11]

At the coronation on 25 July, the Essex faction was thrust to the fore. Charles, in his full regalia, was one of fifteen earls who unrobed the king. 'Little Robin' Devereux, now Earl of Essex, proudly acted as sword-bearer, and Penelope's eldest son, Robert Rich, was knighted. In view of an outbreak of plague, the coronation was a low-key affair with James anxious 'to prevent all occasions of dispersing the infection among our people'. The Venetian Ambassador reported that 60,000 died, and 'the stench of death was everywhere'.[12] Invited guests were told to limit their escorts. A further problem was that Anne refused to take communion during the Protestant ceremony.

It was concerns about James's suitability to be king that led to plots for his (and that of his sons') assassination, so that Arbella Stuart could be placed on the throne, although she was probably completely unaware of them. There were various unconnected schemes all with the same intent and all having the promise of Spanish funding. On 15 July, Cobham confessed to being the leader of the 'main' of these plots and also implicated Raleigh, who was placed under house arrest in Fulham. Raleigh hotly denied involvement, and given his anti-Spanish 'discourse' so recently provided to the king, it must seem unlikely. He made the mistake of admitting he had had suspicions about Cobham, but then contacted him to say that he had said nothing to incriminate him. On hearing this, Cobham provided a written confession that he and Raleigh had planned to visit Flanders, where they were promised 600,000 crowns, before meeting in Jersey, although thereafter the detail becomes hazy. Cobham also admitted that there were secondary or 'bye' plots to force James to offer religious toleration to both Catholics and radicals, with one initiated by English Jesuits and another by English Puritans, who had support from Grey de Wilton.

Apart from Cobham's written confession, there was no evidence to implicate Raleigh, and Cobham almost immediately retracted it. Even if tabled at a trial, Raleigh could not be incriminated under statute law on the evidence of a single witness. Despite Cecil's efforts, no further evidence against him was unearthed. Having supported Cecil to bring down Essex, Raleigh had fully expected his help, but Cecil did not want attention being drawn to his hostility to Essex and failed to recommend a reprieve.[13] On 19 July, Raleigh was moved to the Tower, where he tried to stab himself with a table knife, but enemies thought this was for show, and he soon became more stable. He was also at risk from the plague, writing to Bess that death was the only honourable remedy, providing her with instructions on how to cope without him. She wrote to Cecil to defend her husband, but Howard told her that she needed to provide proof of his innocence. James, who was paranoid of assassination attempts, called for Cecil to press charges. Cecil considered Cobham's retraction 'so blemished' that the outcome would be a formality.[14] Bess provided £5,000 to allow the trial to be heard by privy councillors in the Star Chamber, where, despite a presumption of guilt, no death sentence could be imposed.

With Raleigh remaining unpopular for his perceived betrayal of Essex, the trial was moved to Winchester to avoid mob violence and the continuing threat of plague. James had left London beforehand to stay with the Bishop of Winchester at Farnham Castle, where, on 13 August, Charles was appointed Master of the Ordnance, the army's highest rank. This role had been left unfilled since Essex's death. Four days later, Penelope was given the status of the Earl of Essex in her own right, taking precedence over all barons (including Rich). Among ladies, only the Countesses of Oxford, Arundel, Northumberland (Dorothy) and Shrewsbury were senior to her. The court then moved on to Woodstock, where Cecil, who was trying to prepare for the trial, quipped that they might end up in York. As it turned out, their next move was to Wilton, still occupied by Mary Sidney.[15]

On 17 November, Raleigh was brought for trial to the Bishop's Palace at Winchester. No longer was it to be a 'Star Chamber' trial before privy councillors, but before a jury. Bess worked tirelessly to find sympathetic jurymen, installing two of her connections, only to find them being changed at the eleventh hour. Charles was appointed as one of the trial's commissioners with Coke again appointed as the chief prosecutor.

Although the verdict was a foregone conclusion, in legal terms the case against Raleigh was very doubtful, based as it was on Cobham's retracted testimony. Arbella Stuart was required to attend but was an innocent party and mortified at the whole proceeding. Raleigh exuded confidence and conducted a brilliant defence, challenging every point and branding the prosecution a mockery. There was no doubting that he had made unflattering remarks about James, but there was no evidence of his involvement in the 'main' plot. Given the weakness of the prosecution case, Coke focused his attack on Raleigh's character. He also argued that, as the statutes under which Raleigh was being charged had lapsed, then 'common law and common sense prevailed', and common law required only one witness.[16] Raleigh called for Cobham to be asked to confirm the testimony that he had retracted. When this was refused, Raleigh provided a letter of exoneration, which Cobham had smuggled to him. Unfortunately, Coke provided a second letter from the two-faced Cobham confirming his accusations and citing Raleigh as the ringleader. Although Raleigh's responses won the moral high ground, it took the jury only fifteen minutes to find him guilty, and he was condemned to be hanged, drawn and quartered, with his 'privy members' to be cut off before his eyes, with all his estates being forfeited.[17] Nevertheless, his performance had suddenly transformed him into a popular hero, causing James to dither about carrying out the sentence.

At the trials of Cobham and Grey de Wilton which followed, they were both found guilty of treason. The only issue was whether James would reprieve them. Raleigh and his fellow defendants were twice led to the scaffold before James ordered a temporary stay on their execution. On 10 December, Grey de Wilton and Cobham were once more brought to the scaffold. Surrounded by his Puritan friends, Grey knelt to pray, but the sheriff said that the king's instructions were for Cobham be executed first. He now read a 'short speech' outlining their offences, and then announced: 'See the mercy of your prince, who of himself hath sent to countermand and give you of your lives.'[18] Their sentences were commuted to life imprisonment. (Grey died in the Tower in 1614, and Cobham was released in 1618, but died shortly after.) Charles was one of many who had called on the king to revoke the death penalty, and Raleigh, who had watched at a window, learned that he too was to be reprieved and returned to the Tower.

The court returned to Wilton, where James rehabilitated Arbella, despite her distaste for what had happened. She was excited by life at court with entertainments by Shakespeare and John Dowland, but disapproved of the ladies' lax morals and their gossip about Elizabeth's faults. Everyone now returned to Hampton Court, which was within reach of London, for Christmas and the New Year, and James laid on banquets for visiting ambassadors. Penelope and Charles were in attendance, and she loved all the Christmas festivities organised by Anne despite her being pregnant. Shakespeare performed *A Midsummer Night's Dream,* but Anne particularly enjoyed masques with their 'mixture of music, dancing, fantastic costumes and magical transformation scenes', raising them 'to a new level of sophistication, beauty' – and expense![19] The festivities continued until long after Twelfth Night.

On 8 January, there was a performance of *The Vision of the Twelve Goddesses,* especially written by Samuel Daniel (for whom Charles had been a patron) and dedicated to the favoured Lucy Bedford, whose idea it seems to have been. There was a fight for places, but James was able to sit in state with the Spanish and Venetian ambassadors beside him. With the goddesses parading in threes to stunning effect, each 'wore a mask and a different coloured costume made of richly embroidered satins'.[20] Anne led the way, dressed as Pallas Athene with Catherine Howard (née Knyvett), Countess of Suffolk, another famous but slightly faded beauty as Juno, and Penelope as Venus, on each side wearing dove-coloured mantles embroidered with silver. Each group was led by young pages wearing 'white satin loose gowns', with the three graces below them dressed in silver robes and carrying bright white torches. Anne thought nothing of raiding Elizabeth's wardrobe to chop up historic garments, some to knee-length, to show off both feet and legs. With the participants in masks, the audience had to guess who the legs belonged to. Even Charles played a small part in a role for men, after which the goddesses chose their dancing partners.

These extravaganzas cost an astronomical £3,000, and the privy council baulked when Anne planned another, but she was not to be curbed. Having at last returned to London, there were entertainments by Thomas Dekker and others. She saw so many new plays that Richard Burbage had to dust down *Love's Labours Lost,* confident that it would amuse her. (In 1605, to universal horror, she spent £50,000 on entertainment, leaving her continuously in debt.) The royal couple now embarked on 'their long-delayed triumphal [six-hour] procession' through 'decorative arches' from the Tower to Whitehall, 'pausing for music, speeches and presentations'.[21] James was mounted on a small white Spanish horse with a rich canopy of state held over him by senior noblemen. Anne 'and her ladies rode in open chariots, waving to the crowds'.[22]

On 6 January 1604, Charles was reappointed Captain of the Town, Island and Castle of Portsmouth, and on 30 March, he and Southampton were granted a joint commission of the Lieutenancy of the County and Town of Southampton. On 5 February 1605, Charles was one of seven lords granted the office of Earl Marshal, as 'the office was too great to be entrusted to any single subject'.[23]

When it came to reforming the Church of England, James wanted Charles involved but left him little to do. He disagreed with all the other participants over the form of the sacrament and book of Common Prayer and, after his long-running battle with the Scottish Reformers, was determined to enhance the authority of bishops. Although his accession had seemed to offer an olive branch for Catholics, the main and bye plots left him in no mood to offer concessions, and the Roman Catholic clergy were expelled.

As a 'man of peace', James was strongly supported by Buckhurst and Cecil (now created Lord Cecil) to end the war with Spain. The Spanish also wanted a formal end to hostilities, although no military conflict had taken place since Kinsale. In August 1603, Philip III had sent his envoy, Don Juan de Tassis, Count of Villa Mediana, to begin the discussions. With James sheltering from the plague at Woodstock, preliminary talks began in Oxford. On 2 September, Charles greeted Mediana at Henley to escort him on the last stage of his journey to lodgings at Christchurch College. Mediana took it as a great compliment to be met by such a well-respected Englishman.

James's peace initiative was most unwelcome to the Dutch, who were still enjoying military success. Francis Vere was back at The Brill when he learned of Elizabeth's death, but he had immediately called on the magistrates to proclaim James as king, sending Horace to England with a letter to welcome him. Although James wanted an end to war, Francis remained in the service of the States-General as a much revered commander. He was now 43, covered in wounds and riddled with bullets. With his health failing after twenty years of service, it was time for him to retire. Horace was well qualified to succeed him and took command of a force made up entirely of English mercenaries paid by the States-General and was soon involved in recovering Sluis. Although James tried to involve the Dutch in the peace negotiations, they saw it as a betrayal, (as did a large body of English opinion) and refused to participate.[24]

In 1604, Francis returned to live at Tilbury Lodge, which he had acquired in 1598. This was close to Kirby Hall, still occupied by his mother and brother. He had no desire to attend the goings on at court. He still remained Governor of The Brill and sought to return there, but Cecil persuaded him that this was unnecessary. To move him conveniently out of the way, Cecil sent him on 'an honourable mission' to The Hague with letters of friendship from James to the States-General. He only returned in June 1606, by when the Dutch had granted him a pension of £500 per annum. During his time there, he was able to write an account of his military exploits. Although it was not intended for publication, it remains the principal source material for his experiences.

In mid-March, the commissioners for peace with Spain at last reconvened. They met first at the Spanish ambassador's temporary residence in Richmond Park, but the main talks began on 20 May at Somerset House. Although Anne now lived there, she moved with her ladies to Whitehall Palace while the talks continued. When the Spanish delegation approached Somerset House down the Thames on barges, it was greeted by courtiers in a fleet of gondolas. The English delegation was represented by Buckhurst (now Earl of Dorset), Nottingham, Charles, Lord Henry Howard (now Earl of Northampton) and Cecil, who took the lead. The Spanish were led by Mediana with representatives from Spain, the Low Countries and the Holy Roman Empire. Talks continued throughout the summer, but the Spanish needed to come to terms. With their power declining, they were no longer demanding tolerance for English Catholics. Although the English rejected the offer of a Spanish alliance, it was agreed that English troops would no longer be sent to support rebellions by Spanish subjects, but argued that voluntary enlistment by English mercenaries on either side could not be prevented. (This resulted in many English and Irish Catholics enlisting in Habsburg armies.) Blockading of ports in the Low Countries by either side was to end, as was the Spanish Inquisition's questioning of foreign merchants. The only great English disappointment, particularly for the City of London, was an embargo on English trade with Spanish possessions in the New World.

With a copy of the Treaty of London engrossed for signature, the High Constable of Castille, Juan Fernández de Velasco, 5th Duke of Frias, arrived to sign it on Spain's behalf. He was lodged at Somerset House and was entertained with great pomp. On 19 August, Charles headed a retinue of fifty mounted gentlemen to escort him to Whitehall, and, with the treaty being sworn, the ambassadors were feasted by the king.[25] Although peace was proclaimed, London merchants remained disappointed.

Frias had brought between 8,000 and 10,000 crowns to reward the negotiators. Although rewards were the custom, it was a huge sum. Cecil, who had now been created Viscount Cranborne, accepted £1,500 and seems to have received further sums from the Dutch to discourage too generous treatment for the Spanish. Ever grasping, he later negotiated an increase in his Spanish pension to £12,500 per annum. The other English commissioners each received £1,000. Although Charles had played little active part, he was happy to accept any means to maintain his lifestyle with Penelope at Wanstead.

Although Charles seems to have found court life irksome, he had no intention of settling down to a quiet rural existence. He and Penelope attended the royal banquet for the departing Spanish, sitting with Northumberland and 'Little Robin' at the top table with the king, queen and leading Spanish diplomats. After feasting and dancing, the entertainments included bearbaiting, acrobats on horseback and tumblers. Southampton and Pembroke attended as gentlemen ushers, and afterwards Charles led the guests to their coaches to be escorted to Somerset House by fifty halberdiers with torches.[26]

By now, Cranborne (Cecil) was relying on Charles's judgement as 'the foremost authority on military matters'.[27] The king gave instructions for Cranborne to form an inner cabinet to include Dorset (Buckhurst), Northampton and Charles to handle weighty matters with James, while more mundane affairs were left to the Council, whose Puritan bias was causing him concern. Charles was also appointed to the committee to examine union with Scotland but played little active part in its deliberations.

With Cranborne steadily gaining in standing as James's 'little beagle', he had the knives out for Southampton, unhappy at the royal favours being lavished on him.[28] Although Southampton was considered the most cultured and gifted court member, he was also the Essex faction's senior survivor. Cranborne spread rumours that he was involved in a plot to assassinate several puritanical Scottish courtiers after his reputed criticism of the king's lack of tolerance for Catholics. Although he was arrested, no evidence was found to incriminate him, but it ended any further advancement in James's service. Once more, Penelope stepped in to support Elizabeth Vernon and their children.

Charles and Penelope spent Christmas 1604 at Whitehall, enjoying Shakespeare's plays and other court entertainments. On All Saint's Day, the King's Men performed *Othello,* followed, three days later, by the popular *The Merry Wives of Windsor.* In December, there was *Measure for Measure* and later *The Comedy of Errors.* Samuel Daniel's play *The Tragedy of Philotas,* performed on 3 January, had to be suppressed as it recalled too vividly the career and fate of Essex.[29] When Daniel was called before the privy council, he pleaded that it had been written prior to Essex's revolt, but then admitted having shown it to Charles beforehand. Charles was furious at being linked to 'an unwelcome echo from the past' and called on Daniel to apologise. This did not prevent four editions of the play appearing in the next seven years.[30] On 7 January 1605, a performance of *Henry V* provided another reminiscence of Essex.

The showstopper on Twelfth Night was Anne's *Masque of Blackness* written for the court by Ben Jonson, combining conventional comedy with ballet and pageantry. It was performed by the queen, despite her being six months pregnant, and eleven ladies of the court, dressed identically as blackened nymphs, the daughters of the 'Niger'. They were grouped in six pairs, each identified with a badge painted on fans. Lucy Bedford, who was next to the queen, and Penelope took part, but Dorothy and Arbella Stuart were indisposed with measles. (This did not prevent Dorothy becoming a godmother to Anne's baby, Princess Mary, on her arrival later in the year.) The great chamber at Whitehall was transformed by Inigo Jones into 'a landscape from which 'an artificial sea was seen to shoot forth'. There were Tritons, mermaids and two huge seahorses clad in 'blues and greens, shells and seaweed', demonstrating Jones's 'mastery of stage machinery and décor'.[31] A 'great concave shell, like mother of pearl' seemed to 'move on those waters and rise with the billow'.[32] The queen and her ladies who rode inside it wore dresses 'made from luxurious filmy fabrics in azure and silver, 'best setting off from the black' paint of their arms and faces'.[33] The shell was lit from above with 'a chevron of lights' striking 'a glorious beam upon them'.[34] Beside them, six sea-monsters carried twelve torch-bearers on their backs, with their loose hair garlanded with 'sea-grass', into which were stuck 'branches of coral'.[35]

With 'pretty songs filling intervals of rest', the nymphs came ashore to choose partners from among 'the men of England'.[36]

Despite Ben Jonson's enthusiasm, praise was not universal. The prim Sir Dudley Carleton thought there was too much fish and too little water.[37] Despite the rich costumes, he believed them 'too light and courtesan-like' for great ladies.[38] He also disapproved of the ladies making themselves unrecognisable with their skin blackened. The banquet afterwards turned into a drunken orgy with 'even great persons prostituting their bodies to the intent to satisfy and consume their substance in lascivious appetites of all sorts'.[39] Penelope's aunt, Lady Clifford, had earlier concluded: 'All the ladies about the Court had gotten such ill names that it was grown a scandalous place and the queen herself was much fallen from her former greatness and reputation.'[40]

At last, Charles had time to relax. In March 1605, Cranborne invited him to Theobalds to go hawking, a sport in which he delighted. The other guests were Northampton, Cumberland and, perhaps surprisingly, Southampton. The king does not seem to have been there, but this was a pastime in which he also took pleasure, and Charles accompanied him on other occasions.[41]

James's extravagance and lavish gifts to fellow Scots were already causing dissent, only adding to feelings of betrayal by Catholics at his religious stance. Living in constant fear of assassination, he shunned public appearances and took his pleasures privately with his favourites. In the autumn of 1605, 'resentment revealed itself in a plot to blow up the houses of Parliament while he was in attendance', initiated by a group of Catholics who had received no relief from the heavy fines which had been imposed for their part in Essex's rebellion. Six of them, led by the charismatic and well-connected Robert Catesby, turned to a Yorkshire-born mercenary, Guido Fawkes, to undertake the crime. When the undercroft of the Houses of Parliament was searched at midnight on 4 November, Fawkes was found holding a smoking fuse next to thirty-six barrels of powder. Although he is now remembered as the culprit, Catesby had been the ringleader, and Cranborne, who had infiltrated spies into the conspiracy, probably allowed it to develop to its dramatic denouement to remind everyone of the threat posed by Essex's rebellion.

Efforts were made to assess the extent of foreign support for the plot. As a privy councillor and Master of the Ordnance, Charles was given instructions to lead 1,200 gentlemen to find the conspirators who had fled 'to those countries where the Robin Hoods are assembled, to encourage the good to terrify the bad'.[42] With Cranborne (now raised to Earl of Salisbury) having established their whereabouts, he concluded that Charles's force would not be required. The plotters were arrested before Charles could catch up with them but he was one of the seven commissioners appointed to examine them. Being the king's military adviser, he wrote to James: 'God preserve you ever, and be not too careless of yourself, since God hath shown himself so careless of yourself.'[43] Northumberland, whose agent and distant relative Thomas Percy was one of those implicated, was also arrested and held at Lambeth Palace.

Chapter 40

Charles and Penelope's home life and her divorce from Rich, 1603–06

Charles's and Penelope's lives were certainly full, but Charles was unwell and his letters make frequent reference to fevers, migraines which lasted for several days, 'desperate sickness' (presumably vomiting), and lameness, a legacy of the wound that he had received at Arnhem twenty years earlier. He was never in robust health and his stint in Ireland had taken its toll. In its latter stages, his illness was often referred to as pneumonia, implying that cancer had taken a hold over his lungs. Despite his joy at being back with Penelope, he was deteriorating. They spent the summer of 1603 relaxing with their children at Wanstead. Although he continued to supervise Irish affairs, he 'delighted in study, in gardens, a house richly furnished and delectable rooms of retreat'.[1] He played shovelboard or cards, read books, built up his library and fished in his ponds.[2] He was now the natural successor to Leicester as the literary patron of his age, with numerous dedications alluding to his financial support. These often cited his military achievements and depicted him as Sidney's courtly successor.[3] Works by John Florio and Thomas Campion were dedicated to Penelope, harking back to her days as Astrophil's lover, whose dulcet voice now bewitched the ruler of the Irish.[4]

Charles enjoyed expensive food and wines, drinking 'plentifully but never to great excess'.[5] The king and queen visited him at Wanstead as did the Spanish peace negotiators, who 'made a merry journey' there after calling on Cranborne at Theobalds. Moryson reported that Charles 'crammed their stomachs with all manner of dainties' before returning them to London.[6]

After their three-and-a-half year separation, Charles and Penelope, now aged 40, had time to renew their love affair. She was still considered a beauty, and rumours that he had strayed elsewhere cannot be confirmed. It was hinted that he had affairs with Ormonde's daughter and heiress, Elizabeth Butler, and even with Arbella Stuart, but both seem pure gossip.[7] His relationship with Penelope seems to have gained general acceptance at court, despite their increasingly prominent positions. After having nursed Rich at Leighs in the autumn of 1600, Penelope had lived apart from him, but they became formally separated after Essex's execution.

Following Sir Christopher Blount's execution, Lettice retired to Drayton Bassett but needed Penelope's help in fighting a legal challenge from Leicester's illegitimate son, Robert Sheffield, now calling himself Robert Dudley. Although he was one of his father's principal heirs, his socially ambitious wife, Alice Leigh, persuaded him to claim that his parents were legally married, making him rightfully both Earl of Leicester and Warwick's heir, although their inheritance had already passed to Leicester's nephew, Robert Sidney. By implying that Leicester's marriage to Lettice had been bigamous, Dudley could claim both Essex House and Wanstead. This may have been in retaliation for an attempt by Sir Christopher to claim Kenilworth on Lettice's behalf, even though the remainder had been entailed to Dudley on Warwick's death. With Sir Christopher having made forcible entry, 'it took an order from the Privy Council to dislodge him'.[8]

In 1603, Dudley went to court to prove his legitimacy. Although Elizabeth would have dismissed such a plea during her lifetime, Lettice was obliged to file a bill in the Court of Star Chamber against his claim and against his mother, Douglas, and stepfather, Sir Edward Stafford. Penelope was able to use her influence to establish that Dudley's procedure in bringing the action was unlawful, thereby ending it before it began. Even so, an examination of the court papers shows that his case was highly suspect. He left his wife in disgust and was given leave to travel, accompanied by his beautiful cousin Elizabeth Southwell dressed as a boy. After settling in Italy, they never returned.

Penelope's next project was to plan the marriage of her eldest son, Robert Rich, to Frances Hatton, the only child and heiress of the wealthy Sir William Hatton. She was a great catch and Penelope seems to have needed all her considerable charm to win her over. Despite his wealth and prospects, her son seems to have lacked charm, and the Hattons disapproved of his puritanical bent. Although the marriage went ahead, it did not prove a success. In June, it was the turn of Penelope's nephew, Essex's 'Little Robin'. He married Frances Howard, daughter of the Earl of Suffolk. This, too, was famously unhappy.

On 14 November 1605, Penelope went to court to seek a divorce from Rich. There has been considerable debate on what prompted this, but its timing seems to have been designed to avoid attention during the height of the Gunpowder Plot crisis. She managed to gain Rich's cooperation to prevent Charles's name being cited. 'After a week-long hearing in the ecclesiastical court of London, a divorce decree was passed on Penelope and her husband. Lord Rich had sued for it on the grounds that his wife had committed adultery with a stranger – a man she would not name – and Penelope had confessed.'[9] She provided enough evidence for the judges to find her guilty, despite this causing Rich to be labelled a cuckold. The court agreed a legal separation, not an annulment, which would have required an act of parliament and would have made all her children illegitimate. Nevertheless, under its terms neither party could remarry during the lifetime of the other, and the court warned them to live celibately. Although Archbishop Bancroft of Canterbury, as one of the judges, criticised Rich's puritanism and was won over by Penelope's charms, the legal action severely dented her reputation.

Despite being branded as the disagreeable party in the divorce proceedings, Rich gives every appearance of having acted extraordinarily reasonably. He was granted custody of their children, but 'did not attempt to file a civil suit in the Court of King's Bench or Common Pleas for damages against his wife's lover, as he was entitled to'.[10] He had no immediate plans to remarry and had lived for years with the embarrassment of his wife having a lover, but his marriage to her had had its compensations, gaining him James's favour as a member of the Essex faction.

Six weeks later, on 26 December, Charles and Penelope married in a quiet ceremony at Wanstead, just as her mother and Leicester had done thirty years earlier. Charles's chaplain, William Laud, officiated. They all knew that it was illegal, and any hope of 'burying' it beneath the drama of the Gunpowder Plot completely failed. Laud seems to have been placed under great pressure by Charles and was not won over easily, but believed it was reasonable in 'a court of conscience'.

Charles tried to imply that he had already entered into a pre-contract with Penelope before her marriage to Rich. If true, it would have made her marriage to Rich invalid and his children illegitimate, but they had probably not even met at this time. He described how in 1581, Penelope:

> being in the power of her friends, was by them married against her will unto one against whom she did protest at the very solemnity, and ever after; between whom from the first day there ensued continual discord, although the same fears that forced her to marry constrained her to live with him.[11]

He claimed that, instead of being her 'comforter', Rich 'did study in all things to be her tormenter'.[12] He even suggested that it was 'awe of her brother's powerfulness' that kept Rich from 'any open wrong', and that after Essex's death he 'abandoned her and cheated her out of her dowry'. There was no truth in any of this, or in his claim that it was Rich who had initiated the divorce using threats to force her to confess to adultery. The whole idea seems to have been dreamt up by William Heylin, Laud's secretary and biographer, who was trying to protect Laud after officiating at the illegal marriage ceremony. This had severely dented Laud's reputation in the eyes of James I. He remained penitent about the deception for the rest of his life.

The marriage of Charles and Penelope was not undertaken on a whim. They had been planning it as soon he returned from Ireland. Being illegitimate, their children could not inherit his titles, which became extinct on his death, but their marriage would greatly facilitate their inheritance of his wealth and estates. Charles knew that his days were numbered and, at the age of 42, Penelope was again pregnant. They were hoping that any illegality would be conveniently brushed to one side, as had often happened during Elizabeth's reign, particularly as James had showered them with honours and 'winked' at their 'sinful' existence.[13]

The couple 'underestimated James's pedantry'.[14] He 'reacted with moral indignation, deeply offended by their breach of the law'.[15] Their marriage challenged his authority by flouting his newly passed Bigamy Act. If Elizabeth had been lax in enforcing divorce laws, James would not be.[16] Charles wrote a *Discourse or Apollogie*, using 'every possible legal, moral and religious argument' to gain James's acceptance.[17] The king was unimpressed and probably showed Rich what Charles had written about him. 'No amount of intellectualising, subtle arguments from scripture or pathetic pleas would persuade James to tolerate non-conformity to *any* of his decrees.'[18] He undoubtedly saw Penelope as the guilty party, dominant and manipulative. He told Charles: 'You have won a fair woman with a black soul.'[19] In early 1606, she was dropped from Anne's list of ladies-in-waiting and was no longer welcome at court.[20]

Charles remained in favour because of his indispensable role in bringing the conspirators in the Gunpowder Plot to trial, and his official business was often transacted in James's company.[21] In March 1606, they even went hawking together, giving him an opportunity to explain his predicament.

Laud admitted that officiating at an illegal marriage ceremony was a poor career move, which delayed his appointment as Archbishop of Canterbury. 'James considered that [he] was not fit for high office' because he had 'a flagrant crime upon him', and was still reminding him of it ten years later.[22] Laud bitterly repented his action, humbling himself before God and fasting on its anniversary ever after. He saw Penelope as 'a lady in whom lodged all attractive graces of beauty, wit and sweetness of behaviour which might render her the mistress of all eyes and hearts'.[23]

James was also critical of those addicted to tobacco. A part of its popularity was a belief that it was an antidote to syphilis.[24] His *Counterblast to Tobacco*, published anonymously, considered 'it as "a custom, loathsome to the eye, hateful to the nose, harmful to the brain, dangerous to the lungs". No "learned man ought to taste it".'[25] He claimed that its effect on 'inward parts' was 'soiling and infecting them with an unctuous and oily kind of soot', which ruined 'the sweetness of man's breath'.[26] Charles's lungs were already damaged. In the autumn of 1565, the Oxford academic and physician Richard Andrews joined his household and only returned to the university after his death.[27]

Sally Varlow believes that James's reaction against the couple was more than a legal nicety and 'went beyond even his usual pedantry'.[28] She argues convincingly that with Salisbury's esteem growing, he was determined to destroy all of Essex's former allies. She cites Northumberland's imprisonment after the Gunpowder Plot as another example of his vindictiveness. Although his agent, Thomas Percy, had indisputably been involved and had visited Syon House briefly on the day before the plot's discovery, he was now dead and could not be examined. Northumberland showed that he was not a practicing Catholic and had planned to attend parliament on the day scheduled for the explosion. He also provided evidence that Thomas Percy had stolen £3,000 from the earldom's rental receipts to fund the plot. None of the surviving conspirators named him when interrogated under torture. Even though all the evidence against him was circumstantial, this would not have prevented Salisbury from poisoning his name privately with the king.[29] His family did not enjoy an unblemished record of loyalty to the Crown. He was unpopular and was known to have voiced his disapproval of James. Nevertheless, Dorothy plucked up courage to tell the king that only he could divert 'the ill will of a certain great personage', but James would not listen.[30] When Northumberland's case was heard in the Star Chamber on 26 June 1606, he was committed for life and fined £30,000. James and Salisbury saw him as a leading Catholic and Dorothy could do nothing to sway them otherwise.

By the beginning of 1606, only Penelope and Charles among the old Essex faction remained unsilenced. Salisbury must have seen their illegal marriage as a heaven-sent opportunity to reduce their standing with James. It is difficult to judge how far Rich was involved, but Margaret Hoby, Penelope's former sister-in-law, reported that he accused Charles of having lied in front of the king. Charles, who was 'weary and melancholy', rapidly lost both friends and influence.[31] Fynes Moryson reported him as 'a man broken by disappointments' with 'a countenance sad and dejected'.[32]

Chapter 41

Charles's tragic end, 1606 onwards

On 25 March 1606, Charles and Fynes Moryson left Wanstead for London to attend the trial at the Guildhall three days later of Father Thomas Garnet, who had admitted hearing the secrets of the Gunpowder Plot conspirators, which the confidentiality of the confessional forbade him from revealing. He was found guilty and died when the crowd yanked down on his legs to break his neck as he was being hung to prevent him suffering disembowelment, despite him having pleaded with the plotters to pull back from their plan.

Charles never reached the Guildhall. He had become feverish with what seemed to be pneumonia. Fynes Moryson described it as a 'burning fever, whereof the first fit being very violent, he called to him his most familiar friends' and his lawyer Joseph Earth, to prepare his will, after being moved to the Savoy in the Strand, where he could be nursed. He was determined to leave his possessions to Penelope and his children but had to be sure that the wording of his will was watertight. There was a huge amount at stake. Lands and fishings granted to him in Ireland had multiplied in value following the end of hostilities and he held property all over England. His common law kinsmen were very likely to squabble to obtain a share. As soon as she heard that he was ill, Penelope, despite her pregnancy, set out with their eldest son, Mountjoy, and arrived to find him calling for his doctor. Blood was let, which probably only hastened his inevitable death.

A complex trust was now set up to prevent his estate passing to some distant kinsman. The trustees were Sir Edward Blount of Kidderminster (Sir Christopher's elder brother), Sir William Godolphin, Henry Berkeley (probably Sir Henry Berkeley of Yarlington – Charles's second cousin), with his two lawyers, Earth and John Wakeman. Suffolk, Southampton, Salisbury, Sir William Knollys and Danvers were appointed overseers. (The inclusion of Salisbury implies that Charles still trusted him, and he certainly supported Penelope's rights under the will.) Earth, whose advice on the divorce and remarriage had not had a happy outcome, was determined to ensure that Charles's wishes could not be challenged. 'A procession of witnesses, lawyers and scribes arrived to prepare and validate his various papers.'[1] Although Charles began to show signs of recovery, he relapsed. Southampton (who was to become his children's guardian) appeared, and was followed by Danvers and others involved. Within a week, Charles was failing fast, but the will was signed and witnessed by Southampton, Laud and Sir Oliver St John (who had served under Charles at Kinsale). Penelope was with him while he died on 3 April. Moryson wrote: 'I never saw a brave spirit part more mildly.'[2] According to a disapproving Father Gerard, Charles's last words called for his 'angel' and not for his God.[3] A contemporary historian, Robert Johnston, 'described the earl dying in Penelope's arms while her tears flowed and she kissed his dear hands and face'.[4] By all accounts he died smiling and peaceful, but she lay weeping in a corner and soon lost her baby.[5]

Charles's body was taken to Wanstead for his funeral, 'wrapped in a winding sheet and strewn with sweet herbs'.[6] Although Penelope's friends came to support her, her remarriage had faced much criticism. The Blount kinsmen were soon attempting to sway public opinion against her with rumours that Charles's will only catered for three of his five children, implying that he was not the father of the other two, but it had, in fact, catered for all of them.

Although the will requested 'an honourable funeral but without superfluous pomp and expense',[7] Charles was granted 'a state funeral and a grand tomb in Westminster Abbey'.[8] John Coprario wrote his *Funeral Tears*, a sequence of exquisitely sad songs as a tribute for Penelope to sing on the lute, employing melodies to evoke those used by Shakespeare in Hamlet, with its perceived evocation of Essex. His words complain at Charles having been slandered by 'the busy ape, the envious bold wolf, and the spiteful snake', before he was cold in his grave.[9] Having been his protégé, John Ford's *Fame's Memorial or The Earl of Devonshire Deceased,* is provocatively dedicated to The Lady Penelope, Countess of Devonshire, and '[deplores] the way his life was unjustly termed disgraceful'.[10]

Before Charles's state funeral, the heralds disputed whether Penelope's arms could be quartered with his. It took until 2 May to establish that they should be excluded. James still considered the marriage unlawful, and she remained a victim of his 'self-righteous prudery'.[11] Daniel's long and fulsome funerary poem avoided mentioning her name.[12] On 7 May, Southampton was chief mourner, assisted by Suffolk and Northampton, at his interment as a bachelor in St Paul's Chapel at Westminster Abbey. Henry IV sent condolences to commiserate with Salisbury over his loss! Even Tyrconnell claimed that his grief was 'intolerable'. Charles's experience in dealing with Irish affairs would be difficult to replace.[13]

In June 1606, Francis Vere succeeded Charles as Governor of Portsmouth and became actively involved in improving the town's defences. He also turned his thoughts to marriage. On 26 October 1607, he espoused the 16-year-old Elizabeth Dent, a stepdaughter of Sir Julius Caesar, with whom he broke his journeys to Portsmouth from Essex. He must have seemed a daunting prospect for a young bride. Nevertheless, she was grief-stricken by his sudden death in London only twenty-two months later at the age of 49. He too was interred at Westminster Abbey, where a handsome monument was erected to his memory. There were no children, but Elizabeth remarried in 1613.

England was a lesser place without the likes of Charles and Francis, who had battled on Elizabeth's behalf. When Anne's brother, King Christian of Denmark, visited London in August, the court was involved in another round of riotous boozing. Although Shakespeare may have provided the first performance of *Macbeth*, no members of the Essex faction were there to see it. When Salisbury entertained the royal party at Theobalds, ladies of the court were rolling around 'sick and spewing' in intoxication.[14]

Penelope spent the summer with her mother at Drayton, taking some of her children with her.[15] With Salisbury having been unwell, she wrote solicitously after his health, but gave no hint of her personal sorrow, although she determinedly signed herself, P. Devonshire. She was also most attentive to her mother who walked for a mile in her park every day for the rest of her long life. Nevertheless, her principal preoccupation was in shouldering the challenge to Charles's will from his Blount kinsmen.

Despite the meticulous drafting of the will and the deed of trust, this did not phase the Blount relations, who challenged everything: the marriage, Penelope's character, the children's paternity and their rights to inherit.[16] In June it was proved in the Prerogative Court of Canterbury, but a complaint was registered on behalf of Charles's second cousin, Sir Richard Champernowne. When the appeal was heard in the Court of Arches, Earth produced eight witnesses to Charles's signature, who also confirmed his 'good and perfect memory'.[17] Although the appeal was thrown out, it was challenged in both the Court of Wards and Court of King's Bench. In December, when these were rejected, Champernowne instituted criminal proceedings against Penelope in the Court of Star Chamber, charging her with forgery and fraud. If she lost, she would face imprisonment, but Earth defended her stalwartly, as did the eight witnesses (including Laud), who hotly denied that Charles was 'crazed, feeble, incoherent, senseless' when he had signed.[18] Accusations that his illness was brought on by grief at his illegal marriage were also dismissed. Penelope denied every slanderous charge, particularly that her pregnancy was fabricated, responding as The Lady Penelope, Countess of Devonshire. Yet again, the will was upheld. Her only concession was to drop the Devonshire title for both herself and her son, being henceforth known only as 'The Lady Penelope'.

Penelope had no hope of making a come-back at court. According to Camden, who wrote on Salisbury's instruction, she had 'violated her husband's bed', and that was an end to it.[19] James became ever closer to Salisbury and was so enamoured of Theobalds and its deer parks that Salisbury offered it to him, being granted the 'clapped-out' Hatfield Palace in place of his 'glorious, gilded mansion'.[20] Although he remained in James's service trying to moderate the crown's expenditure, he was frail and exhausted and died in May 1612.

Anne remained on friendly terms with Dorothy, who shared her Catholic sympathies, visiting her at Syon with its magnificent gardens, whose planting was supervised by Northumberland from the Tower. Penelope probably did not attend, and certainly Anne never visited her at Wanstead. Nevertheless, her own latent Catholic sympathies were again rekindled. She was not without visitors. Frances Walsingham came after remarrying Clanricarde. With Penelope having supported her during her earlier pregnancies, it was now Frances's turn. Despite approaching 40, Frances provided Clanricarde with three children, and the couple were converted to Catholicism by Father Gerard.[21] Even now, Clanricarde remained on good terms with James, who greatly respected his insight into Irish affairs.

Penelope remained close to her children. Charles's eldest daughter, Penelope, was now 15 and would soon need her promised dowry. She also had their second daughter, the 12-year-old Isabella, to consider. Southampton proved a model father-figure to the three boys, having been a close friend to Charles, while Elizabeth Vernon was always more of a sister to Penelope than a cousin.[22]

In early July, Penelope came to London to attend the end of the Star Chamber trial but she too became unwell. Her illness was described as a fever with the symptoms of a summer cold, from which she had suffered previously. This may have turned to pneumonia. It has also been suggested that her miscarriage had caused complications, although she had seemed to make a good recovery. Whatever the cause, she died on 6 July 1607 aged 44. There is no official record of where she was, but was reported to have called for Dr Layfield, the rector of St Clement Danes, which suggests that Dorothy may have been caring for her at Essex House. This had become a papist enclave occupied by Northumberland's brothers. Gerard later claimed that Penelope converted to Catholicism on her deathbed. If so, calling for Layfield may have been a fabrication unless it was to confirm her death officially.

Despite the many compliments showered on Penelope in her lifetime, it is not known where she was interred. There is no record at St Clement Danes and her death caused a 'posthumous silence'.[23] Although Thomas Campion referred to her as 'Stella, Britanna, Penelope', other comments were more ribald.[24] An anonymous author wrote:

> She shuffled, she cut, she dealt, she played,
> She died neither wife, widow nor maid.

Penelope's reputation was tarnished, and no one was defending it.

It was not until 1616 that Rich remarried the wealthy Frances Wray, the widow of Sir George St Paul of Snareford, although this does not seem to have provided him with consolation. In 1618, with Warwick having died without issue, Rich bought the Earldom for £10,000 to assist James's impoverished Exchequer but survived for less than a year. His son Robert, who inherited as the 2nd Earl, remained a confirmed Puritan, later becoming Admiral of the Fleet in the Parliamentary forces. In contrast, his brother Henry, who inherited Penelope's charm and good looks, became a Royalist, with 'a penchant for political intrigue, passionate affairs and characterful women'.[25] He married the wealthy Isobel Cope, through whom he inherited half of Kensington and was later created Earl of Holland. He was executed by the parliamentarians in 1649.

With both Charles and Penelope dead, it was Lettice at Drayton Bassett who lived on as the family matriarch, much cherished as a 'highly thought of old lady'. She was 'a brisk and benevolent grandmother to 'the grandchildren of her grandchildren', enjoying their company on their regular visits. Her grandson, 'Little Robin', became an active parliamentarian, but after two failed marriages and with doubtful sexual orientation, lived nearby at Chartley, spending a part of every winter with her. She died in 1634 aged 91 and was buried at Warwick, next to her adored Leicester. Her epitaph states that 'the poor that lived near, death nor famine could not fear'.[26]

Dorothy battled bravely to gain Northumberland's release from the Tower, although he lived there in some style while conducting his scientific experiments in apartments which he redecorated in the Martin Tower. In 1618, six years after Cecil's death, she negotiated a reduction in his fine from £30,000 to £11,000.[27] Northumberland seems to have enjoyed an affair during his incarceration and, in his last few years there, Dorothy rarely visited him.[28] Nevertheless, he was 'inconsolable' on her death in 1619, and she was buried with full ceremony at Petworth. (Petworth House had always been the Percys' principal southern residence, although they occupied Syon or Essex House, if needing to be closer to court.) He was eventually released from the Tower in 1621 and moved to live at Petworth, where he died in 1632.

This leaves Raleigh, whose final years are a story on their own, and are outlined in Endnote 5.

Endnotes

Endnote 1

The parentage of Catherine Carey

Several eminent historians have suggested that Mary Boleyn's daughter, Catherine Carey, was an illegitimate child of Henry VIII as perhaps was her brother, Henry Carey. This is by no means certain but, if so, it will have had a bearing on Elizabeth's attitude to Penelope's mother, Lettice, who was described by her as a 'she-wolf' for having married Leicester. It is worth exploring this in more detail.

Mary Boleyn was the daughter of the able but ambitious diplomat Sir Thomas Boleyn and his wife Elizabeth Howard, and a grandchild of the 2nd Duke of Norfolk. She was born in about 1499. Having remained in England until 1514, her father secured her a position as maid-of-honour to Henry VIII's sister, Princess Mary, when she travelled to France to marry the elderly Louis XII. When Louis died on 1 January 1515, Princess Mary, now dowager queen of France, returned to England after hastily marrying Henry's close friend, Charles Brandon. With her father being appointed the English ambassador, Mary Boleyn remained behind at the French court in the service of Francis I.

During her period in France, Mary Boleyn is reputed to have been involved in several affairs – one with Francis I. The French king reportedly referred to her as 'The English Mare'[1] and 'una grandissima ribalda, infame sopra tutte [a very great whore, the most infamous of all]'.[2] These quotations must be considered doubtful. They were first reported in 1536, when Henry was seeking a divorce from her sister Anne. Furthermore, Mary did not become pregnant at a time when there was no satisfactory method of birth control.

In late 1519 Mary returned to England, and was married to William Carey on 4 February 1520. Carey was one of the squires of the body of

Henry VIII and a Beaufort connection of the king. During 1526, when Henry was seeking a divorce from Catherine of Aragon to enable him to marry Anne Boleyn, he told his kinsman Reginald Pole, who at that time was Dean of Wimborne Minster, that he had conducted an affair with her sister Mary in 1519, but that it had been of short duration. The implication is that this was before her marriage to Carey. As his illegitimate son Henry Fitzroy was born on 15 June 1519, it is thought that Henry ended his relationship with Bessie Blount at about this time, after which, in 1522, she married Gilbert Tailboys. It is not known if her departure was hastened by Henry having a new relationship with Mary after her return from France.

By 1526, Henry wanted a divorce from Catherine of Aragon and was seeking assistance from Pole to intercede with the Papacy. As Pole was studying abroad from 1521 to 1526, he would not have had first-hand knowledge of Henry's liaisons, and Henry will have fed to him what he wanted him to believe. Henry's great concern was that an earlier relationship with Mary Boleyn might prejudice the legitimacy of his marriage to her sister Anne. He certainly would not want to admit to having had children by Mary, when his objective was for Anne to provide him with a legitimate male heir.

Mary is known to have had two children, Henry and Catherine. Henry 'Carey' was born in 1526 and it had been thought that Catherine was younger. However, the births of Catherine's children recorded by her husband Sir Francis Knollys in his Latin Dictionary show that the eldest, Harry, was born on Easter Day, 1541. It also records his marriage to Catherine on 26 April 1540.[3] As it would be unusual for a woman to give birth under the age of 17, this makes it more probable that Catherine was born between 1521 and 1523. Furthermore, it would be surprising if her mother had to wait for six years of marriage before producing a child.

Is there a possibility that either of Mary's children were by Henry VIII? We do not know, and Henry never acknowledged her children or provided for their education as he had for Henry Fitzroy. Nevertheless, there is a reasonable explanation for this. While Bessie Blount remained unmarried during her affair with the king, Mary was married to William Carey and any relationship with the king would contravene the sanctity of marriage and the Ten Commandments. With Henry wanting a son, he would have had no interest in announcing the birth of a daughter by Mary. By the time of Henry Carey's arrival, he was already seeking a divorce from Catherine of Aragon to marry Anne. If he could not admit paternity, he would hardly provide financial support, although he asked Thomas Boleyn to do so and Anne Boleyn, once she was queen, helped her sister.

The evidence for the Carey children being by Henry is based on several factors:

1. Henry made a series of grants of land to William Carey between 1522 and 1525, which looks like a pay-off. It was not unusual for favoured courtiers to receive grants, but their timing in this instance seems to be more than a coincidence.

2. In 1539, as has been explained in the main text, Catherine Carey was appointed by Henry VIII to the coveted role as maid-of-honour to Queen Anne of Cleves, a position, generally reserved for a princess of the royal blood.

3. Elizabeth always showed great deference to both the Carey children. This may have been because they were her Boleyn cousins, but Catherine was given an exalted role as her senior Lady of the Bedchamber, and Henry was created Lord Hunsdon, the name of which was taken from a royal palace, well before he had made his mark as a soldier.

4. During Mary Tudor's reign, Francis Knollys and Catherine escaped England as determined Protestants to live in Frankfurt. At Elizabeth's request (as has been shown), Lettice remained with her at Hatfield and was there from the age of 10 to 16. This was a singular honour for Lettice during a stressful period for Elizabeth.

5. In 1565, Catherine's eldest son, Henry Knollys, married Margaret Cave of another respected court family. As a mark of signal royal respect, the wedding programme included 'a supper, a ball, a "tourney" and two masques, the feasting ending at half past one'. This was one of only three such wedding 'tourneys' during Elizabeth's reign, the other two being for earls.[4]

6. Catherine bears a strong likeness to Henry VIII in the painting of her. This is not so true of Henry Carey. While it is possible that by the time of his birth the royal affair was over, there is still evidence to suggest that he was Henry VIII's son. Of course, the Boleyns and the Careys were related to Henry down several lines, but there is nothing in their respective pedigrees to justify the sort of likeness that could exist between father and daughter.

7. Elizabeth, who was never noted for her generosity, paid for Catherine's magnificent funeral ceremony after her death in 1569, as she was later to do for Hunsdon's in 1596. This was a grand occasion at Westminster Abbey. Would she have done this for her cousin? Is it more likely, as Varlow suggests, that he was her half-brother? The tomb makes no mention of his father's name, and the massive cost of £800 eclipsed what she paid for her other 'cousins', Margaret Douglas, Countess of Lennox, and Frances Brandon, Duchess of Suffolk.

8. It has also been suggested that Elizabeth's hatred of Lettice, after her secret marriage to Leicester, was influenced by her recognition that Lettice was of royal blood. She never seems to have been similarly jealous of Douglas Howard.

On balance, I believe that Hunsdon and Catherine Carey were Henry VIII's children.

Endnote 2

The date of birth of Robert Dudley ('The Noble Imp')
Varlow (p.77), Tallis (p.189) and Veerapen (p.36) record that the Noble Imp was born on 6 June 1581 at Leicester House. This is based on records identified by Simon Adams of the University of Strathclyde in *The Papers of Robert Dudley III*. These imply that Lettice suffered two failed pregnancies before achieving the birth of Robert's son. As she was wearing a loose-fitting gown at the time of her two marriages to Robert in April and September 1578, it is assumed that she was pregnant then and that this precipitated their decision to marry. Varlow also records that the French Ambassador reported her as being pregnant in February 1579 while staying at Grey's Court. (p.78) Wilson says that the child was born before the end of 1579, which presumably was designed to tie in with the Ambassador's report. Jenkins says that the Noble Imp was born 'at the end of 1579, or the beginning of 1580' (p.252), which does not fit with her already being pregnant in the previous February. Stewart claims that he was born in April 1581. (p.235) We also know that before the child's death on 19 July 1584, he had been strong enough in the spring of that year to climb on a stool and to deface a picture of a lady 'in a

petticoat of yellow satin'. (Tallis, p.206) If he were still not yet aged 3, would he have been able to do this? It may seem more likely that he was born earlier.

The significance of the timing of the Noble Imp's birth is that it ended Philip Sidney's expectation of becoming Warwick's and Leicester's heir. On 15 May 1581, Philip took part in a lavish pageant at court to entertain a French delegation which had arrived to promote Anjou's marriage to Elizabeth. It is thought that Philip was heavily involved in writing it. Camden claimed that Philip used the opportunity of the pageant to demonstrate that his hopes of inheritance were blighted as a result of the birth of the Noble Imp. Instead of using his usual motto of SPERO (I hope), he used SPERAVI (I used to hope) with a line through it, to show that his hopes had been dashed. This would suggest that the Noble Imp was born before the pageant, although the record identified by Simon Adams says that his birth was on 6 June. If Simon Adams's record is correct, Philip might still have believed that he had the prospect of making an appropriate spouse for Penelope. The child might not have survived its birth or might have been a daughter.

It is, of course, entirely possible that the change in the motto had nothing to do with the Noble Imp's birth. It would be equally applicable, if Philip had realised that his hopes of marrying Penelope were dashed by her engagement to Robert Rich.

Endnote 3

Elizabeth's appearance when older

Elizabeth is often depicted in old age with heavy white makeup giving her a clown-like appearance to cover the blemishes caused by her smallpox, and with blackened teeth, which made her repellent to her younger favourites. The Ditchley portrait of 1592, when she was aged 59 shows no hint of her being haggard or grotesque. She was of course carefully made up and coiffed to look younger and her magnificent dress shows off her fine figure. It has been suggested that talcum powder was rubbed into her skin with cheeks and lips being blushed.[1] Nevertheless, there is no contemporary evidence that she was pockmarked. There can be little doubt that her teeth were very poor by this stage, like most contemporaries of her age. Poor oral hygiene and a diet of sugary sweetmeats caused dental decay. In all her portraits, even when a young girl, her mouth remains tightly shut. Nevertheless, this did not prevent her from making eye-catching appearances, as she did at Tilbury in 1588, when aged 55.

Endnote 4

Penelope's children by Charles

Details of Penelope's five children by Rich have been outlined on pages 24 and 25 but she then produced a further five by Charles, who initially took the surname 'Rich', in addition to a miscarriage shortly after Charles's death. After the birth of Penelope 'Rich' at Leicester House on 30 March 1592, there is a baptismal record for Isabella 'Rich' at St Clement Danes in January 1595. She was followed by Mountjoy in 1596; St John, for whom there is a baptismal record as 'Scipio Rich' at St Clement Danes in December 1597; and Charles who was born in 1600.

The eldest daughter, Penelope, was 15 when her mother died, and her dowry was not available to her until she was 18. In 1608, when she was 16, she married Sir Gervase Clifton, a Royalist politician, who was created a baronet in 1611. She probably added a couple of years to her age to allow the marriage to go ahead and seems to have got away with it. They had a son, also Sir Gervase, born in 1612, but she died in the following year. Isabella, who reportedly looked like her mother, married Sir John Smythe, who became a member of parliament, but she died in 1632 after having two children. Her son, Robert Smythe, married Dorothy, a great niece of Sir Philip Sidney. Her daughter Letitia Isabella, born in 1630, married first John Robartes, 1st Earl of Radnor, and second Charles Cheyne, 1st Viscount Newhaven. Mountjoy Blount, who inherited the principal parts of his father's estate, remained for some years in the cloud caused by Penelope's disgrace. This did not prevent him from coming to court and becoming a favourite of James I. He was created Earl of Newport in 1617 but was required to hand over Wanstead to the Exchequer in compensation. His politics became uncertain, and he teetered between Parliamentarian and Royalist affiliation during the Civil War. St John Blount became a knight of the Bath in 1625 at the coronation of Charles I. His daughter, Penelope, married Dr Stephen Goffe, a royal chaplain. Very little is known about the youngest son, Charles Blount, who appears to have been killed in 1627, possibly in action on the Ile de Ré.

Endnote 5

Raleigh's final years – 1604–18

'Raleigh spent ... twelve years in the Tower of London in considerable comfort' with 'his books and chemical experiments'.[1] Bess wrote to Salisbury to seek compassion for her husband, but her letters went unheeded, and she had to pawn her jewels to provide for her family and she took on his business commitments. Nevertheless, they both believed that Salisbury would honour the trust protecting their ownership of the Sherborne estate. Having spent some time with him in the Tower, the 39-year-old Bess found she was pregnant and, to avoid the plague, moved out to a house at Tower Hill, where her son Carew was born in February 1605. Five months earlier, Raleigh had suffered a stroke, causing temporary loss of feeling in his limbs. After being permitted to build a little room in the garden at the Tower to provide him with warmer accommodation, he rapidly recovered. Being connected to many of the Gunpowder Plot conspirators, he found himself placed under a more stringent regime closely watched by Salisbury. Despite his efforts to develop a rapport with the king by proposing a more belligerent policy against Spain (notwithstanding that he had been imprisoned for having supported the Spanish), these proved counterproductive.

While imprisoned he wrote *The History of the World*, sourced from his library of 500 books, but it was suppressed in the light of its criticism of past monarchs and his calls for freedom of speech. James retaliated by reclaiming the Sherborne estate for his mignon, Robert Carr, when a defect was found in the trust deed protecting its ownership, but Bess was able to claim compensation.

In 1607, Raleigh approached Salisbury with an offer to fund another expedition to 'Guiana', promising the king untold wealth in return for his freedom. Both James and Salisbury were sceptical, and it was not until Salisbury's death in 1612 that Raleigh renewed his efforts with Bess's help, after gaining support from James's new favourite, Robert Villiers. Although he was released from the Tower in March 1616, he remained unpardoned. Despite facing great difficulties in organising the voyage, he set out fifteen months later with 500 men, including his son, Wat (who was already showing signs of waywardness and aggression), and his old friend Keymis, on seven men-of-war and three pinnaces. The estimated cost of £10,000 was principally funded by Bess out of the compensation from Sherborne. His objective was to find a gold mine near San Thome in the Orinoco delta, to where he was returning after an absence of twenty years.

After facing heavy weather, in which one of their pinnaces was lost, he put into Cork to make repairs, eventually setting out again on 19 August 1617. He was now in his early sixties. He had considerably embellished his account of his previous voyage and seemed to be seduced with a 'fatal amnesia' of the riches available. After a short stop for provisions in the Canaries, where a small Dutch flotilla joined his little fleet, they headed for the Orinoco but endured hurricane weather which caused sickness on board and several deaths. Four smaller vessels were lost, and a man-of-war deserted. With water in short supply, Raleigh was incapacitated by fever and was stuck in the 'filthy stench' of his ship. On reaching the Orinoco, he was at last able to land and a former native servant appeared with bread and local produce.

On 10 December, Raleigh sent Keymis and Wat with 400 men and a month's supply of provisions in five small boats for the three-week journey to San Thome. On arrival, Wat was killed after hot-headedly attacking the Spanish garrison, which had received warning of their arrival. Having established control, Keymis plundered goods worth 30,000 ducats, including tobacco, and set off with a smaller party into the interior. Despite travelling 180 miles upstream, he found nothing. On his return, he set light to San Thome in reprisal for Spanish guerrilla attacks on the men he had left there, before rejoining Raleigh to break the news of Wat's death.

With most of the other ships having deserted him, Raleigh returned to England, where he complained that James had revealed his destination to the Spanish (which may have been true). With news of the attack on San Thome reaching England before him, Raleigh was arrested and his ship impounded. He now wrote his *Apology* to provide a fanciful account of the expedition. On reaching London, he had become genuinely ill with a ruptured hernia and constipation and was permitted to occupy Bess's house in Broad Street, from where he contemplated escaping to France. With the Spanish seeking his head, he recognised that he was doomed when James returned him to the Tower.

Although Raleigh was suffering from malaria, James gave instructions for him to appear before commissioners to approve a warrant for his execution, being still under sentence for his perceived part in the 'main' plot. He was accused of lying to the king about the promised goldmine and of attempting to incite war with Spain. When condemned, he was moved to the Gatehouse prison at Westminster Abbey and was told that he would be executed at a scaffold in the Old Palace Yard on the following day, 29 October 1618. Bess was able to visit him and it was after midnight when she left. He now hoped to have an opportunity to vindicate his actions. The large crowd who came to see him executed were able to hear his forty-five-minute speech. This was a triumphant performance. He refused to admit his guilt and provided his own account of the Guiana voyage. He challenged the king's divine right, and denied having played any part in bringing down Essex, but had shared his desire to destroy Salisbury. He then prayed for fifteen minutes and submitted to execution. It took two blows of the axe.

Truth is stranger than fiction.

Bibliography

Adams, Simon, *The Papers of Robert Dudley, Earl of Leicester,* London Archives ('Adams')

American Musicological Society, Journal of

Archer, Dr Ian, *London-Derry Connections; The early years, 1613–1640,* Gresham College lecture, 2013 ('Archer')

Bardon, Jonathan, *The Plantation of Ulster, The British Colonisation of the North of Ireland in the Seventeenth Century,* Gill & MacMillan, Dublin, 2011 ('Bardon')

Beer, Anna, *Patriot or Traitor – The Life and death of Sir Walter Ralegh,* Oneworld Publications, 2018 ('Beer')

Bentley, Sir Henry, *Original Letters Illustrative of English History,* Letter CCXIII The Earl of Essex to Lord Burghley, London, 1827 ('Bentley')

Birch, Thomas, *Memoirs of the Reign of Queen Elizabeth,* II, A. Millar, London, 1754 ('Birch')

Black, J.B., *The Reign of Elizabeth (Oxford History of England),* Clarendon Press, Oxford, 1963 ('Black')

Broughton, Richard, *Devereux Papers,* ed. H.E. Malden, Camden Miscellany, NS, XIII, 1923 ('Broughton')

Devereux, Walter Bourchier, *Lives and Letters of the Devereux Earls of Essex,* John Murray London, 1853 ('Devereux')

Camden, William, *The Historie of the Most renowned and Victorious Princess Elizabeth, late Queene of England,* London 1630 ed. W. T MacCaffrey, 1970 ('Camden')

Campion, Thomas, *Umbra,* from Campion's Works, ed. Vivian, Percival ('Campion')

Canny, Nicholas, *The Elizabethan Conquest of Ireland: A Pattern Established, 1565–76,* Hassocks, Sussex, 1776 ('Canny')

Bibliography

Cheyney, Edward P., *A History of England from the Defeat of the Armada to the Death of Elizabeth*, Longmans, Green and Company, New York, 1926 ('Cheyney')

Collins, Arthur, *Memorials, Actions and Lives of the Sidneys,* Vol. I, London, 1746 ('Collins')

Croft, Pauline, *The Reputation of Robert Cecil: Libels, Political Opinion and Popular Awareness in the Early Seventeenth Century,* Transactions of the Royal Historical Society, 1991 ('Croft')

Curl, James Stevens, *The Londonderry Plantation, 1609–1914,* Philimore and Co. Limited, Chichester, 1986 ('Curl')

Falls, Cyril, *Mountjoy – Elizabethan General,* Odhams Press Limited, 1955 ('Falls')

Feuillerat, Albert (ed.), *The Prose Works of Sir Philip Sidney,* OUP, 1912 ('Feuillerat')

Fitzwilliam Virginal Book, 1610–25, First published 1899

Fraser, Antonia, Mary Queen of Scots, *Weidenfeld & Nicolson, 1974* ('Fraser')

Froude, James Anthony, *Life and Letters of Erasmus,* Charles Scribner's Sons, New York, 1895 ('Froude')

Geni

Gerard, John, *The Autobiography of an Elizabethan,* trans. from Latin by Philip Caraman, Longmans, Green & Co., 1956 ('Gerard')

Goodman, Dr Godfrey, Bishop of Gloucester, (ed.) Brewer, John S., *The Court of King James the First,* Richard Bentley, London, 1839 ('Goodman')

Harrison, G.B., *The Life and Death of Robert Devereux Earl of Essex,* Henry Holt & Co., New York, 1937 ('Harrison')

Hentzner, Paul, *England as seen by Foreigners,* 1598, John Russell Smith, 1865 ('Hentzner')

Hume, Martin Andrew Sharp, *The Great Lord Burghley; A Study in Elizabethan Statecraft,* Longmans, Green, and Co., New York, 1898 ('Hume')

James VI of Scotland, *Correspondence of, with Sir Robert Cecil and Others in England,* Camden Society ('James VI correspondence')

Jenkins, Elizabeth, *Elizabeth & Leicester,* Victor Gollancz, 1961 ('Jenkins')

Jones, Frederick M., *Mountjoy, 1563–1606:the last Elizabethan Deputy,* Clonmore & Reynolds Ltd. Dublin/London,1958 ('Jones')

Kearsley, C. and G., *A Selection from the Harleian Miscellany of Tracts,* London, 1793 ('Kearsley')

Knox, Thomas Francis, *Letters and memorials of William, Cardinal Allen, 1882* ('Knox')

Lacey, Robert, *Robert, Earl of Essex: An Elizabethan Icarus,* (Phoenix Press, London, 1971 ('Lacey')

Lodge, Edmund, (ed.), *Illustrations of British History, Biography, and Manners,* II, G. Nicol, London, 1791 ('Lodge')

Madden, Richard Robert, *The United Irishmen, their lives and times,* J. Madden & Co. London, 1842 ('Madden')

Markham, Sir Clements R., *Sir Francis Vere, Elizabeth I's Greatest Soldier and the Eighty Years War,* Leonaur, 2016 originally published as *The Fighting Veres,* Sampson Low Marston, Seale and Rivington (1888) ('Markham')

Milton, Giles, *Big Chief Elizabeth,* Hodder & Stoughton, London, 2000 ('Milton')

Moryson, Fynes, *An Itinerary,* 1617 ('Moryson')

Motley, John Lothrop, *History of the United Netherlands,* 1860 OUP ('Motley')

Murdin, William, *A collection of state papers relating to affairs in the reign of Queen Elizabeth,* transcribed from originals at Hatfield House ('Murdin')

Naunton, Sir Robert, *Fragmenta Regalia,* 1642, Arber's English Reprints ('Naunton')

Neale, Sir John E., *Queen Elizabeth I,* Jonathan Cape, 1934 ('Neale')

Prior, F., (ed.), *Elizabeth I: Her life in Letters,* Berkeley: University of California Press, 2003 ('Prior')

Rawson, Maud Stepney, *Penelope Rich and her Circle,* 1911 ('Rawson')

Salmon, Thomas, (ed.), *State Trials,* London 1738 ('Salmon')

Sidney, Sir Henry, *Memoir of his government in Ireland 1583,* The Ulster Journal of Archaeology, 5, 1857

Stedall, Robert, *Elizabeth I's Secret Lover – Robert Dudley Earl of Leicester,* Pen & Sword Books Limited, 2020 ('Elizabeth I's Secret Lover')

Stedall, Robert, *The Survival of the Crown,* The Book Guild Limited, 2014 ('The Survival of the Crown')

Stewart, Alan, *Philip Sidney – a double life,* Chatto & Windus 2000, Pimlico edition 2001 ('Stewart')

Strachey, Lytton, *Elizabeth and Essex,* Chatto & Windus, London, 1928 ('Strachey')

Strafford, Sir Thomas, *Paccata Hibernia,* London 1633 ('Paccata Hibernia')

Tallis, Nicola, *Elizabeth's Rival – The Tumultuous Tale of Lettice Knollys, Countess of Leicester,* Michael O'Mara Books Limited, London, 2017 ('Tallis')

Trotter, Stewart, *Just how gay was Henry Wriothesley, the Third Earl of Southampton?* theshakespearscode.blog, ('Trotter')

Tunzelmann, Alex von, Review of the film version of *The Other Boleyn Girl: Holyoaks in Fancy Dress,* 2008 ('von Tunzelmann')

Varlow, Sally, *The Lady Penelope,* André Deutsch, London, 2014 ('Varlow')

Veerapen, Steven, *Elizabeth & Essex, Power, Passion and Politics,* Sharpe Books, 2019 ('Veerapen')

Vere, Sir Francis, *Commentaries,* John Field, 1657 ('Vere')

Warnicke, Retha M., *The Rise and Fall of Anne Boleyn,* Cambridge University Press, 1989 ('Warnicke')

Wikipedia

Wilson, Derek, *Sweet Robin: A Biography of Robert Dudley Earl of Leicester 1533–1588,* Allison & Busby, 1981 ('Sweet Robin')

Wotton, Sir Henry, *A parallel between Robert late Earle of Essex, and George, late Duke of Buckingham,* London, 1641 ('Wotton')

Papers

Acts of the Privy Council ('Privy Council')

BL MS, Lansdowne

Brewer, John Sherren, and Bullen, William, (eds), *Calendar of Carew Manuscripts,* Lambeth Palace Library and Longmans, Green & Co., 1867–73 ('Carew Manuscripts')

D'Ewes, Sir Simonds, Diaries ('D'Ewes')

CSP Domestic 1581–94 ('CSP Dom.1')

CSP Domestic 1595–7 ('CSP Dom. 2')

CSP Domestic 1603–10 ('CSP Dom.3')

CSP Elizabeth, 1580–86 ('CSP Elizabeth 1')

CSP Elizabeth 1587–1603 ('CSP Elizabeth 2')

CSP Foreign Vol XXI, IV ('CSP Foreign')

CSP Holland

CSP Ireland

CSP Simincas 1568–1579 ('CSP Simincas')

Essex Letter Book among Aylesford Papers

Folger Shakespeare Library, Washington ('Folger')

Harington Papers, *Nugae Antiquae,* 1779 ('Nugae Antiquae')

HMC 9, Cecil, IV ('HMC Cecil')

HMC, De L'Isle and Dudley Papers, II, Collins, 1746 ('De L'Isle and Dudley')

HMC 58, Bath V ('HMC Bath')

HMC, 7th Report – Rutland Papers ('Rutland')

HMC, 7th Report – Salisbury Papers ('Salisbury')

Hotman Letters at Teyler's Museum, Haarlem ('Hotman letters')

PRO, SP 84/49, f. 241 ('PRO')

References

Introduction

1. Beer, p.75
2. Markham, p.282

Background

1. Beer, p.132
2. ibid. p.14
3. Veerapen, p.70
4. Beer, p.73
5. ibid. p.74
6. ibid. p.27
7. Devereux, p.3; cited in Tallis, p.53
8. Varlow, p.24
9. ibid. p.23
10. ibid. p.24
11. ibid.
12. Camden, p.80; cited in Tallis, p.55
13. Varlow, p.26
14. ibid. p.27
15. ibid. p.29
16. Shakespeare, William, *I Henry IV*, Act V, Scene III
17. Froude, p.42; cited in Falls, p.16
18. Rutland, p.45; cited in ibid.
19. Camden, p.117: cited in Falls, p.19
20. Falls, p.13
21. ibid.
22. ibid. p.20

PART I: THE DUDLEYS AND THE DEVEREUXES
Chapter 1: Leicester's flirtation with Lettice Knollys

1. Hume, p.174
2. Wikipedia
3. Jenkins, p.185
4. Wikipedia
5. Varlow, p.47
6. CSP Simincas 1568–1579, p.511; cited in Varlow, p.46
7. Jenkins, p.203
8. ibid. p.202
9. Devereux, p.120

Chapter 2: The 1st Earl of Essex's death and his children's education

1. Falls, p.55
2. Sweet Robin, p.227
3. Tallis, p.155
4. Broughton; cited in Varlow, p.49
5. Sir Henry Sidney's Memoir, 5, p 314; cited in Stewart, p.162
6. Canny, pp.90-1; cited in Bardon, p.4
7. Varlow, pp.50-1
8. Tallis, p.143
9. ibid. p.153
10. Varlow, p.51
11. ibid. p.52
12. ibid. p.51
13. Devereux, Vol. I, p.166; cited in Veerapen, p.16
14. Veerapen, p.19
15. Devereux, Vol. I, p.166; cited in ibid. p.16
16. Veerapen, p.16
17. ibid.
18. ibid. p.19
19. Broughton, letter from Richard Bagot February 1578; cited in Veerapen, p.8
20. Varlow, p.56
21. Veerapen, p.18

Chapter 3: Philip Sidney – the moulding of a renaissance diplomat

1. Stewart, p.212
2. ibid. p.213
3. ibid. p.229

Chapter 5: Penelope's arrival at court and marriage to Lord Rich

1. Varlow, p.61
2. ibid. p.65
3. Falls, p.56
4. Cited in Varlow, p.65
5. Varlow, p.73
6. ibid. p.83
7. ibid. p.65
8. Cited in Stewart, pp.239-40
9. Sweet Robin, p.249
10. Varlow, p.78
11. ibid. p.85
12. ibid.
13. ibid. p.80
14. ibid. p.85
15. ibid. pp.86-7
16. ibid. p.86
17. ibid. p.87
18. ibid. p.86
19. Hotman letters No. 43; cited in ibid. p.86
20. Varlow, p.87

Chapter 6: Dorothy Devereux

1. Adams, III, p.3; cited in Varlow, p.88
2. CSP Elizabeth 1, III, p.451, cited in Tallis, p.196
3. Varlow, p.89

Chapter 7: Robert Devereux, 2nd Earl of Essex

1. Wotton, p.1; cited in Tallis, p.211
2. Bentley pp.80-1; cited in Veerapen, p.35
3. Veerapen, p.35
4. Varlow, p.94

PART II: DEVELOPMENT OF MILITARY AND COURTLY SKILLS
Chapter 8: Raleigh's arrival at court and his project to colonise 'Virginia'

1. Beer, p.77
2. ibid. p.130
3. ibid. p.77
4. ibid. p.28

5. ibid. p.41
6. ibid. p.28
7. ibid. p.31
8. ibid. pp.33-5
9. ibid. p.43

Chapter 9: Essex's success at court and with Leicester in the Low Countries

1. Tallis, p.212
2. Veerapen, p.39
3. Lacey, p.24; cited in ibid. p.41
4. Veerapen, p.70
5. ibid. p.72
6. ibid. p.73
7. ibid. p.89
8. Varlow, p.126
9. Varlow, p.96
10. Varlow, p.95; Veerapen p.48
11. Folger L, a, 566; cited in Varlow, p.95
12. Veerapen, p.50
13. Motley, pp.32-3; cited in ibid. p.51
14. PRO; cited in Veerapen, p.55
15. Feuillerat, p.316; cited in Veerapen, p.57
16. Veerapen, p.74
17. ibid. p.81
18. ibid. pp.58, 62
19. ibid. p.63
20. ibid. p.64
21. ibid. p.67
22. ibid. pp.65, 66
23. Folger, L, a, 39; cited in Varlow, p.102
24. Varlow, p.103
25. ibid. p.119
26. Veerapen, p.69
27. ibid. p.80
28. ibid. p.83

Chapter 10: Sir Francis Vere

1. CSP Holland, liii; cited in Markham, p.92
2. Markham, p.101

Chapter 11: Sir Christopher Blount

1. Cited in Fraser, p.544
2. Knox, p.434; cited in ibid. p.545
3. Falls, p.26
4. James VI correspondence, p.109; cited in Falls, p.28

Chapter 12: Charles Blount's early life and military initiation

1. Falls, p.29
2. ibid. p.21
3. Varlow, p.126
4. Falls, p.22
5. Varlow, p.125
6. Falls, p.25
7. Moryson, Vol. II, p.265; cited in ibid. pp.29-30
8. Falls, p.30
9. Naunton, p.52; cited in Falls, p.24
10. Falls, p.24
11. Kearsley, p.186; cited in Veerapen, p.73
12. Falls, p.25
13. Moryson; cited in Varlow, p.127

PART III: THE ARMADA AND ITS AFTERMATH

Chapter 13: The Spanish Armada

1. Jenkins, p.347
2. Falls, p.38
3. ibid. p.42
4. ibid.
5. ibid. p.43

Chapter 14: Leicester's Last Hurrah!

1. Sweet Robin, p.289
2. ibid. p.300
3. Neale, p.298
4. Sweet Robin, p.304
5. ibid.
6. CSP Elizabeth 2, IV, p.418; cited in Tallis, p.237
7. Veerapen, pp.88-9 and 107
8. Varlow, p.110
9. CSP Foreign, p.451; cited in Falls, p.27
10. Varlow, p.109

Chapter 15: Raleigh's waning standing at court

1. Beer, p.59
2. ibid. pp.55-6
3. ibid. p.42
4. ibid. p.30
5. ibid. p.32
6. Varlow, p.128
7. ibid. p.135
8. Beer, p.275
9. ibid. p.41
10. Veerapen, p.127
11. Beer, p.97
12. Veerapen, p.70
13. ibid. pp.71-2
14. Beer, p.134
15. ibid. p.100

Chapter 16: The Expedition to Portugal

1. Veerapen, p.90
2. ibid. p.154
3. Varlow, p.116
4. Devereux, p.206; cited in Veerapen, p.90
5. Veerapen, pp.91, 93
6. ibid. p.109
7. Wikipedia
8. Veerapen, p.95
9. Devereux, pp.205-5; cited in Veerapen, p.96
10. Collins, p.377; cited in Varlow, p.112
11. Devereux, p.208; cited in Veerapen, p.107
12. Milton, p.271

PART IV: HONING DEVEREUX AMBITIONS

Chapter 17: Building bridges with James VI

1. Varlow, p.169
2. ibid. p.144
3. Veerapen, p.98
4. ibid. p.99
5. ibid.
6. Varlow, p.118
7. ibid. p.113

8. Veerapen, p.100
9. ibid.

Chapter 18: Devereux romances and unrest in France

1. HMC Bath, p.223; cited in Varlow, p.118
2. Veerapen, p.101
3. ibid. p.102
4. Varlow, p.132
5. Veerapen, p.103
6. ibid. p.104
7. Varlow, p.119
8. ibid. p.86
9. ibid. p.120
10. ibid. p.122
11. ibid. pp.122-3
12. ibid. p.128
13. Cited in Falls, p.33
14. Naunton, p.58; cited in Falls p.34
15. Falls, p.34
16. CSP Dom. 1 pp.152, 367; cited in Falls, p.35
17. Cheyney, Vol. I, pp.299-303; cited in Falls, p.34

Chapter 19: Essex's support for Henry IV

1. Varlow, p.132
2. ibid.
3. ibid.
4. HMC Cecil, p.169; cited in Varlow, p.132
5. ibid.
6. Prior; cited in Veerapen, p.116
7. Veerapen, p.113
8. ibid.
9. Varlow, p.134
10. Murdin, p.651; cited in Varlow, p.134
11. Devereux, p.244; cited in Veerapen, p.118
12. Veerapen, p.119

Chapter 20: Devereux marriage difficulties

1. Lodge, p.422; cited in Varlow, p.117
2. Varlow, p.129
3. ibid.

4. Birch, p.218; cited in Varlow, p.180
5. Varlow, p.135
6. Geni – Southwell, Elizabeth
7. Varlow, p.132

Chapter 21: Essex's attempts to develop his political standing

1. Black, p.423; cited in Varlow, p.178
2. Veerapen, p.101
3. Varlow, p.137
4. Veerapen, p.136
5. Varlow, p.138
6. ibid. p.171
7. ibid. p.165
8. ibid.
9. ibid. p.170
10. ibid.
11. ibid.
12. ibid.
13. ibid. p.166
14. Fitzwilliam Virginal Book; cited in Varlow, p.167
15. American Musicological Society; cited in Varlow, p.167
16. Varlow, p.168
17. ibid.
18. ibid. p.162
19. ibid.

Chapter 22: The Devereux flirtation with Catholicism

1. Varlow, p.151
2. ibid. p.152
3. Gerard, pp.33-5; cited in Falls, p.65
4. Varlow, p.156
5. ibid.
6. ibid. p.161
7. ibid. p.144

Chapter 23: Essex's efforts to focus attention on the growing Spanish threat

1. Falls, p.69
2. Varlow, p.172
3. ibid. p.174

4. ibid. p.143
5. ibid. p.145
6. ibid. pp.178-9
7. ibid. p.146
8. ibid.
9. Essex Letter Book, No. 45; cited in Varlow, p.145

PART V: FURTHER CAMPAIGNS AGAINST THE SPANISH

Chapter 24: The continuing campaign in the Low Countries

1. CSP Holland, lxx, lxviii; cited in Markham, p.111
2. Markham, p.118
3. ibid. p.140
4. ibid. p.150
5. ibid. p.164

Chapter 25: Charles's appointment as governor of Portsmouth

1. Falls, p.73
2. Salisbury, IV, p.440; cited in Falls, p.75
3. Falls, p.71
4. Privy Council, XXV, p.31; cited in Falls, p.77
5. Varlow, p.162
6. ibid.

Chapter 26: Raleigh's first expedition to 'Guiana'

1. Beer, pp.101-2
2. ibid. p.115
3. ibid. pp.103-4, 115
4. ibid. p.104
5. ibid. p.109
6. ibid. p.110
7. ibid. p.111
8. ibid. p.112
9. ibid. p.113
10. ibid.
11. ibid. p.115
12. ibid. p.114
13. ibid. pp.128, 114
14. ibid. p.126
15. ibid. p.128
16. ibid. p.127
17. ibid. p.138

Chapter 27: Drake's expedition to Puerto Rico

1. Falls, pp.69-70

Chapter 28: The attack on Cadiz

1. Beer, p.64
2. Beer, p.142
3. Varlow, p.178
4. Markham, p.171
5. Strachey, p.106; cited in Varlow, p.176
6. Veerapen, p.163
7. Varlow, p.176
8. ibid. p.179
9. Falls, p.78
10. ibid. p.79
11. ibid.
12. ibid.
13. Birch, II, p.195; cited in Falls, p.80
14. Varlow, p.182
15. Veerapen, p.187
16. ibid. p.164

Chapter 29: The 'Island Voyage' to the Azores

1. Veerapen, p.167
2. Falls, p.81
3. CSP Dom.2, pp.441, 352; cited in Falls, p.81
4. Falls, p.81
5. ibid.
6. Vere; cited in Falls, p.82
7. De L'Isle and Dudley, p.389; cited in Falls, p.82
8. Falls, p.82
9. ibid. p.85
10. ibid.
11. ibid.
12. Essex Letter Book, II, No. 52, p.447; cited in Varlow, p.185
13. Veerapen, p.169
14. Falls, p.88
15. CSP Dom. 2, p.479; Salisbury, VII, p.361; cited in Falls, p.89
16. Falls, p.89
17. ibid. p.90
18. ibid. p.92

19. Markham, p.187
20. Falls, p.98
21. ibid. p.96
22. ibid.
23. ibid. p.97
24. ibid.
25. Veerapen, p.176
26. Falls, p.99
27. Veerapen, p.177
28. ibid. p.182

Chapter 30: Further action in the Low Countries

1. Markham, p.201
2. ibid. p.206
3. ibid. p.224
4. ibid. p.231
5. ibid. p.232
6. ibid. p.234
7. ibid. pp.236-7
8. L'Isle and Dudley, II, cited in Markham, p.237
9. Markham, p.251
10. ibid.
11. ibid. p.252
12. ibid. p.253
13. ibid.
14. ibid. p.257
15. ibid. p.260

PART VI: CAMPAIGNS IN IRELAND

Chapter 31: Background to efforts to pacify Ireland

1. Curl, p.3
2. Falls, p.102
3. ibid.
4. Curl, p.13
5. Falls, p.101
6. ibid. p.106
7. Bardon, p.23
8. Beer, p.150
9. ibid. p.151
10. ibid. p.152

Chapter 32: Re-establishing Devereux influence

1. Varlow, p.186
2. ibid. pp.186-7
3. Veerapen, p.192
4. Varlow, p.188
5. ibid.
6. ibid.
7. ibid. p.189
8. Trotter
9. Veerapen, p.195
10. Varlow, p.190
11. ibid. p.191
12. ibid.
13. ibid. p.176
14. Essex letters Book, No. 38; cited in Varlow, p.190
15. Varlow, p.190
16. Veerapen, p.195
17. ibid.
18. ibid. p.196
19. Essex Letter Book, No. 16; cited in Varlow, p.191
20. Varlow, p.187
21. ibid. p.192
22. Devereux, p.496; cited in Veerapen, p.197
23. Falls, p.105
24. Beer, p.145
25. ibid.
26. Veerapen, p.198
27. Beer, p.145
28. Veerapen, p.204
29. Nugae Antiquae, II, p.29; cited in falls, p.106
30. Varlow, p.198
31. Cited in Trotter
32. Falls, p.107
33. Jones, p.46; cited in Varlow, p.197
34. Falls, p.70

Chapter 33: Essex's campaign in Ireland and its aftermath

1. Archer, p.3
2. Bardon, p.27
3. Veerapen, p.107

References

4. Carew Manuscripts 1589-1600, pp.314-25; cited in Varlow, p.108
5. ibid. 1601–1603, p.lx; cited in Veerapen p.207
6. Veerapen, p.208
7. Falls, p.128
8. ibid. p.129
9. Veerapen, p.209
10. Falls, p.110
11. ibid.
12. Veerapen, p.199
13. ibid. p.209
14. ibid. p.208
15. Varlow, p.198
16. Veerapen, p.213
17. Varlow, p.199
18. ibid.
19. Veerapen, p.214
20. Varlow, p.201; Falls, p.114
21. Varlow, p.200
22. ibid.
23. Veerapen, p.215
24. Varlow, p.201
25. Hentzner, p.103; cited in Varlow, p.119 and in Beer, p.146
26. Beer, p.147
27. ibid.
28. Varlow, p.201
29. ibid.
30. Birch, II, p.442; cited in Falls, p.115 and in Varlow, p.202
31. Croft, I, pp.43-69; cited in Veerapen, p.216
32. Varlow, p.203
33. Beer, p.153
34. Harrison, p.263; cited in Veerapen, p.218
35. Falls, p.135
36. Veerapen, p.221
37. Varlow, p.207
38. ibid. p.208
39. Moryson, Vol. 2, p.316; cited in Varlow, p.205
40. CSP Ireland, 1600, p.346; cited in ibid.
41. HMC Cecil, X, pp.167-8; cited in Varlow, p.206
42. Varlow, p.206
43. Falls, p.155
44. Camden, IV, p.171; cited in Varlow, p.207

Chapter 34: Essex's rebellion

1. Beer, p.153
2. Veerapen, p.231
3. ibid.
4. Varlow, p.208
5. Falls, p.112
6. ibid. p.114
7. ibid. p.113
8. Varlow, p.203
9. Falls, p.143
10. Ibid. p.135
11. Beer, p.153
12. Falls, p.150
13. Varlow, p.207
14. Beer, p.153
15. Veerapen, p.232
16. ibid.
17. ibid.
18. Varlow, p.210
19. Veerapen, p.233
20. Varlow, p.210
21. ibid. p.211
22. ibid. p.210
23. ibid. p.211
24. ibid.
25. Veerapen, p.239
26. ibid.
27. ibid. p.241
28. Varlow, p.213
29. ibid.
30. Salmon, I, p.170; cited in Varlow, p.213
31. Veerapen, p.254
32. Falls, p.153
33. ibid.
34. ibid. p.154
35. Varlow, p.220
36. ibid.
37. Beer, p.154
38. Varlow, p.221
39. ibid.
40. Beer, 155
41. Varlow, p.212

42. Goodman, Vol. 2, pp.18-19; cited in ibid. p.215
43. Varlow, p.219
44. ibid. p.229

Chapter 35: Charles's arrival in Ireland

1. Falls, p.119
2. ibid. p.120
3. ibid. p.117
4. Paccata Hibernia; cited in Madden, pp.362-3
5. Falls, p.121
6. ibid. p.122
7. ibid. p.120
8. ibid. p.125
9. Varlow, p.223
10. ibid.
11. Falls, p.125
12. ibid.
13. ibid. p.123
14. ibid. p.124
15. ibid. p.129
16. Bardon, p.25
17. Falls, p.136
18. ibid. p.137
19. CSP Ireland, Mar.-Oct. 1600, p.223; cited in Falls, p.139
20. Carew Manuscripts 1589–1600, p.439; cited in ibid. p.143
21. Falls, p.144
22. ibid.
23. Carew Manuscripts 1589–1600, p.481; cited in ibid. p.146
24. Falls, p.146
25. ibid. p.147
26. ibid. p.148
27. ibid.
28. ibid. p.156
29. ibid.
30. ibid. p.151
31. Cited in ibid. pp.152-3
32. Cited in ibid. p.153
33. ibid. p.153
34. Varlow, p.219
35. Falls, p.154
36. ibid. pp.157-8
37. ibid. p.154

Chapter 36: La Jornada de Irlanda

1. Bardon, p.28
2. ibid. p.30
3. Curl, p.1
4. ibid.
5. ibid.
6. Varlow, p.223
7. ibid.
8. Carew Manuscripts, 1601–3, p.181; cited in Falls, p.170
9. Falls, p.174
10. ibid. p.178
11. ibid.
12. ibid. p.180
13. ibid.
14. ibid.
15. ibid.
16. Bardon, p.36
17. Falls, p.183
18. CSP Ireland, 1601-03, p.242; cited in Falls, p.182
19. Curl, p.16
20. Falls, p.188
21. ibid. p.187

Chapter 37: Settling Ireland

1. Falls, p.193
2. ibid. p.197
3. CSP Ireland, CCXII, p.118; cited in Falls, p.196
4. Falls, p.196
5. ibid. p.198
6. Curl, p.16
7. Varlow, p.224
8. Moryson, Vol. III; cited in Falls, p.208

PART 7: WITH JAMES I AS KING
Chapter 38: The end of the Elizabethan era

1. Veerapen, pp.259-60
2. Beer, p.163
3. ibid. p.165
4. ibid. p.162
5. Varlow, p.224

6. Beer, p.170
7. ibid. p.171
8. ibid. pp.170-1
9. Varlow, p.226
10. ibid. p.227
11. Beer, p.170
12. Varlow, p.229
13. ibid.
14. ibid.
15. Lodge, III, p.88; cited in Varlow, p.231
16. Varlow, p.228
17. ibid. p.229

Chapter 39: Life under James I and Queen Anne

1. Varlow, p.226
2. Falls, p.209
3. Varlow, p.232
4. Falls, pp.209-10
5. Varlow, p.230
6. Falls, p.212
7. Varlow, p.230
8. Falls, p.210
9. ibid. p.211
10. ibid.
11. ibid. p.219
12. Varlow, p.232
13. Beer, p.173
14. ibid. p.177
15. Varlow, p.233
16. Beer, p.180
17. Varlow, p.233
18. Beer, p.188
19. Varlow, p.235
20. ibid. p.236
21. ibid. p.238
22. ibid. pp.237-8
23. CSP Dom. 3, pp.64, 89, 192; cited in Falls, p.219
24. Falls, p.214
25. ibid. p.216
26. Varlow, pp.239-40
27. Falls, p.217

28. Varlow, p.240
29. Falls, p.224
30. ibid.
31. Varlow, p.241
32. Falls, p.222
33. Varlow, p.242
34. Falls, p.222
35. ibid.
36. ibid.
37. ibid.
38. ibid.
39. D'Ewes; cited in Varlow, p.242
40. Cited in Varlow, p.242
41. Falls, p.220
42. Falls, p.218; Varlow, p.245
43. Rawson, p.275; cited in Falls, p.218

Chapter 40: Charles and Penelope's home life and her divorce from Rich

1. Moryson; cited in Varlow, p.238
2. Varlow, p.239
3. Falls, p.223
4. Falls, pp.224-5
5. Moryson; cited in Varlow, p.239
6. Varlow, p.239
7. Falls, p.213
8. Jenkins, p.367
9. Varlow, p.246
10. ibid. p.248
11. BL MS Lansdowne 885, f.86b; cited in Stewart, p.239
12. Varlow, p.250
13. ibid. p.247
14. ibid.
15. ibid.
16. ibid. p.250
17. ibid. p.249
18. ibid. p.250
19. ibid. p.247
20. ibid. p.248
21. Falls, p.227

22. Varlow, p.250
23. ibid.
24. ibid. p.247
25. ibid.
26. ibid.
27. ibid. p.249
28. ibid. p.250
29. ibid. p.251
30. ibid.
31. ibid. p.252
32. ibid.

Chapter 41: Charles's tragic end

1. Varlow, pp.253-4
2. ibid. p.254
3. Falls, p.234
4. Varlow, p.254
5. ibid.
6. ibid.
7. Falls, p.236
8. Varlow, p.255
9. ibid. p.256
10. ibid.
11. ibid.
12. ibid. p.255
13. Falls, p.239
14. Varlow, p.258
15. ibid.
16. ibid. p.259
17. ibid. p.260
18. ibid. p.261
19. ibid. p.272
20. ibid. p.263
21. ibid. p.264
22. ibid. p.266
23. ibid.
24. Campion; cited in Varlow, p.266
25. Varlow, p.269
26. Tallis, p.202
27. Varlow, p.271
28. ibid.

Endnotes

Endnote 1: The parentage of Catherine Carey

1. von Tunzelmann
2. Warnicke
3. Varlow, pp.21-2
4. ibid.

Endnote 3: Elizabeth's appearance when older

1. Veerapen, p.123

Endnote 5: Raleigh's final years

1. Varlow, p.234

Index

Fleet prison, 28, 160, 164
Fleet Street, 184
Flores, 69, 134
Florio, John, 92, 237
Flota, The, 135, 137-8, 158
Fluellen, 40
Flushing, 36, 40-1, 107, 113, 121, 128, 141, 143-4
Ford, John, 46, 244
Fowler, Thomas, 59, 74
Foyle, Lough, 193, 195, 202, 213
Francis I of France, 249
Frankfurt, xxxiv, 251
Frederick II of Denmark, xxxii
Friesland, 105, 106, 108
Frobisher, Sir Martin, 63, 69
Fulham, 227
Funeral Tears, 244

Galway, 9, 195, 213, 215
Gamage, Barbara, 113
Gardiner, Sir Robert, Chief Justice in Ireland, 203, 207
Garland, 131-2, 135, 138
Garnet, Father Thomas, 243
Garter, Order/Knight of the, xxxv, xxxvi, 4, 13, 16, 39, 139, 162, 173, 191, 221, 225-6
Gascoyne, George, xxx
Gatehouse prison, Westminster Abbey, 257
Gelderland, 103, 109
Gentleman of the Bedchamber, 222
Gerard, Father John, 94-5, 244, 246-7
Gerard, Sir Thomas, 94
Gertruydenburg, 107-8, 141
Geule, The, Ostend, 149-51
Ghent, 16, 144
Giffard, Roger, 89
Glenconkeyne, Forest of, 212
Globe theatre, 183

Glyde, River, 172
Godolphin, Sir William, 192, 243
Goffe, Dr Stephen, 254
Gomez de Toledo, Don Diego, xxxvi
Gontaut, Charles, Duke of Biron, 188
Goodwin Sands, 122
Gordon, George, 6th Earl of Huntly, 72
Gorges, Sir Fernando, 138, 184-6
Gould, Alice, 61
Gournay, 82-3
Graciosa, 135
Graeme, Sir Richard, 208-9
Grand Canary, 167
Grave, 152
Gravelines, 54
Great Chamberlain, xxxii
Greenwich, 14, 16, 38
Grenville, Sir Richard, 32-4, 70
Greville, Fulke, 131
Grey, Lady Catherine, 72
Grey, Lady Jane, xxxiii, xxxiv, 33
Grey, John, 2nd Lord Grey of Groby, xxxiii
Grey, Mary, of Groby, Viscountess Hereford, xxxiii, xxxiv
Grey, Thomas, 2nd Marquess of Dorset, xxxiv
Grey de Wilton, Arthur, 14th Lord, xxx
Grey de Wilton, Thomas, 15th Lord, 165, 173, 179-80, 227, 229
Grey's Court, Henley-on-Thames, xxxiii, 11, 13, 29, 86, 252
Grolle, 109
Groningen, 105-8
Guadaloupe, 119
Guarás, Antonio de, Spanish ambassador, 6
'Guiana', 115-8, 255-7
Guildford family, 43
Guildhall, 243
Guise family, 5, 76

Metz, 109
Meurs and Nieuwenaar, Adolf, Count of, 103
Meyrick, Gelli, 29, 66, 134, 166, 178, 184, 187
Meyrick, Rowland, Bishop of Bangor, 29
Middelburg, 149
Middle Temple, xxx, 45, 128
Midsummer Night's Dream, A, 230
Mile End, 62-3
Moleyns, Sir Barentine, 85
Monaghan, 7, 202, 213-4
Monasteravin Abbey, Kildare, 199
Moncontour, xxx
Mondragón y Mercado, Cristóbal de, 107, 109
Monson, Sir Richard, 135
Montgomery, Count of, *see* Lorges, Gabriel de
More, Sir Thomas, xxxvii, 21
Morgan, Colonel Thomas, 41-2
Morgan, Thomas, Spy, 43-4, 47
Morley, Thomas, 92
Moryson, Fynes, 45, 191, 200, 237, 242-4
Moryson, Sir Richard, 192-217
Moselle, 109
Mother Hubbard's Tale, 33
Mountjoy, Lords, *see* Blount
Mountnorris, 198
Mousehole, Cornwall, 98
Moyry Mass, 194, 196, 198
Munns, John, 110-1
Munster, xxx, 34, 157, 170, 177, 192-3, 196-7, 199, 203-4, 206, 210, 212-4, 217, 226
Munster, President of, xxxi
Murray, Sir Alexander, 141

Naunton, Sir Robert, 48
Navarre, 67

Neagh, Lough, 202
Neville, Charles, 12th Earl of Westmoreland, 4
Newbolt, Sir Henry, 120
New Exchange, 224
New Forest, Keeper (Warden) of, 55, 139
Newlyn, Cornwall, 98
Newport, Christopher, 69
Newry, 156, 194, 196, 198, 213
Nieuport, 144-8
Noble Imp, The, *see* Dudley, Robert
Nonpareil, 123
Nonsuch Palace, 35, 85, 164, 172
Norfolk, Duke of, *see* Howard, Thomas
Norman Conquest, xxxiii, xxxvi
Normandy, 81, 83, 107
Norreys, Sir John, 36-7, 47, 57, 66-9, 79-80, 105, 156, 198
Norreys, Sir Thomas, 192
Northampton, Earl of, *see* Howard, Lord Henry
Northern Rebellion/Rising, 4
North of Kirtling, Roger, Lord, 162
Northumberland, Duke of, *see* Dudley, John
Northumberland, Earls of, *see* Percy
Nottingham, Earl of, *see* Howard of Effingham
Nymegen, 104, 106
Ny Park, Castle, 205

O'Brien, Donogh, 4th Earl of Thomond, 193, 195, 204, 206, 208
O'Byrne clan, 170, 199
O'Byrne, Phelim McFeagh, 199
O'Cahan clan, 194, 215
O'Cahan, Donal Ballach, 214
O'Connor clan, 199
O'Connor, Dermot, 196
O'Doherty clan, 194

Persons, Robert ('R. Doleman'), 96
Peter, King of Castile and Leon
 ('the Cruel'), xxxvi
Petworth House, 248
Phelippes, Thomas, 89
Philip II of Spain, 65-6, 68, 88-90,
 126-7, 138, 142-3, 155, 159, 169
Philip III of Spain, 143, 169, 216, 231
Philip, Count of Nassau, 109
Philippe Emmanuel of Lorraine, Duke
 of Mercoeur, 77, 80
Philippine, 144
Picardy, xxxvi
Plague, 63-4, 77, 83, 85, 95, 98, 181,
 194, 227-8, 255
Plantagenet(s), xxxvi, 154, 180
Platter, Thomas, 175
Plymouth, 60, 63, 66-7, 69, 99, 119,
 121-2, 125, 127, 131-3, 137-8, 168
Pole, Reginald, 250
Poley family, 43
Poley, Margery, 43-4
Poley, Robert, 44
Ponta Delgada, Azores, 65, 136
Pope Clement VIII, 73
Pope Gregory XIII, xxx, 4
Popham, John, Chief Justice, 184-5
Portland, 62
Portmore fort, 156
Porto Santo, Madeira, 69
Portsmouth, 82, 110-2, 122, 127, 130,
 139, 194
Power, Sir Henry, 207-9
Prague, University of, 13
Premier Livre de Chansons et Airs, 92
Prerogative Court of Canterbury, 245
President of the Council of the North,
 11, 114, 224
President of the Council of Wales, 8
Privy Council, 5, 15-6, 38-9, 43, 56,
 63, 81, 88, 99, 105, 112, 114, 125,

161-2, 164, 171, 173-4, 177, 183-4,
 186, 200, 215, 217, 222, 226, 228,
 230, 233-5, 238
Protestant League, 8, 13-6
Prothalamion, 91
Puerto Real, 122-4
Puerto Rico, 119-20, 139

Quadra, Alvares de, Bishop of Aquila,
 Spanish Ambassador, 185
Queenhithe, 185

Radcliffe, Henry, 4th Earl of Sussex,
 110-1
Radcliffe, Thomas, 3rd Earl of Sussex,
 10, 15
Ragazzini, Signor, Papal Nuncio, 43
Rainbow, 53-5, 121, 135
'Raleghana', 115-8
Ralegh, The Cittie of, 34
Raleigh, Carew, 255
Raleigh, Damerei, 62-3, 85
Raleigh, Sir Walter, xi, xii, xxvii, xxix,
 xxx, xxxi, xxxii, 32-5, 38, 47, 60-4,
 69-70, 75-6, 115-9, 121-3, 125, 129,
 131-9, 157-8, 161-2, 164-5, 173,
 180, 183-8, 190, 201, 220-2, 224,
 227-9, 248, 255-7
Raleigh, Walter ('Wat'), 64, 221, 255-6
Rape of Lucrece, 160
Ravels, 141
Recklinghausen, 104-5
Recusancy fines, 100
Rees, 103-4
Repulse, 121, 133
Revenge, 32, 69-70
Reynolds, William, 166
Rheinburg, 103-4
Rhine, 103-5, 109
'Rialta, Ernestus and Richardo', 74
'Rich', Charles, 190, 254

Rich, Elizabeth, 25
Rich, Essex, 25-30
Rich family, 57-94
Rich, Henry, later Earl of Kensington,
    25-6, 74, 77, 79, 247
'Rich', Isabella, 112, 246, 254
'Rich' Letitia Isabella, 254
Rich, Lettice ('Lucy'), 24, 216
'Rich', Mountjoy, 1st Earl of Newport,
    128, 243, 246, 254
Rich, Penelope, *see* Devereux,
    Penelope
'Rich', Penelope, 85, 110, 246, 254
Rich, Richard, 1st Lord of Leighs,
    xxxviii, 21, 24
Rich, Robert, 2nd Lord of Leighs, 21
Rich, Robert, 3rd Lord of Leighs, later
    1st Earl of Warwick, xi, xxvii, xxix,
    10, 21-7, 35, 45-6, 56, 66, 69, 74,
    77-9, 85-6, 89, 91-2, 112-3, 122,
    126, 128, 131-2, 160, 162, 165-7,
    173, 176, 179, 186, 188-9, 191,
    222-3, 228, 238-40, 242, 247, 253-4
Rich, Robert, later 2nd Earl of
    Warwick, 25, 227, 238, 247
'Rich', Scipio/St John, KB, 158, 254
Richard II, 177
Richard II, 183
Richmond Palace, xxx, 164, 175,
    221, 232
Rincurren, 205
Roanoke Island, North Carolina, 33-4, 60
Robartes, John, 1st Earl of Radnor, 154
Robsart, Amy, 2
Roscommon, 170
Rouen, 82-3, 87, 126, 192
Rudolf II, Holy Roman Emperor, 13
Russell, Anne, Countess of Warwick,
    75, 159, 175
Russell, Edward, 3rd Earl of Bedford,
    184, 187, 223

Russell, Elizabeth, Lady, née Cooke, 13
Rutland, Earl of, *see* Manners, Roger
Ryswick, The Hague, 148, 152

Sackville, Sir Thomas. Lord Buckhurst,
    later Earl of Dorset, 176, 178-80,
    194, 231-3
St Barbe, Ursula, Lady Walsingham,
    85, 179, 188
Saint-Bartholomew, Massacre of, 5, 8
St Bartholomews, London, 128
St Clement Danes, 62, 85, 112, 158,
    166, 174, 247, 254
Saint-Germain, Peace of, 1570, xxx
St Ives, 138
St John, Sir Oliver, 244
St John's College, Cambridge, 160
Saint-Martin, Jeanne de, 25, 74
Saint-Nazaire, 77
St Olave's, Seething Lane, 78, 96
St Paul, Sir George, of Snaresford, 247
St Paul's Cathedral, 38, 184
Salisbury, Earl of, *see* Cecil, Robert
Samerie, M., Jesuit chaplain, 43
San Andres, 123, 131, 133
San Andres fort, 143-4
San Felipe, 203
San Felipe, Castle of, Cádiz, 124
San Francisco, Convent of, Cádiz, 124
San Juan de Sicilia, 54
San Juan, Puerto Rico, 119-20, 139
San Mateo, 41, 123, 131, 133
San Miguel, 41, 123, 131, 133
San Sebastian, Cádiz, 122
San Sebastian, N. Spain, 66
San Thome, 'Guiana', 256
Sandwich, 130
Santander, 66-7, 168
Savage, Sir Arthur, 186-7, 199, 214
Savoy Hospital, The Strand, 243
Saye, Sir William, of Bedwell, xxxvii